Routledge Author Guides

Nietzsche

Routledge Author Guides

GENERAL EDITOR B. C. SOUTHAM M.A. B.LITT. (OXON)
Formerly Department of English, Westfield College, University of London

Titles in the series

Browning by Roy E. Gridley, *Associate Professor of English, University of Kansas*

Byron by J. D. Jump, *Professor of English, University of Manchester*

William Cobbett by James Sambrook, *Department of English, University of Southampton*

Nietzsche by R. J. Hollingdale

Tolstoy by Ernest J. Simmons, *sometime Professor of Russian Literature, Harvard University*

Routledge Author Guides

Nietzsche

by

R. J. Hollingdale

Routledge & Kegan Paul
London and Boston

First published in 1973
by Routledge & Kegan Paul Ltd
Broadway House, 68–74 Carter Lane,
London EC4V 5EL and
9 Park Street,
Boston, Mass. 02108, U.S.A.
Printed in Great Britain by
Cox & Wyman Ltd,
London, Fakenham and Reading

ISBN 0 7100 7562 6 (c)
ISBN 0 7100 7563 4 (p)

Library of Congress Catalog Card No. 72–97947

General Editor's Preface

Nowadays there is a growing awareness that the specialist areas have much to offer and much to learn from one another. The student of history, for example, is becoming increasingly aware of the value that literature can have in the understanding of the past; equally, the student of literature is turning more and more to the historians for illumination of his area of special interest, and of course philosophy, political science, sociology, and other disciplines have much to give him.

What we are trying to do in the Routledge *Author Guides* is to offer this illumination and communication by providing for non-specialist readers, whether students or the interested general public, a clear and systematic account of the life and times and works of the major writers and thinkers across a wide range of disciplines. Where the *Author Guides* may be seen to differ from other, apparently similar, series, is in its historical emphasis, which will be particularly evident in the treatment of the great literary writers, where we are trying to establish, in so far as this can be done, the social and historical context of the writer's life and times, and the cultural and intellectual tradition in which he stands, always remembering that critical and interpretative principles are implicit to any sound historical approach.

BCS

Contents

Preface

Nietzsche is an arena where conflicting opinions have been fighting it out for more than eighty years, and an armistice, a 'general consensus', is not in prospect. The existence of this state of hostilities means that anyone who undertakes a general, unpolemical introduction cannot avoid taking sides: there can be no neutral expounder of Nietzsche. This fact should be kept in mind throughout the ensuing book. I do not know of any satisfactory method of presenting him other than that of making up your mind what you think he means and stating it as clearly as you can: and this is, of course, an 'interpretation'. A book embodying all known interpretations would naturally be possible, but even then the author would find it very difficult to avoid betraying which appealed to him and which he thought misguided or mad, and he would thus be down in the arena in spite of himself.

Here, on the contrary, I pay attention to other interpretations only silently, without acknowledgment, or polemical defences of my own views, and I do so not because I think they require no justification, or want to conceal the extent of my indebtedness, but in the first place because an introduction to Nietzsche must not become an introduction to his commentators and critics. The 'Nietzsche literature' is extensive and growing all the time: but it is something the student ought not to be interested in, or perhaps even have heard of, unless or until he is interested in and informed about Nietzsche himself. First things first applies here as elsewhere. That many differing and often irreconcilable views of Nietzsche do exist is, of course, a fact pertaining to the subject itself, and some discussion of the possible grounds for this variety of attitude and response is justified: but it will not be found until the *end* of the book, which is where it belongs. (The only exception is a brief reference in chapter 4 to the chapter on Nietzsche in Bertrand Russell's

History of Western Philosophy: but this is introduced only because it seems the best way of emphasizing the point I am making there.)

A second reason for refusing to polemicize is that insistence on a particular interpretation is not the purpose of this introductory guide. 'Interpretation' is ultimately no more than a necessary method of presentation: the book's objective is to make the reader want to read Nietzsche for himself. If it succeeds in that objective, the reader will quickly become his own 'interpreter'.

Instead of polemics against other commentators there is plentiful quotation from Nietzsche himself (translation is in every case my own). Some may think there is too much quotation: my view is that you can never have too much direct contact with a writer you are trying to know and understand. This consideration aside, I can see no reason for paraphrase when citing the author will express the point just as well or, as a rule, much better.

One further caution. Nobody thinks a book about a poet is almost the same thing as the poet's collected poems, but many people do think a book about a philosopher is almost the same thing as the philosopher's philosophy. This is an error, even in the case of a philosopher about whose meaning there is little dispute. A book about a philosopher is like a map of a city. You can *know about* a city from a map, and you can learn from a map how to find your way about in it, but you cannot *know* it, because knowing a city involves experiencing it. The life of the place, its feel, smell, colour, three-dimensionality, you can get only by going there and being there. This book is a map of Nietzsche, it is not a substitute for going there and being there.

Notes on the Text

Nietzsche's philosophical ideas are to be found primarily in the series of books he wrote between 1870 and 1888. These books are as follows (the initials by which they are cited in the text are given in brackets):

The Birth of Tragedy (*BT*), published 1872; 3rd edn, prefaced by an 'Essay in Self-Criticism', 1886.

Untimely Meditations. I *David Strauss, the Confessor and the Writer* (1873), II *On the Usefulness and Disadvantage of History for Life* (1874), III *Schopenhauer as Educator* (1874), IV *Richard Wagner in Bayreuth* (1876). (Cited as *UI, UII, UIII, UIV.*)

Human, All Too Human (*HA*), published 1878; 2nd edn, with a new preface, 1886.

Assorted Opinions and Maxims (*AOM*), published 1879.

The Wanderer and his Shadow (*WS*), published 1880; 2nd edn, together with *AOM*, as the second volume of *HA*, with a new preface, 1886.

Daybreak (*D*), published 1881; 2nd edn, with a new preface, 1887.

The Gay Science (*GS*), published 1882; 2nd (expanded) edn, 1887.

Thus Spoke Zarathustra (*Z*). Parts One and Two published 1883, Part Three 1884, Part Four issued privately 1885, published 1892.

Beyond Good and Evil (*BGE*), published 1886.

On the Genealogy of Morals (*GM*), published 1887.

The Wagner Case (*W*), published 1888.

Twilight of the Idols (*T*), written 1888, published 1889.

The Anti-Christ (*A*), written 1888, published 1895.

Ecce Homo (*EH*), written 1888, published 1908.

Nietzsche contra Wagner (*NCW*), written 1888, published 1895.

A secondary source of his philosophical opinions is in his literary remains (*Nachlass*). In the *Gesamtausgabe in Grossoktav* (2nd edn, 1901–13), the *Nachlass* occupies as many volumes as the works (i.e. eight), but its quantity must not be allowed to obscure its subordinate rank. Essentially it is the contents of Nietzsche's notebooks and stands in the same relation to the works he himself published or intended for publication as the litter of a sculptor's workshop does to his finished statues. Nor must it be supposed that the fairly tidy appearance of these notes and jottings when they have achieved print is a reflection of their original state, which is often chaotic.

The key to a balanced understanding of the *Nachlass* is the knowledge that most of Nietzsche's finished works originated in similar notebook entries, and are consequently a selection from that body of material of which the *Nachlass* is the portion not selected. That the *Nachlass* is reject material is the first datum for its assessment. How much weight and authority to give it in an exposition of 'Nietzsche's opinions' must in the last resort remain an interpretative question, but any interpretation which relies heavily on it to the exclusion of the finished works seems to me unsound in principle: such a method has to assume that, since he published what he should have rejected and rejected what he should have published, Nietzsche was unaware of what his opinions really were or deliberately sought to conceal them, and there is no evidence for either contention.

The distinction between the finished works and the *Nachlass* was blurred by the publication in 1901 (and in a greatly expanded edition in 1906) of *The Will to Power* (*WP*), a collection of notes and jottings arranged so as to resemble a finished book. But that *The Will to Power* is an unauthorized compilation is by now fairly well known, and the unfinished character of the material in it ought to be apparent to anyone even slightly acquainted with the style of the finished works.

I

Foundations

I

Every account of Nietzsche is an interpretation. Perhaps students of
him are inclined to forget the extent to which this is also true of every
philosopher, indeed of every imaginative writer of any kind: if so, it is
because the absence of even a broad basis of agreement is particularly
obtrusive in his case. That there is no secure foundation is the first thing
any student is forced to notice.

Every new account has to lay its own foundations; and since, as with
any sort of building, the foundations are what lie under all the rest and
sustain or fail to sustain it, it seems a good idea here too to lay the
foundations first. What follows are the fundamental propositions about
Nietzsche upon which the present discussion is going to be based. They
do not comprise all I think can be said of him: they are an abstract of
the minimum I assert to be true of him and an attempt to supply
foundations which will hold.

II

Nietzsche was primarily a philosopher (and not, for instance, an
aphorist, a poet, or a 'lay prophet') whose distinctive contribution to
European thought was to recognize and face the consequences of a
radical change in Western man's apprehension of and attitude towards
'truth'. Although sometimes credited with having attempted to compel
this change himself, he really claimed no more than to have anticipated
it and to have drawn appropriate conclusions.

Formerly Western man had metaphysical truth, religious truth,
moral truth, rational truth: now he has come to recognize that these
truths are not true; he has seen through them and recognized them as

errors. That element in metaphysical, religious, moral and rational truths the undermining of which has brought about their downfall is their pretension to absoluteness. To believe something true has been to believe it 'absolutely true', true at all times, true for everybody, true whether or not anyone knows it to be true. 'Truth' and 'absolute truth' have been synonyms. What has undermined this attitude towards truth has been the dissemination in simplified form of the philosophy of Hegel and the theory, triumphant in Darwin, of evolution: Hegel and Darwin have accustomed modern man to the idea of *becoming*. Everything evolves – consequently 'truth' evolves: that has been the great change in modern man's attitude towards truth; and, in so far as 'truth' has hitherto been synonymous with 'absolute truth', this change has amounted to a slackening and finally a loss of belief in the truth of truth. 'Everything evolves' has come to mean 'nothing is true'.

The correct way of stating this new insight into the nature of truth is, however, not to say that truth is untrue, which would be only a verbal paradox, but to say that truth is perspectival. Whether a metaphysical, religious, moral or rational statement is true depends upon the perspective of the mind which views it; in themselves, 'absolutely', all such statements are false, and they can usually be shown to be false by the discovery of the perspective from which they appear true. 'Irrefutable truths' – actually 'irrefutable errors' – are truths determined by the perspective of mankind as a whole, an unavoidable consequence of mankind's being in a certain situation and not in a different situation from which its perspective would be different.

Faith in the kinds of truth undermined by evolutionism has been replaced by faith in *scientific* truth. Of this kind of truth it must be said, first, that it is no more objective than any other kind of truth: the 'truths' of empirical science are not discoveries but interpretations. The 'laws of nature', all 'laws' of any sort, are 'interpreted into' the observed phenomena by the mind which observes them: they are an arrangement (*Zurechtmachung* – putting to rights, dressing up) of the world in accordance with those requirements that have to be met if mankind is to 'understand' and live in it. Empirical science is useful; but it is not a means through which the nature of the world can be discovered, since logical inference and mathematical proof are founded upon concepts with which nothing in the world corresponds: they are a human *Zurechtmachung* of an essentially structureless and irrational existence.

The second thing to be said of scientific truth is that it is, or purports to be, exclusively factual: the realms of value and meaning are, in principle, outside the sphere of science. However many 'facts' science may 'discover', and however vast and imposing a logical and mathematical structure it may erect out of them, it can never advance a single step towards bestowing upon this explanation of the world any meaningful significance. Science may announce that this or that *is* the case, but it can never announce what *ought to be* the case: the question of what 'ought to be' is an unscientific question which cannot even be framed in a form amenable to scientific investigation. Ultimately, all scientific explanations are reducible to the form 'If A happens, B happens'; nothing further is implied in any scientific explanation: science sees and has to see the world as a chain of 'causes' and 'effects'. Modern science, having been compelled to deny itself even the limited encroachment on the sphere of 'value' implied in explanations in terms of purpose (teleology), is wholly committed to explanations in terms of cause (mechanism). Science thus has to see the world as a machine, and it is 'scientific' and useful *only* when it sees the world as a machine.

The substitution of scientific truth for all other kinds of truth has therefore deprived the world of *meaning*. The question 'Why?', which has hitherto meant 'to what end?' is now answered only as if it meant 'from what cause?' The question 'to what end?' receives no answer.

III

Nor is any answer to be expected, for the unmasking of truth as error cannot be reversed: mankind knows, or will soon know, that 'life' is a phenomenon that cannot be explained. This state of consciousness, which experiences the world and mankind as facts without meaning and life as senseless, is coming and must come: man has been moving towards it ever since Copernicus, and the momentum of his advance is by now tremendous.

Nietzsche undertakes to experience this coming nihilism experimentally in himself: to produce an anticipatory account of the nihilist state of mind. The task is congenial: necessarily so, for otherwise he would be unable to attempt it. To regard it as possible one has to share Nietzsche's conception of the nature of thought.

The traditional view, to which the general consensus no doubt still adheres, is that thought is an autonomous faculty existing *in* the brains of creatures with brains, a sort of *causa sui* and *primum mobile* whose

3

operations proceed according to laws of their own which are not the laws governing the material world. But the theory that truth is perspectival, not absolute, is unfavourable to the idea of the autonomy of thought: it suggests that thought is a part of the apparatus of the thinking creature in the same way as its arms, legs, and digestion are. In addition, the existence of *any* autonomous faculties is beginning to seem more and more unlikely: to speak of the faculty of will, for example, sounds very much like speaking of the faculty of love or of anger, and reminds one of the primitive notion of humours. An affect is a consequence, something produced; we feel the sensations of love, anger, willing because of events antecedent to them: if these events did not occur, these sensations would not occur. 'Anger', for instance, is not something I do, it is rather something that happens to me, and the same may be true of thinking. Indeed, the strongest evidence that thought is not a faculty which I possess is the fact that thinking is not an act: a thought happens, it 'comes to me', I have no control over the matter. This view of the nature of thought – that it is an end product, not a faculty – was Nietzsche's view of it: he described thought as 'a relation of the impulses to one another' and, like everything else of which we become conscious, a 'terminal phenomenon'. In the light of this idea, his assertion that 'I have at all times written my writings with my whole heart and soul: I do not know what purely intellectual problems are' becomes more than a claim to be involved and committed; it suggests – or is at least consonant with – a conception of the 'heart and soul', in other words the whole organism, as integrated with the 'intellect'.

That Nietzsche was 'temperamentally' attuned to nihilism, that he found that the thoughts which 'came to' him were destructive of former certainties, made him a precursor of the coming general nihilism. That such thoughts are 'dangerous', as he repeatedly says they are, is no objection to them: on the contrary, being constituted as he is, he enjoys the idea that they are dangerous, and in describing the style of Machiavelli as 'protracted, difficult, hard, dangerous thoughts and the tempo of the gallop and the most wanton good humour' (*BGE*, 28), he describes what he takes to be his own style. The dangerous element resides in the fact that they all tend towards the same end: towards demonstrating the existence of a world in which the Assassins' motto 'Nothing is true, everything is permitted' could easily become everybody's motto (see *GM*, III. 24; and cf. *WP*, 602).

To reduce a lengthy, subtle but not very orderly procedure to a single simple formula, his method is to demonstrate that all forms of truth other than scientific truth are errors (perspectival), and then to unmask scientific truth, and especially the processes of scientific reasoning, as errors also (a *Zurechtmachung* and interpretation in the interests of the interpreter): the end result is precisely that 'nothing is true'. It would be right to point out that he also asserts that the latter 'errors' are necessary and ought not to be abandoned; indeed, he insists it is impossible to abandon them, even when they have been recognized as errors; but this saving clause is printed in very small type compared with the gigantic letters he employs for the destructive task of announcing their erroneousness, and people who do not read the small type in this or any other document are likely to overlook it altogether.

Most of his readers, when he finally acquired them, were in the first instance not very interested in logic or theory of knowledge, and not very vitally affected by metaphysics: but they were interested in and vitally affected by morals, and it was as a destroyer of 'moral truths' that Nietzsche at first gained notoriety. There is no 'moral law', no 'moral world-order': this assertion was one which conflicted most violently with current and deeply-felt opinion. In *The Cardboard Box*, Sherlock Holmes voices in the directest way the conventional prejudice and prejudgment in this matter: 'What is the meaning of it, Watson?', he asks. 'What object is served by this circle of misery and violence and fear? It must tend to some end, or else our universe is ruled by chance, which is unthinkable.' What Holmes means by 'meaning' is moral law, as is shown by the immediate reference to misery and violence and fear: and a universe 'ruled by chance' is one in which there exists no moral world-order. But this state of affairs, far from being unthinkable, is, according to Nietzsche, the one which actually obtains. 'Moral meaning', being a value, is outside the scope of science, which has nothing to do with values as a matter of principle. Empirical scientific method can discover why morality exists (that is to say, what causes it), but in doing so it demonstrates the perspectival nature of moral 'truths'; and this demonstration destroys morality, and goes a long way towards suggesting that our universe *is* ruled by chance – or rather that it is a universe in which the word 'chance' is without meaning, since accidents can be recognized only within a regulated system in which they are exceptional.

The elimination of a moral world-order – because of its immediate personal applicability the most famous aspect of Nietzsche's nihilistic philosophy – is in fact only a part of his general elimination of all order: 'the total nature of the world', he writes in *The Gay Science* (109), 'is ... to all eternity chaos.'

The demonstration that nothing is true is paralleled by an account of what must follow from the corollary that everything is permitted. It is in the course of this account that one encounters the hair-raising Nietzsche, the 'prophet of great wars' and of moral anarchy, the herald of convulsions and disasters; likewise the Nietzsche who refuses to flinch at this coming turmoil but goes out to meet it in a spirit of squaring up to the inevitable. Here one encounters too the prognostications of decline: of a collapse of man under the weight of the realization of his senselessness; of his loss of a taste for life; of his efforts to distract and blunt his mind with work, social improvements, anything that will stop him from remembering that life has no meaning; of his self-reduction to a herd animal which limits its drives to those which can be easily satisfied at once and is determined to see no farther ahead than the next day. Contempt for the 'timidity' which refuses to face this prospect is allied to a provocative, 'shocking' directness and frankness in delineating the naive violence and morally unencumbered vitality of those 'strong men and races' to whom the awareness that 'everything is permitted' will open up a boundless area of freedom. This is an aspect of the 'fascist' Nietzsche: a just judgment of him in this role would have to emphasize that he was primarily concerned to describe, in language that left no doubts in the mind of the reader, what he saw coming in any case, and that ultimately this is all he is doing; at the same time the fact could not be suppressed or glossed over that the forcefulness and spirit of these descriptions is such as to give them the character of an instigation to the kind of behaviour described. That they have often been read as incitements to 'immorality' and violence is demonstrably true; that they have ever actually inspired immorality or violence would be harder to prove. A consideration of how wide an intellectual, moral, and stylistic gulf separates *Beyond Good and Evil* from *Mein Kampf* would not be irrelevant. In the end what would be most clearly apparent is that Nietzsche failed to appreciate the depth of sordidness to which Europe would descend. Sometimes one feels that, in his delineation of an age in which everything is permitted, he is on the brink of anticipating Auschwitz and Treblinka: but this feeling is dissipated by his incurable tendency to bestow on all positive, 'strong' action some tincture of nobility. Pursued to its ultimate cause, this tendency might be found to constitute a defensive mechanism: a refusal to look into the *last* depths of the abyss; or perhaps one should

6

say simply that there is in Nietzsche no trace of the pornographer. That twentieth-century Europe would be violent, amoral and nihilist he foresaw quite clearly, but that some of its characteristic features would also resemble those of a pornographic novel was beyond his power of imagination.

IV

It was only after he had applied his analytical and intuitive genius to a delineation of the nihilist world outlook that he was able to understand with his 'whole heart and soul' *how* necessary it was that this outlook should be transcended. The nihilism which was coming and must come would mean that man would be finished as man: he would be faced with a universe of meaningless and purposeless brute facts in which the most meaningless and purposeless fact would be man himself. All 'greatness' in man – which, however defined, had always been a product of self-confidence, self-control, and a faith, even a naive and unjustified faith, in his own rightness and justifiability – would be a thing of the past.

It has to be emphasized, when speaking of Nietzsche's ideas of transcendence, that he never supposed or suggested that nihilism could be transcended without first being experienced. All former modes of transcendence had perished under the impact of science, and any attempt to revive them could only be an artificiality and an all-but-conscious act of self-deception; sooner or later their discredited nature would become apparent, and the believer would be compelled to abandon them. Nihilism was a state of mind to which mankind was, as a matter of incontrovertible fact, being compelled, and nothing that anyone said or did – and certainly not a series of books of philoso-phy – could halt this process. The most he could do was push it forward faster. At the same time, the adoption of a radically new mode of transcendence as an attempt to halt the advance of nihilism would likewise be an artificiality, and one calculated to inspire even less lasting belief than an attempt to revive old modes. Only out of the experience of a total loss of faith – a radical, all-embracing and *real* scepticism, a full realization of what it means that 'God is dead', and with him the whole metaphysical meaning of man, world and life itself – could there come a true, 'heart and soul' realization of the need for a new beginning and therewith also the strength for it. 'Such an *experimental philosophy* as I live anticipates even the possibilities of the most fundamental nihilism, but without this meaning it has to halt at a negation, at a No, at a will to say No. It wants rather to go over to the reverse of this – to a *Dionysian affirmation* of the world' (*WP*, 1041).

The essential insight, without which all endeavour will be in vain, is that the metaphysical is recognized as illusory. There is no 'other world', no 'beyond', no 'real world': the 'apparent world', *our* world, transitory, meaningless, continually becoming, never reposing in being, is the only world. A new mode of transcendence of this world will have to be non-metaphysical. But 'the metaphysical' and 'the transcendent' have hitherto amounted to the same thing. Is a non-metaphysical transcendence possible?

Nietzsche's answer to this question is his theory of 'will to power', the beginning of which is the recognition that the fine and admired attributes of man do in fact exist, and the heart of which is the assertion that there therefore exists *in* the world a means by which the world can be transcended.

V

Consider, as a simple example, the existence of what is called a 'sense of justice'. The world as discovered and disclosed (interpreted) by the 'meaningless' knowledge of empirical science contains no values: consequently the concepts 'just' and 'unjust' are as inapplicable to the world as the concepts 'up' and 'down' are to outer space. But in the human world 'up' and 'down' do mean something, and so do 'just' and 'unjust': there exists in men a sense of justice to which nothing in the non-human world corresponds – definite sensations, unmistakable in character and not to be confused with any other, which when we feel them inform us we are making the value judgment 'this is just' or 'this is unjust'. Such feelings can be crude or sophisticated, but that they are real – that we really feel them – can hardly be denied. Where do they originate? Hitherto their existence has been explained metaphysically: since the rest of the world knows nothing of them they must be part of the 'divine' in man. But if this explanation is pronounced untrue, if they are denied a metaphysical origin, then there is nothing for it but to declare them a 'natural' phenomenon, something existing in man's own nature. And this means that, in so far as the possession of the value feelings 'just' and 'unjust' constitutes a transcendence of the valueless world disclosed by empirical science, a means of transcendence exists in man's own nature.

Assuming that everything has evolved, the question of the origin of a sense of justice should be phrased: 'how has a sense of justice evolved?' The answer to that question would thus entail a search for something that was at first *not* a sense of justice but which became one. Nietzsche proposes that the *idea* of justice originated:

> Among forces of *approximately equal power* . . . where there exists no clearly recognizable predominance and a contest would result in nothing but mutual injury, the idea arises of coming to an understanding and of negotiating over one another's demands: the characteristic of *exchange* is the original characteristic of justice . . . Justice is requital and exchange on the presupposition of an approximately equal power-position: thus revenge originally belonged within the domain of justice; it is an exchange. Gratitude likewise. (*HA*, 92)

This arrangement is of course a consequence of 'a sensible self-preservation', consequently of a natural egoism; but, 'in accordance with their intellectual habit', men have forgotten this origination: 'because children have for millennia been trained to admire and imitate such actions, it has gradually come to appear that a just action is an unegoistic one', and this has led to the high value placed on just actions. The ability to calculate degrees of power which is presupposed by a decision to institute an exchange when they are approximately equal is, according to Nietzsche, the earliest acquirement of mankind, and originates in 'the oldest and most primitive personal relationship that exists' – the relationship between buyer and seller, creditor and debtor:

> It was here that one person first encountered another person, one person first *measured himself* against another person. No grade of civilization has been found in which something of this relationship was not already perceptible. Setting prices, gauging values, contriving equivalences, exchanging – these things preoccupied the earliest thinking of man to so great an extent that in a certain sense they constitute thinking *per se*. (*GM*, II. 8)

From this most rudimentary idea there evolved the sense of 'exchange, contract, debt, right, obligation, agreement', which then transferred itself to the earliest and crudest forms of social order:

> And with that plodding consistency characteristic of the thinking of primitive mankind, which is hard to set in motion but then proceeds inexorably in the same direction, one presently arrived at

the great generalization 'everything has its price; *all* things can be paid for' – the oldest and most naive moral canon of *justice*, the beginning of all 'good-naturedness', all 'fairness', all 'good will', all 'objectivity', on earth. (*Ibid.*)

Rigid and literal application of the dictates of 'justice' is confined to societies still in a relatively weak state: societies in which the power of the individual to harm the whole is relatively great. As the community's power increases and the relative power of the individual diminishes, the community no longer feels the need to defend itself so rigorously: the law becomes more moderate.

A *consciousness of power* on the part of society is not unthinkable at which it could allow itself the noblest luxury that exists for it – letting those who harm it go *unpunished* . . . The justice which began with 'everything can be paid for, everything must be paid for' ends . . . as does every good thing on earth, by *sublimating itself [sich selbst aufhebend]*. This *self-sublimation [Selbstaufhebung]* of justice: one knows by what beautiful name it calls itself – *mercy*; it remains, as goes without saying, the privilege of the man of greatest power, better still his 'beyond the law'. (*GM*, II. 10)

VI

In this thesis, as I have partially quoted it, four characteristics should be especially noted. Firstly, it is an attempt to understand a 'metaphysical' phenomenon in naturalistic terms. Secondly, it involves hypothetical assertions about primitive mankind. Thirdly, it offers the materials for a theory rather than a completed structure (the incompleteness of the above quotation does not affect this: it would still be the case if all Nietzsche's references to justice were quoted). Finally, it is based on and continually returns to power-relationships and power-feelings, and their sublimation, as the essential explicatory principle. These characteristics will be found to predominate throughout his work whenever he functions as an analyst of the phenomena of human life.

The first characteristic is a consequence of the motive for the whole undertaking: it is only because metaphysical explanations have become unacceptable that any new explanation is called for. The second is clearly a reflection of 'evolutionism'; he followed the tendency of his age to render down complex states of mind and 'soul' into simpler ones supposedly characteristic of primitive man and then to trace their 'evolution' back to the complex forms. That all his assertions about 'primitive man' must remain hypothetical is guaranteed by his definition of that term as man as he was 'long before the 4,000 years we more or less know about' (*HA*, 2): any statement about the mental and psychical condition of primitive man can never be accorded a greater degree of certitude than plausibility. His ruling dicta are: that the concepts of primitive man were irreducibly simple; that once primitive man had an idea in his head he held on to it with unbreakable tenacity and drew its consequences with rigid and to us unimaginable consistency; that his memory was weak, so that the origin of an idea and its consequences was soon forgotten (one result being the coming into existence of 'categorical morality', i.e. the transformation of prohibitions and commands with a purpose into absolute prohibitions and commands through a failure to remember their purpose).

The third characteristic defines Nietzsche's *œuvre*: the evidence for this will be found throughout the present study.

The fourth is the thesis by means of which he draws into order threads that would without it lie tangled: it remains a thesis, but there is a determined effort to make it work. In department after department he sought to show that the observed phenomena of human life could have been produced by the drive to enhanced power – more exactly, the *feeling* of the gratification of that drive – which man is posited to share with the animals. Adopting Schopenhauer's terminology of 'will' he referred to a 'will to power' – it was not a good choice of word, since he was later compelled to explain that he did *not* mean 'will' – and tried to understand human behaviour as manifestations of it.

VII

He adopted the concept of 'sublimation', and tried to understand the great and valued achievements of the human race as products of 'sublimated will to power'; he tried to show how the drive to greater power, over the world and over other men, had been sublimated into the capacity for power over oneself. He sought the origin of the capacity for 'sublimation' in the 'intensification and deepening' (*Verinnerlichung*) of the power drive when it was denied outward discharge in aggressive actions by the enclosure of primitive man within the walls of society. He sought the first origin of morality in a power relationship and of antithetical moral judgments in the relative power positions of their originators ('master and slave morality'). He drew on the history of Greece for evidence that a high culture could have been produced by the sublimation of the instincts of aggression.

He was led to approve of 'strong will to power' and to deprecate – to use no stronger word – the enfeeblement of the aggressive instincts ('rather . . . a Cesare Borgia than . . . a Parsifal' (*EH*, III. 1)); he was led to see in conflict, enmity, hardship, suffering, cruelty: in short in 'evil', an essential component of the total economy of man without which a 'great human being' could no more be achieved than a sword could be forged without fire and hammer-blows. He was led to radical repudiation of all desire for 'peace of soul' ('live dangerously').

VIII

In considering the conceptions in which Nietzsche embodied his ideas of transcendence through sublimated will to power I find Karl Jaspers's idea of 'ciphers' useful. A 'cipher' in Jaspers's use of the word is 'the embodiment of transcendence' which cannot be annulled by equating it with the object signified. Science has abolished the embodiments of transcendence in the world produced by the religions but the transcendent ideas remain in the ciphers. The meaning of a cipher is not to be exhausted by any examination of it, for example by discovering its psychological origin: its meaning reveals itself only through existential experience of it. Finally, just as we do not invent the language we use but appropriate it to our use, so we do not invent the ciphers but appropriate them.

In this sense of the word, Nietzsche can be said to have appropriated a number of ciphers in which to embody his conception of transcendence.

The best-known of them is '*Übermensch*' – superman (properly 'supraman', though this piece of etymological purity has now no chance of acceptance). The psychological content of this cipher links it with his psychology of will to power: the superman is the embodiment of sublimated will to power; but the meaning has not been exhausted when the cipher has been elucidated psychologically. The superman is more than the embodiment of a psychological theory: he is also the embodiment of life-affirmation through acceptance of the totality of life, and especially of the suffering entailed in living; in which aspect he is also described by the cipher 'the Dionysian man'. A passage in eulogy of Goethe provides a succinct summary of the meaning of 'superman': 'What he aspired to was *totality*; he strove against the separation of reason, sensuality, feeling, will . . . he disciplined himself to a whole, he *created* himself. . . . Goethe conceived of a strong, highly cultured human being, skilled in all physical accomplishments, who, keeping himself in check and having reverence for himself, dares to allow himself the whole compass and wealth of naturalness, who is strong enough for this freedom; a man of tolerance, not out of weakness, but out of strength, because he knows how to employ to his advantage what would destroy an average nature; a man to whom nothing is forbidden, except it be *weakness*, whether that weakness be called vice or virtue . . . A spirit thus *emancipated* stands in the midst of the universe with a joyful and trusting fatalism, in the *faith* that only what is separate and individual may be rejected, that in the totality everything is redeemed and affirmed – *he no longer denies* . . .' (*T*, IX. 49). A more succinct definition still is essayed in *Ecce Homo* (III. 1): the word *Übermensch* designates a '*Typus höchster Wohlgeratenheit*' – a type that has turned out supremely well.

'Superman' and 'Dionysus' are attended by the grand cipher 'eternal recurrence': Dionysian acceptance of life in its cruellest and most senseless manifestation, a supreme test of one's life-acceptance.

IX

The nihilism the development of which had begotten a counter-will to a new mode of transcendence lost none of its insidious force, but continued its work of undermining: and it is in the tension thus set up that much of what is most individual and, to the casual reader, puzzling in Nietzsche exists. The paradoxes, the contradictions, the deliberately misleading expressions, the wit, even the abnormal punctuation, have their origin in the tension between the positive and negative, between *Ja-sagender* and *Nein-sagender*.

It is this tension and its consequences which prevent 'Nietzsche's philosophy' from attaining any fixed final form and from issuing in anything that could be summarized without falsification as a doctrine. But it is this tension, too, which gives his work its inexhaustibility: the sense one has that the play and counter-play of ideas in it has, even theoretically, no end. And since this is a faithful reflection of what is probably the case – since the problems he treats of probably really are irresolvable – his work has retained its immediacy, freshness and relevance while that of almost all his contemporaries has become of historical interest only.

2

Backgrounds

Having attempted to focus our eyes on what is essential and basic in Nietzsche, we must now widen our view to take in his surroundings and environment.

He was born in 1844 in the village of Röcken, in Prussian Saxony, and died in 1900 in Weimar; his father and both grandfathers were Lutheran clergymen; and his life's work was philosophy. Thus his 'background' consisted of three traditions: the national, religious, and philosophical. We shall outline each of them and then note what his relationship to each of them was.

II

His life coincided with the rule – at first in Prussia, and from 1866 effectively throughout Germany – of Wilhelm I and Bismarck. (Wilhelm was Regent of Prussia 1858–61, King 1861–71, President of the North German Confederation 1866–71, German Emperor 1871–88; Bismarck was Minister-President of Prussia 1862–5, Federal Chancellor 1866–71, Imperial Chancellor 1871–90.) It also coincided with the victory of German nationalism over other forces in German life and the rise of a peculiar form of socialism for which the term 'national socialism' is as good a term as any.

In considering Nietzsche's relation to these forces and to his national background in general we must first note that the fact that he was never a citizen of the *Reich* but for most of his adult life a Swiss, seems to have exercised no influence over him whatever. He was born a Prussian subject, but in 1869 he became a naturalized Swiss in order to assume the chair of classical philology at the university of Basel: he appears to have changed his nationality without any hesitation or reluctance, and to have then put the fact that he had changed it out of his mind.

In the summer of 1870 he applied for, and obtained, permission to join the Prussian army at the front, although the military affairs of Prussia ought no longer to have been of any concern to him. For the remainder of his active life he wrote about Germany as if he was still a German himself: the ferociousness of his attacks on the Germans would, indeed, be inexplicable without the supposition that he continued to feel wholly involved with the *Reich*. He never mentioned Switzerland, or that he was a Swiss; he took no interest whatever in Swiss affairs. In particular he drew no conclusions, favourable or otherwise, from his experience of the form of democratic government established in Switzerland. This is a point worth insisting on. The 'democracy' of his anti-democratic writings is a theoretical construct: you cannot discover from them how, or whether, democracy works in practice, or that its theoretical egalitarianism is in practice constantly circumvented; the most complete realization of the theoretical possibilities of democratic rule appears in his works as normative. One of the implications of this is that the example of Swiss democracy made no impression on him at all.

It would also be as well to mention here that Nietzsche was given to asserting that his ancestors were Polish and that Poles often mistook him for a Pole. That this is part of his anti-German campaign seems fairly clear: when he had come to regard himself as the greatest man living he refused to allow the Germans the honour of having produced him. Max Oehler published during the Nazi era a book in which he traced 200 of Nietzsche's forebears and showed that they were all Germans. Oehler was a descendant of Nietzsche's mother's family and had been curator of the Nietzsche Archive at Weimar, and his desire to establish Nietzsche's racial credentials is comprehensible: this notwithstanding, there is no reason to think that his researches were not in fact genuine. The evidence that Nietzsche himself did not really believe that his family was of Polish origin seems to me to lie in his obsessive anti-Germanism: he attacked other nations, but these attacks are as nothing compared with the blast of his assault on Germany – and this degree of antagonism is consistent only with an inner identification. If he had felt Polish, he would have attacked, if anyone, the Poles.

His national background was, then, exclusively German, and the political form which it assumed during his lifetime had been determined in its essentials by the end of the Napoleonic era: the peculiar form of government and the peculiar form of nationalism whose combined effects produced the Germany he knew were both creations, if at some remove, of the Napoleonic occupation.

III

The German Confederation instituted by the Congress of Vienna and brought into existence by the Federal Statute of June 1815 was an arrangement by means of which the ruling houses in the states established in the German world by Napoleon maintained the status quo. Power was formally vested in a Federal Diet meeting in Frankfurt but actually resided in Vienna, and specifically in the Austrian Chancellor Metternich, the first of the four fatal autocrats of modern Germany. Metternich's policy seems to have been nothing more subtle than a fixed opposition to any alteration to the power position enshrined in the Federal Statute – a policy which cannot properly be called desirable or undesirable but simply doomed to fail. Metternich appears to have realized this but to have believed that change, when it came, would necessarily be change for the worse: in practice, therefore, his policy amounted to putting off the evil day for as long as possible, and to this end he instituted a police state which, while very mild indeed compared with later achievements in this line, had the peculiarly depressing and irritating characteristic of being devoted to nothing but the perpetuation of standstill and inefficiency.

Metternich's empire was formally anti-democratic: its ideal was that the possibility of popular participation in government should be utterly forgotten. The Diet was composed of representatives of the states: it was not a parliament, was not elected, and there was no popular representation at all. Baden, Bavaria, Nassau, Weimar and Württemberg possessed moderate constitutions; Hanover's constitution was a product of its association with the British crown and when that association was discontinued in 1837 the constitution was abolished; throughout the greater part of the German world – including Austria and Prussia, which were by far the biggest states – the populace enjoyed no constitutional rights.

This anachronistic structure began to crack during the 1840s, and when the disturbances of 1848 and 1849 brought the rule of Metternich to an end the inevitable process of change began. The actual concessions into which the ruling houses were panicked may not have been very considerable; even the acquisition by Prussia of a constitution may not in practice have been nearly so revolutionary an innovation as it seemed to be, since it left real power in the hands which had always possessed it; and the failure of the National Assembly to create a single nation, or even to perpetuate its own existence, may have permitted a return of reaction: but the vital fact was that *something* had altered, the stillness had been broken, and forces hitherto paralysed or almost completely frustrated could now move more freely.

In 1851 Bismarck was appointed Prussian envoy to the Federal Diet: he went there with the avowed intention of dethroning Austria as head of the Confederation and substituting Prussia. Later he substituted for this programme the abolition of the Confederation itself and the institution of a new union of which Prussia would be the head and from which Austria would be excluded. Austria was already a paper tiger, but it was not until 1866 that Bismarck felt the time had come for a demonstration of that fact. As Minister-President of Prussia he reorganized the Prussian army; he involved Austria as an ally of Prussia in a war with Denmark; and out of that conflict he engineered a war between Prussia and Austria. At the battle of Sadova (3 July 1866) Austria lost the leadership of the German world and Prussia secured it. The defeated nation was compelled to accept the dissolution of the German Confederation and its exclusion from a new German union, the North German Confederation, which comprised only the states north of the Main (the southern states, with the exception of Austria, were associated with it in a customs union and a uniform fiscal system).

The Bismarckian victory, however, represented something more than the replacement of one dominant power by another. If it had been only that its consequences would have been very different and very much less momentous than they were. By 1866 Bismarck's Prussia had come to stand for an ideal, and its victory was a victory rather of the ideal it stood for than of Prussia as such.

Ideals are things on behalf of which people are willing to sacrifice other things. They may not cease to value these other things, but they do not value them as highly as they do their ideal, and if their ideal makes it necessary they should be sacrificed, then sacrificed they are. After 1866 the German liberals sacrificed liberalism on behalf of the ideal represented by Prussia. In 1933, millions of Germans who valued freedom sacrificed freedom on behalf of the same ideal, then

17

represented by something else. This ideal is not shared by all nations, and we have to exercise our imagination a little if we are to understand how it can be so keenly desired as to make the sacrifice of other desired things seem a small price to pay for it.

I have said that the effects of the form of government experienced by the Germans under the Confederation helped to produce the form of state which existed throughout Nietzsche's adult life; but perhaps one should look even farther back: perhaps the frustrations of the Metternich era did no more than stir up a racial memory of an earlier period in which in a positive sense 'nothing happened', that blank in history during which something resembling primal chaos took over the German world. The effect of the Thirty Years War on the German people has probably never been fully assessed, and possibly never can be assessed: for an entire generation the Germans were merely the occupants of a field over which armies fought one another – how can you count all the effects that is likely to produce in the children and grandchildren of that generation? This much, however, you can say: to have experienced total disorder, total insecurity, is a sure guarantee that one will afterwards value order and security, and their presuppositions, very highly.

During the reign of Metternich the form assumed by this archaic chaos was the civil form of inefficiency: the states of the Confederation were hopelessly, pathetically, one might almost say deliberately, inefficient. Metternich's policy of letting nothing happen, while it did not positively demand administrative muddle, was very favourable to it: one way of preventing change would be to allow it to be thwarted by simple incapacity, by administrative paralysis, by inertia. In the end it became impossible to get anything done – not because the repressive forces at the disposal of the states were overwhelmingly effective (they were, like everything else, very inefficient) but because the machinery for getting anything done seemed not to exist; and thus, in the end, efficiency, that is the ability to proceed from an intention to its realization, that is 'strong will', became not merely an ideal but an ideal the attainment of which was the unspoken common policy of all parties, overriding and demoting to second place their differences as to what was to be attained through the exercise of it.

It was this ideal which was mirrored in the 'Prussian efficiency' demonstrated at the battle of Sadova: the mobilization of Prussia in three weeks and its crushing defeat of Austria before the states allied with Austria had hardly done more than get their riding boots on.

Thenceforward, Prussia stood for the capacity for action, for the possession of 'strong will': and it was as the embodiment of this ideal – which, as I say, may very well have appealed also to the dread of paralysis, of ineffectiveness of the will, which the punishment they endured in the Thirty Years War had implanted in the 'German soul' – that Prussia conquered not merely Austria but precisely the 'German soul' itself. 'Iron resolve', 'unshakeable will': no other modern nation has responded to the promise of these things as the Germans have when they have felt frustrated.

Four years after Sadova, Bismarck's Germany received its final form in the revived *Reich*. The technique by which this was achieved had nothing extraordinary about it, and need not have been consciously formulated. All governments were ready for war on all kinds of pretexts, or on pretexts that were patent fabrications, as was the pretext upon which France and Prussia pushed one another into war in 1870; and the victory of Prussia backed by the other states 'sealed with blood' a union which was already almost a fact.

IV

Bismarck ruled the new Germany for nearly twenty years. His mind was devious and his character complex, but his policy was fundamentally simple: he wanted a strong, independent nation with Prussia at its head. He was an efficient and cunning ruler: the Germans had never been governed by anyone remotely like him before. He made Germany into a 'great power'. What did Nietzsche think of him and his achievements?

> Of all the evil consequences which have followed the recent war with France perhaps the worst is a widespread if not universal error . . . that German culture too was victorious in the struggle . . . This delusion . . . is capable of turning our victory into a complete defeat: *into the defeat if not the extirpation of the German spirit for the benefit of the 'German Reich'*. (*UI*, 1)

This passage from the first paragraph of the first of the *Untimely Meditations* contains in small compass Nietzsche's whole objection to the Bismarckian Empire: its political ambitions, misunderstood as cultural, were in reality inimical to culture, and to German culture in particular. It was diverting and impoverishing Germany in the only sphere that counted. This is a point of view from which he never afterwards deviated: on the contrary, he came increasingly to think that the warning uttered in *David Strauss* had been all too justified, and the fears which inspired it very comprehensively realized.

In *Beyond Good and Evil* there is a dialogue between 'two old "patriots"' in which the specific charge of having corrupted a nation is made against an unnamed statesman who is obviously Bismarck. 'Suppose', one of the patriots asks, 'a statesman were to put his nation in the position of having henceforth to pursue "grand politics", for which it was ill-equipped and prepared badly by nature, so that it had to sacrifice its old and sure virtues for the sake of a new and doubtful mediocrity – suppose a statesman were to condemn his nation to "politicizing" at all, while that nation had hitherto had something better to do and think about and in the depths of its soul still retained a cautious disgust for the restlessness, emptiness and noisy wrangling of those nations which actually do practice politics – suppose such a statesman were to goad the slumbering passions and desires of his nation, turn its former diffidence and desire to stand aside into a stigma and its predilection for foreign things ... into a fault, devalue its most heartfelt inclinations in its own eyes, reverse its conscience, make its mind narrow and its taste "national" – what! a statesman who did all this, a statesman for whom his nation would have to atone for all future time, assuming it had a future – would such a statesman be *great*?' 'Undoubtedly!' the other retorts: 'otherwise he would not have been *able* to do it! Perhaps you may say it was mad to want to do such a thing? But perhaps everything great has been merely mad to begin with!' 'Misuse of words!' cries the former: 'strong! strong! strong and mad! *Not* great!' Nietzsche, who overhears the argument, consoles himself with the thought that 'when one nation becomes spiritually shallower there is a compensation for it: another nation becomes deeper' (*BGE*, 241).

The other nation, it also seems obvious, is France – that nation whose culture, he had said in 1873, had *not* been defeated by Germany in 1870. The main question, here as everywhere in his writings on the subject, is whether a nation has a high culture, not whether it is a 'great power'; and the German state – or, as he later came to believe, any state – is inimical to a high culture. In so far as this view of the relationship between culture and politics applies to Germany he acquired it by comparing the age of Goethe with the contemporary age: for in the 'classical era of German culture', Germany was politically a nonentity in both the literal and the figurative senses of the word. He may also have acquired it directly from Goethe himself, with whose opinion in this matter his own corresponds. 'Suppose we had had for centuries in Germany only the two capitals, Vienna and Berlin, not to speak of only one, I should like to know how German culture would have fared!' Goethe said to Eckermann (23 October 1828); and after enumerating the cultural advantages of political diversity, concluded by asking whether the 'great and glittering' cities of Frankfurt, Bremen, Hamburg and Lübeck would still be what they then were 'if they should lose their own sovereignty and become incorporated into some great German *Reich*?' Goethe opposed the demand for German unity because he had no reason to think German culture would benefit: to him, as to Nietzsche, culture was the main consideration, and not a 'strong, united Germany'.

It might also be remarked that the most powerful nation in the world throughout Nietzsche's life was England, but his references to England are almost all concerned with the alleged aridity and plebeianism of English culture, and never with the British Empire, which he finds no occasion for mentioning. Evidently the admiration for 'power' with which he is popularly credited does not include admiration for powerful nations.

His final thoughts on the subject of the new *Reich*, assembled in the chapter of *Twilight of the Idols* called 'What the Germans Lack', are consistent with the foregoing. 'The new Germany represents a great quantity of inherited and inculcated ability', but it is '*not* a high culture which has here gained ascendancy'. There exists a 'good deal of courage and respect for oneself ... self-confidence ... industriousness ... endurance'; and in Germany 'people can still obey without being humiliated by obeying'. On the other hand, the Germans have become stupid: 'once they were called the nation of thinkers: do they still think at all? Nowadays ... politics devours all seriousness for really intellectual things – *Deutschland, Deutschland über alles* was, I fear, the end of German philosophy.' The 'seriousness ... profundity ... *passion*' in spiritual things which formerly characterized the Germans is on the decline, and the reason for it is obvious:

No one can spend more than he has ... If one spends oneself on power, grand politics, economic affairs, world commerce, parliamentary institutions, military interests – if one expends in *this* direction the quantum of reason, seriousness, will, self-overcoming that one is, then there will be a shortage in the other direction. Culture and the state . . . are antagonists . . . The one lives off the other, the one thrives at the expense of the other. All great cultural epochs are epochs of political decline: that which is great in the cultural sense has been unpolitical, even *anti-political* . . . The moment Germany rises as a great power, France gains a new importance as a *cultural power*.

That 'education, *culture*, itself is the end – and *not* "the *Reich*"' has been forgotten in Germany (*T*, VIII).

This seems sufficiently comprehensive: one must add, however, that Nietzsche was determinedly opposed to national divisions of any kind in Europe, and therefore especially opposed to any policy which strengthened them.

Thanks to the morbid estrangement which the lunacy of nationality has produced . . . between the peoples of Europe [he wrote], thanks likewise to the shortsighted and hasty-handed politicians who are with its aid on top today and have not the slightest notion to what extent the politics of disintegration they pursue must necessarily be only an interlude – thanks to all this . . . the most unambiguous signs are now being overlooked, or arbitrarily and lyingly misinterpreted, which declare that *Europe wants to become one.* (*BGE*, 256)

In antithesis to the already current phrase 'good German', he called himself a 'good European', and deprecated 'that pitiable European petty-state politics and nervousness which with the foundation of the German *Reich* has entered a critical phase' (*T*, IX. 39).

V

The views we have been examining, whether one agrees with them or not – and when they were written most people, and certainly most Germans, did not agree with them – are all of the sort one might call reasonable and moderate: but Nietzsche is well known to have harboured very unreasonable and immoderate views about Germany too, and to discover the source of these we must turn to the other element which moulded the nineteenth-century German state: its peculiar form of nationalism.

Bismarck was not wholly devoid of national feeling, but he was emphatically not a 'German nationalist': it was with Wilhelm II that

German nationalism came to power, and in order to do so had to dispose of Bismarck. It was not a case of a headstrong younger man growing impatient with a more cautious older one: when Wilhelm II 'dropped the pilot' it was because he wanted to steer the ship in a different direction.

German national consciousness and a feeling of patriotism was created, so far as modern times are concerned, by the Napoleonic occupation. That it came into existence as a reaction to French domination was a fatality, since the German people were already victims of a strong sense of inferiority to the nations of the West and had developed a powerful *ressentiment* against them.

The recent era of German expansion stands between us and that earlier era, and makes us forget there was a time when the West regarded the Germans as being, above all, quaint. Little duchies and grand duchies; medieval towns, baroque palaces, 'fairy castles of the Rhine', and Gothic ruins; Nuremberg toys, Dresden shepherdesses, and 'German professors'; funny names like Ulm, Worms, and Polkwitz; three hundred different kinds of sausage: that was 'Germany'. The Germans were an amusing and lovable people, but very old-fashioned and provincial. In questions of grand politics they did not come into consideration. And the Germans themselves to some extent shared this judgment, because it was of course to some extent true; they too considered Germany a backwater where nothing happened, and for many years so it was. But there were other factors, less securely based in reality, which assisted to give the Germans a low opinion of themselves: the degree to which the German lands were integrated with the Latin West during the Middle Ages, for example, had become forgotten almost as completely inside Germany as outside, and many Germans believed, quite wrongly, that they had been deprived of the benefits of 'Latin civilization'.

As a consequence of these, partly real, partly imaginary grounds for feeling inferior, German nationalist sentiment had in it a number of corrupting and self-destructive elements, and was, in its typical manifestations, unlike any other. It was reactive: it arose, not out of a feeling of national strength and self-identity, but out of a consciousness of not possessing those things. It was rooted ultimately in a feeling of self-contempt, and when it attained to a position of power, its over-riding characteristic was therefore an over-compensatory self-assertion. Its message to the rest of Europe was that the rest of Europe should be afraid of it. This desire to inspire fear was rationalized into the principle that every nation must, by its nature, be hostile to every other; but the unconquerable sense of grievance which lay behind it betrayed itself in a continual complaining and protesting at foreign hostility and 'unfriendly acts'.

The spirit of German nationalism became morally bigoted and made grandiloquent claims on behalf of its own genius; but the more intensely it desired to think well of itself, the more urgent became the need to account for the long obscurity and failure of the German nation, and this need was met by the theory – soon accepted in many quarters as a known fact – that the Germans had been corrupted by 'the infiltration of alien elements'. German racism, the most sinister product of German nationalism, was, like that nationalism itself, reactive: it is perhaps not going too far to say that German racism did not *become* anti-Semitic but originated in anti-Semitism; that it defined itself in terms of that which it resented and reacted against. It had from the first no positive basis; it lacked plausibility and achievements; consequently it had to seek its justification in something which contradicted appearance, in something invisible and impalpable which actuality could not refute: German racial superiority had to be derived from the hidden constitution of the German himself, from biological structure, from 'blood'.

The development of the German idea of nationality was paralleled by the development of the 'German idea of the state' – an idea which would permit the creation of a German nation answering the requirements of German nationalism. This idea was that of *Volksgemeinschaft*.

The Romantic Movement, which displaced the Enlightenment in Germany and influenced many spheres of life beyond those of art, was led, for reasons intimately connected with the contemporary helplessness of Germany, into an idealization of the Middle Ages. In this era, it was asserted, the peoples of Europe were 'one' in a single community of faith. This community is not to be identified with 'believing in the same religion': it is a mystical belonging-to-one-another, a sharing of a common consciousness, a state of 'perfect communion'. In the German lands – understood to constitute the heartland of Christendom – the term for this subliminally united community was the *Volk* – the people, the 'folk'. The *Volk* constitutes the nation: in any other sense a 'nation' is nothing very meaningful, a mere political unit, something temporary and capricious: a true nation is a mystically-at-one folk community, a *Volksgemeinschaft*.

This community needs no laws, for its members love one another in purity of heart and act accordingly: anyone who fails to do so is thrust out in case he corrupt others. 'Virtue' means feeling with one's *Volksgenossen*, loving what they love and hating what they hate. 'Freedom' consists in entering into the spirit of the folk with all one's heart, soul, and mind: in any other sense, freedom is merely a cover for a fall from virtue. To feel differently from the community, to oppose it, is proof of depravity. The *Volksgemeinschaft* determines of itself how it shall live: it does so, not by voting at elections or framing resolutions at town meetings – these operations being entirely superfluous in a community already profoundly at one on all possible questions – but through one of its own members, who embodies in his person the desires and will of the whole. Opposition to this chieftain is the same thing as opposition to the whole: that is to say, depravity. His commands are not 'laws', any more than a father's commands to his sons are laws: they are expressions of the true needs of the community in this or that situation; consequently the entire community – its depraved and outcast elements excepted – will wholeheartedly desire to obey them.

This 'Romantic' image of a state, founded not on any rational idea of the functions and purposes of a state but on love and perfect communion, is of course a formula for totalitarianism: and it was towards a state modelled on this formula that German nationalism continually moved.

For an idea of the remoteness from reality of the German nationalist criteria of the state a comparison with the simple formula proposed by the young Hegel is instructive. Hegel defined the essence of a state as its power over individual citizens and its ability to defend itself against other states: if these conditions are met, a state exists; if they are not, it does not. These may or may not be sufficient criteria, but they are a rational attempt to define a state in terms of the functions it must perform. Compare with them the criteria proposed by Arndt, whose long life spanned the whole era of the rise of German nationalism: according to Arndt the essentials of the state are racial and linguistic purity. To foreign contemporaries this seemed a typical piece of 'German innocence' – for what could be more innocent than purity? – but it is in reality a piece of irrationalism of a 'folkish' tendency, pure race and pure language as criteria of a state being of the same type as the Romantic criterion that all its members love one another. The nationalism of Arndt is typical in other respects too: he held that the national state was good as such, and cosmopolitanism wicked; he habitually coupled the words 'cosmopolitan' and 'Jew'; and he was obsessively Francophobe.

Arndt was influential. Even more influential was the nationalism of 'Father' Jahn, who flourished in the 1830s and 1840s. Jahn's political philosophy consisted essentially in the proposition that everything German is inherently superior to everything not. In Jahn's view, France was an implacable enemy of Germany, was corrupt, and ought to be destroyed; cosmopolitanism and 'leagues of nations' were Jewish devices for weakening Germany; Germany needed a 'German war' because it was only in the crucible of war that the German people would rediscover its 'folkdom'. And so on. The whole scenario existed already in the days of Arndt and Jahn: Nazism merely put it on the stage. Nationalism as over-reactive self-assertion; racism grounded in anti-Semitism; opposition to cosmopolitanism, whether that of communism or of 'international Jewry', as a trick to keep the Germans down; advocacy of international hostility as a law of nature; a paranoic sense of grievance to which genuine grievances were as fuel to a fire; the idea of the state as a *Volksgemeinschaft* with one leader and no law: to these Nazism also managed to add a few characteristics which recalled Bismarck's Prussia – its socialism, for example, which was socialist to just the degree and for just the reason Bismarck's regime had been 'socialist'. In his public hysteria, blood-curdling phraseology and pompous display, Hitler resembled Wilhelm II rather than Bismarck: but his employment of the terms 'iron resolve', 'unshakable will', and the like, to characterize his attitude towards every difficulty and danger, was calculated to produce upon a later generation of Germans an effect similar to that produced on an earlier by the battle of Sadova.

Since the last war there have been efforts, the need for which one can well understand, to show that the Nazi era was an aberration, an exceptional state of affairs, and not an integral part of German history. Aside from the inherent improbability that so popular a regime as the Nazi could have been an aberration only afterwards recognized as such, an appreciation of the nature of the nationalist spirit which struggled for domination under Bismarck and came to the throne in the person of Wilhelm II must, I am afraid, defeat such efforts.

To be fair to the German nationalist movement – to see it in the most favourable possible light – I think one has to describe it in Adlerian terminology (which is, of course, the terminology I have been using). Because of the circumstances attending its inception, it drew certain conclusions as to the meaning of life and fashioned its life-style accordingly. Its conceptions and actions were irrational only from the point of view of a different life-style: given the presuppositions behind them, German nationalism behaved correctly. After all, whatever one may think of the Germans now, one is unlikely to think of them as quaint: and inasmuch as one of its objectives was to stop people thinking of Germans as quaint, German nationalism may be said to have succeeded. Its error, clearly, was the typical neurotic's error of solving a problem in a useless and unconstructive way. If immediately I lie down in bed at night I am every time seized by the thought that I have left the front door open, I can solve the problem presented by this thought in various ways. One way would be to get up and spend the rest of the night sitting awake before it so as to *see* that it was shut. This would be a real solution to my problem: I would no longer be worried by the idea that the front door was standing open; but it would also be a perfectly unconstructive one: I should have solved my problem without having in any way improved my life. (A constructive solution would, for instance, be to train myself not to worry whether the front door was open or not.) German nationalism solved its problems in a way comparable to sitting up all night to make sure the front door is shut: the solution was real but unconstructive – it made things far worse than they were before.

VI

Now, it was German nationalism, and not in general the Bismarckian *Reich*, which irritated Nietzsche into the outbursts of Germanophobia for which he subsequently became notorious. In *Ecce Homo*, he wrote:

> It is even part of my ambition to count as the despiser of the Germans *par excellence* . . . the Germans are impossible for me. Whenever I picture to myself a type of man that goes against all my instincts, it always turns into a German – or an anti-Semite [the last phrase is to be found in the manuscript but not in the text printed after Nietzsche's death] . . . the Germans are *canaille* . . . The Germans have no idea whatever how common they are; but that is the superlative of commonness – they are not even *ashamed* of being mere Germans. (*EH*, III: section on *W*, 4)

This is, of course, grotesque; but *Ecce Homo* also furnishes some examples of what specifically Nietzsche had against the Germans:

I speak of their indecency *in historicis*. German historians have not only altogether lost the *grand view* for the course, for the values of culture ... they have even *outlawed* this grand view. One has first of all to be 'German', to have 'race', then one can arbitrate over all values and disvalues *in historicis* ... 'German' is an argument, '*Deutschland, Deutschland über alles*' a principle ... There is a *reichsdeutsch* historiography, there is, I am afraid, even an anti-Semitic one. (*Ibid.*)

What is attacked in passages of this sort is at bottom the 'German national' prejudice and programme. The *Volk* is always referred to merely as a mob or a rabble, certainly not as a 'community', and the claim that it constitutes the basis of a nation is dismissed with such aphorisms as: 'A *Volk* is a detour of nature to get to six or seven great men. Yes, and then to get round them' (*BGE*, 126). The assertion that the Germans are a uniquely gifted race is countered with: 'as far as Germany extends it *ruins* culture' (*EH*, II.3,5). Anti-Semitism is characterized as an 'obscenity' (*HA*, 475). A longer representative passage will give an idea of how completely contrary his outlook was to that of the rising nationalist movement:

If a people is suffering and *wants* to suffer from nationalistic nervous fever and political ambition, it must be expected that all sorts of clouds and disturbances – in short, little attacks of stupidity – will pass over its spirit into the bargain: among present-day Germans, for example, now the anti-French stupidity, now the anti-Jewish, now the anti-Polish, now the Christian-romantic, now the Wagnerian, now the Teutonic, now the Prussian ... About the Jews, for example ... I have never met a German who was favourably inclined towards the Jews; and however unconditionally all cautious and politic men may have repudiated real anti-Jewism [*Antisemiterei*], even this caution and policy is not directed against this class of feeling itself but only against its dangerous immoderation, and especially against the distasteful and shameful way in which this immoderate feeling is expressed ... That Germany has an ample *sufficiency* of Jews, that the German stomach, German blood has difficulty ... in absorbing even this quantum of 'Jew' ... that is the clear declaration and language of a universal instinct to which one must pay heed ... 'Let in no more Jews. And close especially the doors to the East (also to Austria)!' – thus commands the instinct of a people whose type is still weak and undetermined, so that it could easily be effaced . . . by a stronger race. The Jews, however, are beyond all doubt the strongest, toughest and purest race at present living in Europe; they know how to prevail even under the worst conditions . . . by means of virtues which one would like to stamp as vices – thanks above all to a resolute faith which does not have to be ashamed before 'modern ideas' . . . A thinker who has the future of Europe on his conscience will . . . take the Jews into account as he will take the Russians, as the immediately surest and most probable factors in the great game and struggle of forces . . . That the Jews *could*, if they wanted – or if they were compelled, as the anti-Semites seem to want – even now predominate, indeed quite literally rule over Europe, is certain; that they are *not* planning and working towards that is equally certain. In the meantime they are, rather, wanting and wishing . . . to be absorbed and assimilated by and into Europe . . . one ought to pay heed to this inclination and impulse . . . and go out to meet it: for which it would perhaps be a good idea to eject the anti-Semitic ranters from the country . . . the stronger and already more firmly formed types of the new Germanism could enter into relations with them with the least hesitation; the aristocratic officer of the March [of Brandenburg], for example: it would be interesting . . . to see whether the genius of money and patience (and above all a little mind and spirituality, of which there is a plentiful lack in the persons above mentioned) could not be added and bred into the hereditary art of commanding and obeying, in both of which the above mentioned land is today classic. (*BGE*, 251)

The outlook implied in this passage is repeated in dozens of places: 'The anti-Semites do not forgive the Jews for having "spirit" – and money. Anti-Semite – another name for the "underprivileged"' (*WP*, 864); 'To enthusiasm for the "German national character" I have indeed attained very little, but even less to the wish to keep this "glorious" race *pure*. On the contrary, on the contrary . . .' (letter of 21 March 1885 to his mother); 'I find life in present-day Germany altogether unwholesome, it has an enervating effect upon me; and every time I go there my cynicism [*Menschenverachtung*] grows to dangerous proportions' (letter of 'summer 1886' to Franz Overbeck). In what were probably the last lines he wrote for publication, after a hit at 'Europe's flatland, Germany', he warned the Italians against persisting in the Triple Alliance: 'with the "*Reich*"', he said, 'an intelligent people can make only a *mésalliance* . . .' (*NCW*, Foreword).

VII

Nietzsche spent the first four-and-a-half years of his life in a Lutheran parsonage. His mother, with whom he lived until he left for boarding school at the age of fourteen was, as one might expect of a woman whose father and husband were clergymen, intensely pious; and also members of the household until their death were two aunts, unmarried sisters of his late father, and both unswerving believers. His own sister, who was only eighteen months younger than he, was also one of the faithful. With this background it is perhaps not surprising that he should have forsworn Christianity at quite an early age: some commentators, indeed, have found the existence of such a home life entirely sufficient to account for the subsequent existence of *The Anti-Christ*. An examination of his life and thought reveals, however, that some of the specifically Lutheran feelings remained with him to the end, while his critique of the conceptual basis of Christianity as such was in fact far more radical than can possibly be accounted for by any theory of 'revolt' against an oppressive family background.

Lutheranism is a form of Protestant Christianity in which fatalism and sentimentality are the dominant affects: the belief that whatever happens is the will of God, and the belief that the will of God corresponds with one's own will, that is to say, that what one would like to be the case, God too would like to be the case. It is a sort of pleasant determinism which has an ameliorating effect on the sin-and-damnation aspect of the Christian faith: for if God directs all things, and if God feels as I do, then God will never damn me: dear God, '*der liebe Gott*', would not be capable of such a thing. This idea of God lies at the heart of Lutheran sentimentality and tends to exclude the other objects of Christian devotion: there exists a tendency to ignore, not only the Virgin, but Jesus as well, and to speak only to the Father. There is in Lutheran piety a manliness in love of which Jesus is not mature enough to be the object: resembling a son's love for his father – or, to come closer to its historical origin, a vassal's love for his lord – it requires in its Lord a combination of reliability, wisdom and loving kindness which cannot easily be imagined in anyone under forty.

Whatever may be said against this conception of Godhood, it at least makes its devotees happy and not miserable, and a child will find it an easy conception to grasp. Nietzsche had no piercing-eyed Christs to give him nightmares, or any horrific pictures of a possible hellish afterlife to keep him awake. God was like his father, the pastor of Röcken; or rather, since his father died at the age of thirty-six when Nietzsche was only four years old, he was like his father as he loved to remember him: 'Gifted with spirit and a warm heart, adorned with all the virtues of a Christian, he lived a peaceful, simple and happy life, and was loved and admired by all who knew him' (*From my Life*, 1858, by thirteen-year-old Nietzsche); 'a tall, slim figure with delicate features and of a kind and pleasing demeanour. Liked and welcomed everywhere, as much for his witty conversation as for his kindly sympathy, honoured and loved by the peasants as a parson whose words and deeds were alike beneficial, the most fond husband and loving father, he was the perfect model of a country parson' ('The Course of my Life', 1861).

A perfect model of a country parson is, of course, what he is describing. German literature of the 1820s to 1850s is full of model country parsons; the Vicar of Wakefield was their ancestor, and Mr Pickwick their lay contemporary; and the source of their hold on the imagination of German readers was their likeness to the Lutheran God, of whom they are little domestic reproductions. This is the other side of the Lutheran coin: the degeneration of God to Mr Pickwick is inherent in an idea of God in which the quality of loving kindness is emphasized at the expense of every other; and where the relationship between man and God is fundamentally that of loving vassal to loving liege lord, man degenerates to Sam Weller, *ein treuer Diener seines Herrn*.

This was Nietzsche's idea of God when he was a child; and the autobiography he wrote at the age of thirteen therefore ends with the following confession of faith:

> I have already experienced so much – joy and sorrow, cheerful
> things and sad things – but in everything God has safely led me
> as a father leads his weak little child . . . I have firmly resolved
> within me to dedicate myself for ever to His service. May the
> dear Lord give me strength and power to carry out my intention
> and protect me on my life's way. Like a child I trust in His grace:
> He will preserve us all, that no misfortune may befall us. But His
> holy will be done! All He gives I will joyfully accept: happiness

and unhappiness, poverty and wealth, and boldly look even death in the face, which shall one day unite us all in eternal joy and bliss. Yes, dear Lord, let Thy face shine upon us for ever! Amen! ('From my Life')

It is a fine expression of Lutheran sentimentality: but I ask whether the feelings expressed in it are not precisely the same feelings as those expressed in this confession of faith made thirty years later in another autobiography: 'My formula for greatness in a human being is *amor fati*: that one wants nothing to be other than it is, not in the future, not in the past, not in all eternity. Not merely to endure that which happens of necessity, still less to dissemble it . . . but to *love* it' (*EH*, II. 10). Affectively the two passages are, surely, very similar, and we shall discover other affective similarities between Lutheranism and Nietzsche's mature conceptions: but this ought not to surprise us if we reflect that the affective aspect of religion is its superficial aspect, and the affects which become attached to a religious belief can equally well attach themselves to something else.

VIII

For every institution, from a universal religion to a poker game, presents a twofold aspect: the affective and superficial, and the rational and structural. It is the affective element which ensures the existence of the institution in fact: if nobody wanted it, it would not exist; but it is the rational element which makes its existence possible in principle. The affective element is superficial because it does not determine the structure, which exists independently of it, and the institution could in principle exist without it. The structure, on the other hand, is altogether free of affective connotation, is not the object of any affect, and depends upon nothing external to it but only upon its own internal rationale.

Consider the case of a poker game. Poker games exist in fact, let us say, because of the existence of faith (in the honesty of the participants), hope (of winning), and love (of gambling): in any event, they exist in fact because they are wanted. But their existence would be impossible in principle but for the existence of the rules of poker. Love of gambling is the affective and superficial aspect of a poker game, the rules of poker are its rational structure. The rules could in principle exist even if nobody had ever wanted to gamble; conversely, although a love of gambling may exist, nobody loves the rules of poker, which do not engage the affects at all. These rules are a set of requirements consistent with one another and with reality: if any of them were impossibilities – for example, if a player were required to lay down his cards and at the same time retain them in his hand – the game of which they are the structure could not be played (could not exist), no matter how great was the love of gambling which brought the players together.

If you now apply these considerations to a universal religion, you will see that sentiments, of whatever kind, are not the materials from which it is constructed; you will see that its structure is not affective but rational. The rational structure of a religion is called its dogmatic theology: a dogmatic view of the nature of things which must hold together if the religion is to exist.

Here again you must distinguish between essential and non-essential: there are clearly elements in the structure of every institution which could be other than they are and elements which could not if the institution is to exist. Reverting to the example of poker, we can see straightaway that the rule laying down the method of scoring is different in kind from the rule stipulating that the participants must act one after another; and that a similar distinction exists between the absolute value of a card and its value relative to the other cards. Distinctions of this type apply equally to universal religions: the dogma of the Holy Trinity, for example, is of the same type as the rule that a certain card is the ten of spades. Even the facts of the life, death and resurrection of Jesus as taught by the Christian churches are not fundamental to the Christian religion, since the asserted true nature of God thus revealed could have been revealed in quite other ways ('advanced' theologians of course recognize this and do not defend the authenticity of the story of Jesus as if the survival of Christianity were at issue).

Now, there are three essential Christian dogmas relevant to a consideration of Nietzsche's critique of Christianity: three assertions about the nature of things which belong to the structure of the Christian religion and whose removal would bring the building down.

Reality is unchanging   God is from everlasting to everlasting, to endless years the same. This is the ground of all Christian faith, and not only of the faith in immortality. If God could change or were capricious all Christian dogmas would be provisional. Good and evil would no longer be good and evil if God's will could alter. The worst consequence of all is that, if God could change, he could 'wither and perish' as we do: reality could pass into nonentity. The mere possibility of this is sufficient to negate Christianity.

History is a process God, eternally the same, therefore outside time, created time as the mode through which to reveal himself to his creation. This revelation had a beginning and will have an end: the period between is occupied and caused to exist by the progressive (temporal) unfolding of the nature of God. This vast drama is the means through which God and man are brought into contact with one another and the life of man furnished with a meaning; without it, God and man would exist on different planes of reality. Life would make no sense if God were not 'working his purpose out'; prayer, worship, praise, the whole apparatus of 'divine service', the whole conception of 'serving God', would likewise be senseless: God would be a being with whom man had nothing to do. The church, the priest, the parson would have nothing to offer if history were not the process of divine unfolding.

Man has free will The creator is perfect, but the creation is imperfect: if the creation were not imperfect it would not need the creator: if the creation did not need the creator it would have no need of a 'mediator', a 'redeemer', a 'church'. But how can a perfect creator create an imperfect creation? When the creative will created all things except itself it also created will, which meant that the creation could go its own way: only thus would it be a true creation and not merely the creator over again. And the creation has exercised this will to act in a way counter to the creator's will: an eventuality which was part of the creator's design, even essential to his purpose, yet none the less and necessarily 'a fall', a deviation from perfection. Thus the distance between creator and creation is explained by the existence of human free will: without free will in man this distance would not have arisen and the 'mediating' church would have had no function to perform.

It was at the destruction of these three dogmas that Nietzsche worked for most of his life: his polemics against Christian morality and the allegedly fatal role played by Christianity in world history, important though they are, are relatively specialized aspects of his philosophy compared with his denial of the existence of an unchanging reality, of a linear temporal process, of purpose or meaning in life, and of freedom of will. His positive philosophy is, indeed, in large part an attempt to formulate how one would have to live if existence were governed by chance, if there were no purpose or moral order in the world, and if man were actually the 'supreme being'.

In all these respects he became and remained radically anti-Christian – far more radically so than is realized by those who see him as having been merely 'in revolt' against the religious sentiments of his home. This 'revolt', indeed, was never really accomplished: the sentiments remained, and returned in disguised form. In terms of the analogy we have been using, he retained a love of gambling but rejected the rules of poker.

IX

In a passage which he subsequently had second thoughts about and revised, and then had third thoughts about and crossed out – which did not hinder the editors of *The Will to Power* from publishing it as section 749 of that book – Nietzsche wrote:

> The princes of Europe ought in fact to consider whether they can do without our support. We immoralists – we are today the only power which needs no allies in order to come to victory: we are thus the strongest of the strong by far. We do not even require the lie: what other power can do without it? A powerful seduction fights on our side, the most powerful perhaps that exists: the seduction of truth ... 'Truth'? Who puts this word into my mouth? But I remove it again: but I disclaim that proud word: no, we do not need that either, we shall come to power and victory even without truth. The enchantment which fights on our side, the eye of Venus that charms even our opponents and makes them blind, is the *magic of the extreme*, the seduction exercised by everything extreme: we immoralists – we are *the most extreme* ...

Much could be written about this passage, and especially about the fact that Nietzsche erased it. The only part of it which concerns us here is the suppressed confession of extremism: the boast that, quite apart from the question of truth or falsehood, 'the immoralist' has at his disposal the powerful seduction exercised by all extreme positions.

Nietzsche was conscious of his extremism, but he also knew how much could be argued against extremism: its seductive power itself is, when viewed in the light of his own criteria, an argument against it. The above note cannot be dated more exactly than some time between the spring and autumn of 1887, with revision some time between the spring and autumn of 1888; but in a long note dated 10 June 1887, we read the observation: 'Extreme positions are not succeeded by moderate ones, but by *contrary* extreme positions'; and later on in the note the question, 'who will prove the *strongest*' in the coming crisis of nihilism receives the answer: 'The most moderate – those who do not have *need* of any extreme articles of faith' (*WP*, 55).

Again we must bear in mind that this note, although it was allowed to stand in his notebook, was also left unpublished; but a sort of objection to extremism does appear among his published writings of this late period as aphorism 30 of the first chapter of *Twilight of the Idols*: 'One seldom commits only one rash act. In the first rash act one always does too much. For just that reason one usually commits a second – and then one does too little.'

Extremism appears in both these passages as an emotional over-reaction, that is to say as an aspect of weakness, of inability for rational self-control; and it was perhaps because Nietzsche came to see that that was what it was that he crossed out the passage in which he boasted of his own extremism and drew attention to that in it which possesses strength, namely its power to seduce others – a power which it possesses independently of whether it embodies truth or falsehood.

For, his insight into the nature of extremism notwithstanding, Nietzsche constantly tended towards extremes: this conflict is an aspect of the complexity of his mind and one reason every construction of his philosophy will be in some ways an oversimplification; but it also means that his relationship to his immediate background can be accurately depicted in relatively few and simple lines, for here the dominant impression is always one of extreme antithesis. We have seen already that he stood opposed to the principal political currents in the Germany of his time, and that his attitude towards the fundamentals of the religion in which he was raised was one of complete denial; and we shall now see that he differed just as radically from the third tradition relevant to a consideration of his thought, the philosophical.

X

Everyone who discusses Nietzsche discusses his 'precursors', and one can derive a lot of pleasurable instruction from discovering the threads with which he is connected to this or that philosopher of the past. Unfortunately, so many names have been named that the whole procedure is likely to become confusing rather than instructive until one has undertaken something fundamentally far simpler: an investigation of his relationship to the totality of his philosophical background – that is to say, to the state of philosophy as it was when he first became an independent mind.

From short histories of philosophy you will learn that Nietzsche 'came after' Schopenhauer. This is true chronologically, and in so far as Schopenhauer certainly directed Nietzsche's mind, as he did many other minds, towards the irrational and 'subconscious' as the source of human motivations; but in any other sense it is a statement more likely to obscure than illuminate Nietzsche's relationship to his predecessors.

The effect on Nietzsche's thought of Schopenhauer's metaphysical philosophy was certainly far less than that of 'evolutionism', and it would therefore make more sense to say that, philosophically, he 'came after' Darwin. But Darwin's specific contribution to the theory of evolution influenced him only in a negative sense – he denied the validity of 'natural selection' and a 'struggle for life' – and Darwin was in any case too recent to constitute part of his 'tradition'.

If one is to stick to the 'came after' form – which does have its uses – one would do better to say that Nietzsche came after Hegel, inasmuch as Hegel summarized and brought to completion a tradition which had lasted two millennia, and it was this tradition which constituted his real 'predecessor'.

When he was born, Western philosophy was something relatively complete. Plato was the first real philosopher, Hegel the last: before Plato there had been only the rude forefathers, after Hegel there could be only *epigoni*. A certain way of looking at things had attained the theoretical limit of its development: during two thousand years the fundamentals of this outlook had not changed; modifications, new insights, disagreements, novel theories had not affected the basic suppositions, and in Hegel's philosophy even these modifications and disagreements had been accounted for and incorporated within the grand design.

Of the basic suppositions which distinguish Western philosophy from Plato to Hegel it will again be useful to select the three most relevant to a consideration of Nietzsche's thought and to an understanding of how extreme his rejection of his tradition was.

Belief in a correspondence between reality and reason The undertaking was, as a whole, an attempt to subject the world, 'reality', 'being' as we experience it, to rational explanation, and that implies a belief that the attempt may succeed: without a belief in some sort of correspondence between reality and reason, Western philosophy would not have come into existence. Statements of this belief, or statements which imply it and would make no sense without it, are to be found, not only within the period Plato to Hegel, but during the age preceding it, when philosophy in the full meaning of the word was, according to traditional understanding, in course of preparation. 'Everything that is has always been and always will be', said Melissus of Samos, speaking in accents he had learned from Parmenides. 'For if it had come into being there must necessarily have been nothing before it came into being. But if there was nothing – something could under no circumstances come into being out of nothing.' The statement attempts to describe, not what is as a matter of fact, but what is because it has to be; it attempts to lay down the law as to the necessary character of things, and does so by ascribing to reality the property of according with the rules of reason. The question 'Why is the nature of being as it is?' is answered with 'Because reason cannot have it otherwise'. At the other end of this two-thousand-year period, Hegel asserts that 'the real is the rational and the rational the real', and that 'reason is the sovereign of the world', which is again an iteration of the same belief that the structure of reason and the structure of reality are identical.

Belief in degrees of reality There is a sense of the word 'real' in which everything that is, is real; but there is another sense of it in which some things are real and other things only appear to be. The distinction between 'appearance' and 'reality' is again as old as Parmenides – indeed, as old as recorded Western thought – and is to be found throughout the entire period. 'Now One grows up out of Many to exist alone,' said Empedocles, 'now it divides itself to become Many again ... This constant changing never ceases: now everything is united into One by Love, now it separates again in the enmity engendered by Strife.' This sounds less like the beginning of science than the continuation of mythology by other means: in fact, it is an attempt to describe the 'real' nature of the world in terms of hidden entities. The eyes of Empedocles saw earth and sky and sea, but his mind saw 'behind' these phenomena: the senses, one understands, are necessitated to error; only the mind can know what 'really' is. This division of the world into appearance and reality was from the beginning a radical division: the 'real world' was from the first totally different from the apparent, and every characteristic of the 'apparent world' was demonstrated to be inapplicable to the real. In Plato and in Hegel, the world we know is in some sort an inferior or partial world: only Plato's Forms or Eternal Ideas, of which the phenomena of the perceived world are imperfect reflections, and Hegel's Absolute Spirit, of which the perceived world is the dialectical unfolding, are fully and wholly 'real'.

Belief in the ethical significance of the world The universe we observe, from the galaxies hurtling through space to the sub-microscopic world of the bacteria, seems to lack all ethical significance, yet Western philosophy has insisted from the very first that its ethical conceptions belong to the heart and nature of things. The earliest complete sentences of Western philosophy are these of Anaximander of Miletus: 'The beginning and origin of the things which are is the *apeiron* [that which is undetermined, formless, and boundless]. Into that from which the things that are arise, however, they pass away again, as they are obliged to do; for they give satisfaction and reparation to one another for their injustice, as is appointed according to the ordering of time.' Anaximander probably conceived of the *apeiron* as material, as formless matter, for early Greek science was firmly materialist; and Burnet (*Greek Philosophy*) understands the above proposition as belonging to the realm of physics. 'This conception of justice and injustice recurs . . . in Ionic natural philosophy and always in the same connection,' he writes. 'It refers to the encroachment of one opposite "element" upon another.' Russell (*History of Western Philosophy*) is willing to grant the conception a little more breadth of reference, and says that the 'idea of justice . . . played a part in Greek religion and philosophy which is not altogether easy for a modern to understand', but was associated with the idea of 'not overstepping eternally fixed bounds'. An idea, belonging to physics, in this development of it becomes metaphysical, and is attached to religion as well as philosophy. Gomperz (*The Greek Thinkers*, I) goes further still: he says that, whatever Anaximander's view of the origin of things may have been, there is no doubt that 'he was quite clear that every created thing is doomed to destruction', and that this 'conviction afforded him a satisfaction which we may character-ize as a moral or religious sentiment.' Gomperz even goes so far as to suggest that Anaximander's view of life might have been the same as that of the Mephistopheles of Goethe: '*alles, was entsteht, ist wert, dass es zugrunde geht.*' This suggestion, still in the last resort tentative, that Anaximander's proposition is at heart an ethical one ('*ist wert*'), is the

39

same as that which the early Nietzsche had already made, not at all tentatively, in his most fully developed interpretation of the 'pre-Socratic' philosophers: in *Philosophy in the Tragic Age of the Greeks* (1873) he calls Anaximander 'a true pessimist', illumines his proposition by comparing it with 'a similar reflection' of Schopenhauer's – 'The correct standard by which to judge every human being is that he is really a creature which ought not to exist at all, but which expiates its existence by manifold suffering and death ... We expiate our birth firstly by living and secondly by dying' – and interprets Anaximander as seeing 'all becoming as a punishable emancipation from being ... as an injustice to be atoned for with destruction' (section 4).

This last interpretation ought not to seem at all far-fetched, since it merely ascribes already to Anaximander a tendency, inherent in almost all his successors, to bestow upon all activity an *ethical* meaning. In Plato's philosophy there exists an Eternal Idea of justice in the same way as there exists an Eternal Idea of a horse; all the virtues are reflections of the Ideas of them; and the supreme Idea is the Idea of 'the Good', which may fairly be taken to mean what the Christian means by God in his ethical aspect. Thus to Plato 'good and evil' exists in the nature of things, and the highest task of reason is to discover it; thus 'knowledge makes virtuous', and philosophy is not only 'science' but also the road to the good life.

It is this aspect of philosophy which has done more than any other to enhance its *value* and to render its value apparent: it dispelled the suspicion that philosophizing might be an *idle* occupation, and without it Hegel could hardly have set philosophy formally at the apex of human culture as the supreme activity of mankind.

The hold of these three beliefs on the Western mind has been and is very strong; strongest, perhaps, in the case of those people – who are, of course, the great majority – who hold them without ever consciously formulating them: but Nietzsche consistently denied them all. That, fundamentally and in brief, is his relationship to his philosophical background.

XI

Reading German literature is often a dismaying study. More of it is dead than ought really to be possible in the literature of a living language. Inferior imitation of foreign models is endemic and seemingly ineradicable: A is the *German* B, X is the *German* Y. Original creations are often parish-pump affairs not at all likely to grip the attention of anyone except a 'student of German life and letters' and not always his.

In a passage with the ironical title *The treasury of German prose*, Nietzsche wrote: 'Apart from Goethe's writings, and in particular Goethe's Conversations with Eckermann, the best German book there is, what is there really of German prose literature that it would be worthwhile to read over and over again? Lichtenberg's aphorisms, the first book of Jung-Stilling's autobiography, Adalbert Stifter's *Nach-sommer*, and Gottfried Keller's *Leute von Seldwyla* – and that for the present is all' (*WS*, 109). In the same volume (125) he says that, of the six 'great ancestors' of German literature, Goethe belongs 'in a higher order of literatures than "national literatures"', and the other five – Klopstock, Herder, Wieland, Lessing and Schiller – 'are unmistakably becoming or have already become antiquated'. To the question whether there exists such a thing as a 'German classic', he answers in effect 'No'. This is to be very critical and selective, yet on the whole it would be hard to argue against him.

German literature, in short, is often provincial and inept and seems to lack continuity, not to speak of organic development. For these things you have to look elsewhere. Goethe, the tremendous, dis-couraging presence of Goethe, drove many of the best and most original minds out of 'literature' into other fields (this, at least, is my theory). There is no Tolstoy or Dostoyevsky, no Balzac or Flaubert, no Dickens or Mark Twain, in nineteenth-century German literature: instead there is Hegel and Schopenhauer, Marx and Freud. It is in German philosophy that you will find 'development', one thing leading to another, and a consistently high level of performance. (And, of course, in music, in which form alone the stream of German lyricism can become audible to the non-German reader: German music as a branch of literature, with Wagner simply as the most obvious case, the German composer whose music is palpably conceptual, musical sounds 'standing for' extra-musical qualities, ideas, things.)

Now where, within this context, can you 'place' Nietzsche? At a unique junction between German philosophy and German literature. He is the most signal instance of a German philosopher who is also a master of 'style', a technician who need not fear comparison with any writer, whether of German or of any other language. (The union of philosophy and literature also takes place in Schopenhauer, but at a lower level of achievement on both counts.) As a philosopher, Nietzsche belongs to the native tradition which started with Leibniz; as a writer of German prose he is arguably the best craftsman since Luther. He is one of the few German writers who offer something which cannot be obtained as well or better from another literature: you can miss ninety per cent of 'German literature' and miss only that; but if you miss Nietzsche you miss an area of human sensibility.

3

Development

Nietzsche's philosophy is not to be found in any single book, nor in the books of any single period of his life. It is, rather, an aggregate of all his books. It is a process of development, not a body of propositions.

To 'know' his philosophy therefore amounts to experiencing this development. There exists a widespread belief that it is a matter of indifference which of his books you read first or in what order you read them: but the opposite is the case if your intention in reading them is to understand his philosophy, for his philosophy is, so to speak, his mind's autobiography of which each book is a chapter. You will get far more out of him if you regard the entire series of books as if it were *one* book.

This philosophical development does not, however, proceed in an unbroken rising curve: it appears as a series of fairly straight lines broken off and resumed higher up. Biographically, it can be viewed as a number of situations which became intolerable and whose intolerability propelled the philosopher into action; or as a career punctuated by crises precipitated by a deeply-felt sense of frustration and attended by physical and 'psychical' symptoms. So viewed, his active life falls into four periods.

To 1865 Nietzsche lived at the parsonage at Röcken until the death of his father in 1849; the family then moved to Naumberg, where he attended the town boys' school and subsequently high school. In 1858 he won a free place at Pforta school, the Prussian Rugby, and from there he went on, in October 1864, to Bonn university as a student of theology and classical philology. He subsequently abandoned theology

and after transferring, in August 1865, to Leipzig, he read Schopenhauer's *World as Will and Idea* and was converted to 'Schopenhaueranism'. This earliest period is thus characterized by the relinquishment of
the religion in which he was born and the acquisition of a philosophy
which amounted to a new religion. During the course of this evolution
he also acquired a knowledge of and then a familiarity with the
principles of philosophical inquiry; and a number of seeds planted at
this time later germinated. The moment of crisis, which came at
Easter 1865, was his abandonment of the study of theology, and
therewith his formal renunciation of his religion.

1865 to 1876   At Leipzig, Nietzsche became a star classical scholar, and
in February 1869 he was appointed to the chair of classical philology
at Basel at the unprecedentedly youthful age of twenty-four, Leipzig
awarding him his doctorate without examination. He had met Wagner
in November 1868 and became a follower of his, and during his first
years at Basel he associated very closely with Wagner and his family
and assisted him in establishing the Bayreuth Festival in 1876. His first
books – *The Birth of Tragedy* and the four *Untimely Meditations* – were
published. During these years his inner life, and a good deal of his
outer life, was dominated by Schopenhauer and Wagner. As Wagner
was also a Schopenhaueran, adherence to Schopenhauer and adherence
to and practical support for Wagner formed in Nietzsche's mind a single
entity; and since Wagner associated or even identified the success of his
artistic plans with the future wellbeing of the German nation,
Nietzsche's involvement with them focused his mind upon 'German
national affairs' more directly in this period than in any other. At the
same time a degree of unconscious resistance to all of this, present from
the first, gradually increased in intensity. Even his earliest publications
were subtly infected with *Untreue*; and the sense that he was making a
false start which came more and more to possess him was strengthened
by the impression made on him by his reading of such 'materialist'
writers as F. A. Lange and Paul Rée, and his growing interest in 'natural
science'. The moment of crisis came in July 1876, during preparations
for the first Bayreuth Festival: he fled from Bayreuth and therewith
from Wagner, and began work on *Human, All Too Human*.

1876 to 1883   The decline in his health, which had begun about 1871,
compelled him to abandon the Basel chair (Easter 1879), and he was
retired on a pension. Thenceforth he lived in lodgings and hotel

rooms mainly in Sils-Maria, in the Ober-Engadine, and in Nice. The condition of total scepticism, inherent in the crisis of Easter 1865 but blocked and held back by Schopenhauer-Wagner, broke through with *Human, All Too Human*; his stylistic genius, likewise held back, also broke through. There is a great feeling of liberation, of the exercise of hitherto unused powers, and of a vast widening of interests. To this period belongs the series of aphoristic books on the pattern established by *Human, All Too Human: Assorted Opinions and Maxims, The Wanderer and his Shadow, Daybreak*, and *The Gay Science*: reflections touching on the whole gamut of European culture whose controlling tendency is a destructive analysis of cultural values. But this analysis is attended by a growing and at last overwhelming awareness of the nihilist and ultimately dispiriting and life-denying effect of such radical scepticism, and consequently of increasingly vehement self-encouragements to find a way out of and beyond it. Biographically, the period was one of mounting ill-health and isolation, and of a continual failure of personal relationships which came to a climax in total disappointment in the one serious 'love affair' of his life, when he tried and failed to win Lou Salomé. At the end of 1882 he was seized by a sense of having reached – emotionally, intellectually and physically – a terminus; and he contemplated suicide. The turning-point of this crisis came with the turn of the year: in the January of 1883 despair gave way to euphoria and 'inspiration', and he began to work furiously on *Thus Spoke Zarathustra*.

1883 to 1889   By now virtually alone, Nietzsche lived only to write. The discovery of a means of transcendence which grows out of total scepticism was proclaimed in *Zarathustra*, where the 'superman', the 'will to power' and 'eternal recurrence' are introduced. *Zarathustra* inaugurated a period of continual inventiveness, in respect both of ideas and of literary style: *Beyond Good and Evil* and *On the Genealogy of Morals* are probably his 'best books' – an incredible display of weightless erudition and solid originality, of new things that are going to last. The former despair had gone, but was replaced by an increasing irritation at being ignored which developed into an overcompensatory 'sense of mission' and at last into a genuine *folie de grandeur*. At the same time – and this is what makes the late Nietzsche unique and in some respects uncanny – there was no decline in intellectual ability or literary mastery: the prefaces to the new editions of his earlier books are among the most beautiful 'pieces of writing' in German, and he had, indeed, become the greatest master of German prose since Luther, although he was still almost unknown. The year 1888 was a climax in every respect: whatever inhibitions he had left he now discarded, and being himself as tense as a tightrope, he tautened his language until it attained what is probably the maximum degree of concentration possible in German. But the 'brilliance' of the language is in places unnaturally bright, and in *Ecce Homo* especially there are clear indications of unbalance. A major work planned during this period – *The Will to Power: an Attempt at a Revaluation of All Values* – was abandoned during 1888, and a shorter work, called *The Revaluation of All Values*, substituted but also subsequently abandoned: the materials for these works – comprising an enormous quantity of manuscript notes, some of them coherent passages, others no more than jottings or lists of themes – are still in course of publication.

The conclusion came at the very beginning of 1889, when he suffered a mental breakdown from which he did not recover and after which he wrote nothing more. During the eleven-and-a-half years between his collapse and his death in August 1900 he became famous and his books began to be bought and read: but of this he knew nothing.

II: To 1865

The nature of the crisis-situation produced by Nietzsche's renunciation of his religion, and something of its lasting effect, can probably best be exposed by considering his emotional relationship with the idea of 'truth'.

To Nietzsche, truth was usually something terrible, difficult and agonizing; it had 'the heart' against it, and the seeker after truth must therefore 'destroy his own humanity'. Referring to the second crisis of his life – that which separated him from Wagner and 'German affairs' – he wrote: 'I took sides . . . *against* myself and *with* everything that was painful and difficult for precisely *me*' (*HA*, II, Preface). In the résumé of his intellectual life in *Ecce Homo*, he said:

> Philosophy, as I have hitherto understood and lived it, is a
> voluntary living in ice and high mountains – a seeking out of
> everything strange and questionable in existence, all that has
> hitherto been excommunicated by morality . . . How much truth
> can a spirit *bear*, how much truth can a spirit *dare*? That has
> become for me more and more the real measure of value. Error
> . . . is not blindness, error is *cowardice* . . . (Foreword, 3)

In *The Anti-Christ* he asserts: 'Truth has had to be fought for every step of the way, almost everything else dear to our hearts, on which our love and our trust in life depend, has had to be sacrificed to it: ... the service of truth is the hardest service' (50).

This is not a particularly common attitude: for, although most people would probably stop short of asserting that beauty is truth, truth beauty, they none the less do incline towards believing in the truth of that which makes them happy. To Nietzsche, however, that something was beautiful or made happy was a reason for suspecting it to be false. 'Error is cowardice' does not make much sense until you realize it means 'Truth is something to inspire fear'.

Let us seek a possible origin of this attitude in the earliest occasion on which he discovered an important new 'truth'. He left his home for the first time in October 1858 to go to Pforta. He was within ten days of his fourteenth birthday. His father had been dead for nine years: to say that he had not been forgotten would be to suggest that he might have been, but to the Lutheran piety represented by Nietzsche's mother and sister, and at the time of his departure by Nietzsche himself, this possibility did not exist, for to them Pastor Nietzsche was not dead at all in any radical sense. He had 'gone before' to a place whither they would all in due course go and be reunited with him. To Lutheran piety – but not of course to that species of piety alone – immortality is a fact: having created a human soul, God the Father will not, or even cannot, uncreate it; and death is, in Nietzsche's words, that 'which shall one day unite us all in eternal joy and bliss' (*From my Life*).

Now, when survival after death is believed in so firmly that it is taken simply for a fact, so that the dead are not really dead at all, denial of this belief may, if your father is dead, become a sort of parricide. If you deny immortality, you deny that the dead are still living: and if you have previously believed in immortality with the intensity of faith demonstrated by the Nietzsche who wrote *From my Life*, the affect attending such a denial may be that you have killed them. On the level of cold rationality, of course, you will argue that what you deny is that there ever has been such a thing as immortality, and that the dead always were dead even when you falsely believed otherwise. But cold rationality is an abstraction, something analysed out of the existential phenomena of the particular thoughts of a particular human being, and this reality is influenced by all sorts of affects – if, indeed, it is not wholly a product of them. In the real situation in which Nietzsche 'intellectually' denied the truth of Christianity, he therefore at the same time destroyed 'in his heart' that which had formerly drawn life from belief in that truth.

If this was, in fact, the pathos attending the first reversal of 'the truth', it would explain why thereafter the pursuit of truth should be associated in his mind with defiance of 'the heart' and sacrifice of 'almost everything else dear to our hearts', and why truth itself should appear to him as something hard or 'immoral'.

His abandonment of Christianity took place gradually during the years he was at Pforta and was complete by the time he left that school for Bonn University in October 1864. Its cause was, perhaps, nothing more remarkable than the acquisition of a 'classical education'. The curriculum at Pforta was heavily weighted in favour of the classics, and Nietzsche quickly became a classical scholar of unusual accomplishment. Only five years after he left Pforta he was recommended for and got the chair of classical philology at Basel at the age of twenty-four, and his doctorate was awarded him by Leipzig without examination. All who had anything to do with him as classicist are agreed that, in his hands, 'classical studies' came to life: when discussing Greece and Rome, it was 'as if he spoke from his own knowledge of things quite self-evident and still completely valid' (Bernoulli: *Nietzsche und Overbeck* I, p. 67). This profound and 'intuitive' understanding of Greek and Roman civilization must have influenced his Christian beliefs, and could very well have been the instrument which destroyed them, through bringing to life in him a whole world *other than the Christian*. Arguments against the Christian outlook would have come later: the decisive *fact* would have been that Hellenic civilization had existed, flourished, and brought forth things considered to be of supreme value in entire ignorance and independence of Christianity – but with that the self-evidence of the Christian outlook upon which all naive faith must depend would have disappeared.

He experienced a recrudescence of Christian feeling at Easter 1861, when he was confirmed; but that was the end, and he never 'felt Christian' again. In a letter of a year later (April 1862), to two boyhood friends, he wrote: 'Christianity is essentially a matter for the heart . . . To acquire bliss through faith is to demonstrate nothing more than the ancient truth that only the heart, not knowledge, can make us happy'. The thought is the same as that expressed twenty-six years later in *The Anti-Christ*: 'The "kingdom of Heaven" is a condition of the heart . . . The "kingdom of God" is . . . an experience within a heart' (34); and already he is saying that truth (knowledge) is not that which makes us happy.

By the spring of 1862 he had definitely ceased to be a believing Christian, but the fact did not yet worry him very much: he was, after all, seventeen years old, and had plenty to occupy his mind and 'heart' other than the niceties of theology. So we find that, in the juvenile essays of this time, Christianity is thrown aside almost carelessly. In *On the Childhood of the Peoples*, for instance, he casually discards the 'next world' because it robs 'this world' of all divinity, and adds: 'That God became man shows only that man is not to seek his bliss in eternity, but to found his heaven on earth; the delusion of a supra-terrestrial world has placed the spirit of man in a false relation to the terrestrial: it was a product of the peoples' childhood.' The certainty of a reunion in 'eternal joy and bliss' had, in the course of three-and-a-half years, become a 'delusion'.

His earliest 'philosophical' essay, 'Fate and History' (March 1862), denounces Christian belief as 'custom and prejudice' imposed on us 'from our earliest days', and says, not without insight into his own future: 'To dare to launch out on the sea of doubt without compass or steersman is death and destruction for undeveloped heads; most are struck down by storms, very few discover new countries. From the midst of this immeasurable ocean of ideas one will often long to be back on firm land . . .'

If we move two years on, to Easter 1864 (Nietzsche now being nineteen), we find that the movement away from Christianity has increased in momentum. A passage in an essay called 'On Moods' is revealing: 'Strife is the perpetual food of the soul, and it knows how to extract the sweetness from it. The soul destroys and at the same time brings forth new things; it is a furious fighter, yet it gently draws its opponent to its side in an inner alliance.' The tendency of the thought expressed here is anti-Christian in one of the specific senses in which Nietzsche's mature philosophy is anti-Christian: it advocates 'strife' (*Kampf*) as a desirable state of the soul.

Six months later he left Pforta for Bonn, which he entered to study theology and philology; six months after going to Bonn he abandoned theology. This was now a serious and considered breach with religion: it had ceased to be an in part uncontrolled and unintentional drifting away and had become a clearly conscious decision and fact. On Easter Sunday 1865 he announced to his mother and sister that he was not coming to communion: there are few ways in which a member of a

Protestant Church can resign, but to refuse to attend Easter Communion is one of them, and in his own mind he was thenceforth, in fact and not only in imagination, 'out on the sea of doubt' without compass or steersman – a situation he had said was 'death and destruction for undeveloped heads'.

His mother and sister were horrified at what had happened: questions of belief and unbelief were realities in this household. There was a domestic scene, tears, recriminations: and after he had gone back to Bonn, his sister Elizabeth wrote him a long letter in which she tried to make him see that he was in error. He replied:

> Concerning your basic principle, that truth is always to be found on the side of the more difficult, I agree in part. However, it is difficult to believe that 2×2 does not equal 4; is it therefore true? On the other hand, is it really so difficult simply to accept as true everything we have been taught, and which has gradually taken firm root in us and is thought true by the circle of our relations and by many good people, and which moreover really does comfort and elevate men? Is that more difficult than to venture on new paths, in conflict with custom, in the insecurity which attends independence, experiencing many waverings of courage ... Is not the true inquirer totally indifferent to what the result of his inquiries may be? For, when we inquire, are we seeking for rest, peace, happiness? No, only for truth, even though it be in the highest degree ugly and repellent ... Here the ways of men divide: if you wish to strive for peace of soul and happiness, then believe; if you wish to be a disciple of truth, then inquire ... (letter of 11 June 1865)

The attitude expressed in this letter, that the search for truth is difficult and truth probably 'in the highest degree ugly and repellent', is a brave one, but of course in a youth of twenty it is a little too brave: it is bravado rather than bravery, or perhaps only one aspect of the state of mind brought about by his relinquishment of religion. Another aspect is revealed in the condition in which Nietzsche describes himself as living five months later, shortly after he had transferred from Bonn to Leipzig. 'I lived then,' he wrote, referring to the end of October or beginning of November 1865, 'in a state of helpless indecision.'

He had been accustomed to certitude, and now he had none: and this sensation must have been the predominating one during the summer of 1865. In due course he learned to tolerate this sensation, but he could not do so yet: he wanted to be back on 'firm land', and this desire rendered him vulnerable to excessive influence from without. That this was the case is revealed in his account, written nine months after it happened, of how he found a new certainty to replace the one he had lost:

> I lived then in a state of helpless indecision, alone with certain painful experiences and disappointments ... Now imagine how the reading of Schopenhauer's chief work must affect a man in such a condition. One day I found this book in ... [a] second-hand bookshop, picked it up as something quite unknown to me, and turned the pages. I do not know what demon whispered to me, 'Take this book home with you'. It was contrary to my usual practice of hesitating over the purchase of books. Once at hime, I threw myself onto the sofa with the newly-won treasure and began to let that energetic and gloomy genius operate upon me ... Here I saw a mirror in which I beheld the world, life and my own nature in a terrifying grandeur ... here I saw sickness and health, exile and refuge, Hell and Heaven. ('Retrospect of my Two Years at Leipzig')

The World as Will and Idea had replaced the Bible. It was not an intellectual decision: it was a conversion, a way out of a crisis.

III: 1865 to 1876

This period will seem a dull one unless you look beneath its surface. Ostensibly Nietzsche was playing a secondary role in his own life: he was a 'follower' of Schopenhauer and Wagner; under the surface, however, there was an intense conflict going on between these dominating influences and all those influences which resisted such domination. It was this conflict – between a too soon attained firm land and the adventurous scepticism which had launched him out on the sea of doubt – which constituted the situation of which the crisis of 1876 was the outcome and temporary resolution.

In later years he recognized that he had been unconsciously resisting Schopenhauer even when he had been calling himself his disciple. In the 'Essay in Self-Criticism' prefaced to the third (1886) edition of The Birth of Tragedy, for instance, he wrote that, even in the foreword to his first book:

Art – and *not* morality – is represented as the actual *metaphysical* activity of mankind; in the book itself the suggestive proposition recurs several times that it is only as an aesthetic phenomenon that the existence of the world is *justified*. The whole book, indeed, recognizes only an artistic meaning and hidden meaning behind all events . . . One may call this whole artist's metaphysics arbitrary, idle, fantastical – the essential thing about it is that it already betrays a spirit who will one day and regardless of the risk take up arms against the *moral* interpretation and significance of existence . . . Here that 'perversity of mind' against which Schopenhauer never wearied of hurling in advance his angriest curses and thunderbolts attains speech and formulation . . . (5)

The use of the word 'anti-Christ' a little further on to designate a non- and anti-moral world-outlook suggests that Nietzsche had in mind this passage from Schopenhauer: 'That the world has no ethical significance but only a physical one is the greatest and most pernicious of errors, the fundamental error, the intrinsically *perverse* view, and is probably at bottom also that which faith has personified as the Anti-Christ' (*Parerga and Paralipomena*, II. 109). At least he had some such passage in mind: and it shows that in this important matter, though not in this alone, a radically different, even antithetical drive was at work from that which propelled him into the ersatz religion of Schopenhaueranism.

Here we are interested in Schopenhauer and Wagner only in so far as Nietzsche was involved with them: we cannot attempt to do justice to them. Schopenhauer was above all a metaphysician and ethical theorist, Wagner above all an artist and a practical organizer: within these spheres they are very great men, outside them they decline to mediocrity or worse. I am not referring especially to their common anti-Semitism. Schopenhauer is great when he denies the faith of the Enlightenment in the autonomy of the mind and sees the origins and motives of human behaviour in an irrational will of which the mind is no more than an instrument; he is not great when, by a tortuous development of this idea, he proves that women are inherently inferior to men. Wagner is great when he organizes the life of an entire town in the middle of mercantile capitalist Germany for the production of a single work of art under ideal conditions; he is not great when he publishes a proposal for a 'controlled migration' of the populations of cold climes to warmer ones in the interest of vegetarianism.

As metaphysician, Schopenhauer substituted for luminous divine intelligence an unconscious will, and for all notions of the ground of being as mind, architect, purposeful intellect, 'divine artificer', the single notion of a blind drive to exist ('will to live'). As ethicist, he asserted the reprehensible nature of this will and sought in this conception an understanding of why life is so much worse morally than our 'moral sense' dictates to us it ought to be. His 'doctrine' – formed by the influence of his ethics on his metaphysics – was that the intellect, created at first by the will as its instrument, is capable of recognizing the reprehensible nature of will and of acting ethically by 'denying' the will. His direct, permanent influence on Nietzsche was limited to the propositions that the world is not the creation of an intellect, that is to say it is not a rational structure, and that the human intellect is not an autonomous entity. The rest of Schopenhauer he subsequently repudiated. To Nietzsche, will is understood, not metaphysically, but physiologically, as a complex of drives and affects which enters the consciousness as a single sensation and is thus designated by a single word: he denies the existence of will in Schopenhauer's sense of it. He also denies Schopenhauer's ethical conclusions by asking whence Schopenhauer thinks he has acquired the moral criteria by which he condemns the world as ethically reprehensible, and then undertaking an examination and analysis of the 'moral sense', and especially of how it was evolved. His conclusions lead him to substitute for Schopenhauer's demand for a denial of the will a demand for the total affirmation of life – though here, it must be conceded, the pathos attending this demand probably owes its intensity to its being the antithesis of Schopenhauer's.

With Wagner, Nietzsche's relationship was much more intense and complicated. He became an intimate of Wagner's household, and Wagner, thirty-one years older than he, became a second and greater father. When Nietzsche turned his back on him it was a second act of parricide. He obtained from Wagner a number of aesthetic theories which he employed in *The Birth of Tragedy*; more importantly, he obtained from him a three-dimensional picture of 'the artist' upon which his subsequent psychological explanations of the artist-nature rely very heavily; most importantly, he obtained from him an idea of 'greatness', of the possibilities still open to the human spirit even in the 'late' nineteenth century. In these respects it would probably be wrong to say that Nietzsche ever 'turned away' from Wagner at all: to the very end he never had any doubt that he was the 'greatest artist' of his time. But by then Nietzsche had redefined both greatness and the nature of the time in which he and Wagner lived, so that he was able to say that Wagner was decadent without denying his greatness.

What he did repudiate was that which united Wagner with German nationalist aspirations and made of him a forerunner, or at least a herald, of the state of things to which these aspirations eventually led. Wagner was Francophobe and an anti-Semitic racist; indeed, most of the fantasies and phobias of the German nationalist movement are to be found somewhere in his writings or recorded utterances. But these traits are epiphenomena, and were more striking to his contemporaries than they can or need be to us: what is more important for an understanding both of him and of the ground for Nietzsche's repudiation of him is something less easy to set down in a few words, though the experience of it is unambiguous enough. There is in fascism a recrudescence of certain affects which, when found in earlier mankind, seem to be signs of strength and 'naturalness', and whose revival in modern times is therefore attended with the sensation of getting back to wholesome and honest fundamentals; but, precisely because earlier mankind is earlier, and modern mankind in many ways a different species, this revival is in reality an atavism, and in the man in whom it takes place a sign of neurosis. Wagner was such a man.

It is customary to think of him as a 'late Romantic', and it is true that the characteristic stigmata of German Romanticism are all to be found in his operas: the folk mystique (*Meistersinger*), *Gemeinschaft* (*Parsifal*), anarchic individualism (*Siegfried*), night- and death-worship (*Tristan*), the rediscovery of German medieval epic poetry (*Tristan, Parsifal*) and lyric poetry (*Tannhäuser, Meistersinger*), belief in the 'redemptive' role of woman (*passim*). But there is also in him that which appears in his predecessors only fitfully, attenuatedly, and in a very unconvincing form when compared with his own miraculous invocation of it: the blood, fire, magic, protracted revengefulness, passion of superhuman duration and intensity, oaths and oath-breaches, and feeling of doom which permeate the world of the *Nibelungenlied* and its sources, and which Wagner brought so vividly alive again that we are likely to give the whole concatenation the name 'Wagnerian' rather than any other. In the *Ring des Nibelungen* strong primitive emotions are made contemporary: but as contemporary emotions they are not strong but neurotic.

Consider the primitive virtue of *Treue* – 'troth', 'trustiness', the loyalty of vassal to liege lord. In the *Nibelungenlied* the central character,

Hagen, is an embodiment of *Treue*: vassal and warrior, and brave to the point of self-destruction, he is inspired wholly and solely by a sense of loyalty to his lord, and this virtue justifies him and all his actions. In Wagner's treatment of him he becomes a villain, but his virtue of *Treue* stays with him as a moral imperative which explains his conduct; and this virtue is bestowed by Wagner on all the characters in whom he wishes to see a trace of moral justification. The fateful quality in his heroes, in Siegfried and Tristan, that which constitutes the tragic element in their destiny, is their involuntary lapsing from *Treue*, their being compelled to become *untreu*. In Wagner's female characters the decisive quality is again *Treue*. What the Flying Dutchman needs for his 'redemption' is a woman '*treu bis in den Tod*': Senta is the required article, and Isolde and Brünnhilde are in this respect only Senta writ larger: they too are *treu bis in den Tod*. Lohengrin's Elsa is not *treu*, and is punished. In his own life Wagner was inclined to set a very high value on *Treue* – on the part of others and towards himself.

Emotional primitivism and a strong emphasis on the primitive virtue of *Treue* – the latter being exaggerated until it overbore every other imperative – were characteristics of 'national socialism'; and inasmuch as Wagner was already a propagator of them, Nietzsche later felt entitled to call him a neurotic and decadent (*W, passim*).

The positive tide which carried him away from Schopenhaueran metaphysics and Wagnerian art was the tide of *science*. He began to ask himself what metaphysical speculation about the ultimate nature of things, pessimistic 'denial of life', sagas of gods and heroes, hours-long surrender to narcotic music, had to do with the real needs of Europe in the last quarter of the nineteenth century. What, come to that, they had to do with his own real needs. The one unmistakable fact about modern life was that 'science' in the most general sense had taken over its direction; and the one unmistakable requirement of philosophy was that it should take that fact into account.

The 'influences' which turned him in this direction were chiefly the facts of life themselves, but a number of specific influences may be stated. In the *History of Materialism* of Friedrich Albert Lange, which he first read in the summer of 1866 and then read 'again and again', he found the 'materialist movement of our times, the natural sciences with their Darwinian theories . . . ethical materialism' (letter of 16 February 1868). He also found in it what he clearly came to regard as the decisive argument against metaphysical presumptions. Schopenhauer's 'will' is a description of ultimate reality, of the 'thing in itself'; but, says Lange, ultimate reality is not only unknowable (as Kant himself had held), the idea of it is part of the phenomenal world: anything that enters our head is proved by the fact to belong to the plane of 'appearance', no 'breakthrough' into any other plane of reality is even imaginable, consequently the distinction between the real and the apparent world is not one we can draw.

The triumph of the theory of evolution in Darwin's theory of natural selection meant to Nietzsche above all that what looked like purpose in the world could be explained as the consequence of random and fortuitous change; and any kind of dualism – of matter and spirit, of that which forms and that which is formed – seemed to have been rendered unnecessary.

Through personal discussion with Paul Rée, and through reading his *Psychological Observations* and later his *Origin of the Moral Sensations* (published in 1877 but discussed with Nietzsche during the course of writing), he became familiar with the idea that religion and morality are subjective phenomena, and their investigation a matter for psychology.

By the summer of 1876 he was ready for a decisive change of direction. The last of the *Meditations* – *Richard Wagner in Bayreuth* – took him an unconscionable time to write and the final product is hardly worthy of him even in his 'early' manifestation. Within a month of the publication of this essay in July 1876 he was at work on *Human, All Too Human*: the fundamental novelty of this book, after you have noted the stylistic transformation and the sense of having come out of a closed drawing room into a cold breeze, is seen to be a drastic difference in subject matter. Metaphysics is spoken of only to be repudiated, Schopenhauer is mentioned only in order to be contradicted, and Wagner is not mentioned by name at all; 'the artist' is no longer rhapsodized over but analysed; generalization is replaced by the examination of small, sometimes minute, particular problems which are asserted to be the only problems that matter. Above all, the profuse employment of the words 'science', 'scientific method', 'scientific observation', and the like, indicates where the interest of the writer now lies. The book, when it appeared in 1878, was dedicated 'to the memory of Voltaire'.

In his account of this time in *Ecce Homo*, he says he 'perceived a total aberration of my instincts, of which the individual blunder, call it Wagner or Basel professorship, was a mere symptom. An *impatience* with myself overcame me . . . A downright burning thirst seized hold of me: thenceforward I pursued in fact nothing other than physiology, medicine and natural sciences . . .' (section on *HA*, 3). The last phrase is a literally false statement designed to send the reader in the right direction: if you read Nietzsche from *Human, All Too Human* onwards as if he were writing about physiology, medicine and 'natural sciences' you will never really misunderstand him.

IV: 1876 to 1883

From here onwards the *ideal* method of studying Nietzsche's development is a command of German, chronic insomnia, and a set of the collected works. The student who read straight through from the beginning of *Human, All Too Human* to the end of Book Four of *The Gay Science* (the fifth book was added later) would need no explanation of how 'scientific scepticism' broke down all the admired and valued things but how all these broken pieces were at the same time being gathered together again by the force of a unifying theory: he would need no explanation because he would see it taking place, and how it was taking place, and would participate in the experience of living through it and suffering from it – for these emotional reactions are set down too. There is no way of faking this experience: to *know* how this philosophical tendency produced 'a crisis situation' you have to enter into the situation yourself.

This situation, which we now have to try to look into from the outside, was a product of an increasing consciousness of the nihilism inherent in sceptical analysis and a somewhat desperate awareness of the need to emerge from it through some form of 'transcendence'. Coincidentally with this there was as it were an undersea current building up and gathering momentum, drawing more and more of the water along with it, until finally it broke surface and reduced the ocean to a single directed stream. This current was the idea of the drive to power as the basic drive in man, and by extension in all other creatures. The point at which it broke surface was the moment, in January 1883, at which Nietzsche realized the possibilities inherent in it, and first became fully aware that the suggestions he had been offering as to the ubiquity of the power drive and the number of 'masks' it assumes did in fact constitute a theory of universal 'will to power'.

This evolution may appear to conflict with the assertion that if you read Nietzsche as if he were writing about physiology, medicine and natural science you would never really misunderstand him; but it does not in fact do so, because to Nietzsche 'will to power' *was* a scientific conception – or, better perhaps, he was anxious to prove that it was. He knew quite well that 'will to power' as an explanation of events is teleology, and that teleology is 'not science'; he was engaged on trying to get round that difficulty when his breakdown cut short his speculations. His notes were published in *The Will to Power*: some of them come close to identifying 'power' with 'energy', and to understanding 'energy' as *'quanta* of power'. These developments are not especially well known even to those who know Nietzsche well, so it is important to give them proper emphasis. But it must also be emphasized that, when employed as an explanation of human behaviour, 'will to power' is not identified with a 'force' of any kind, and that the need for such an identification emerged only when the principle was extended beyond man to the whole world – which may suggest that this extension is ill-considered and impermissible. In any event, these developments show that in formulating a theory of will to power Nietzsche was not relapsing into metaphysics but, in intention at least, still pursuing a 'scientific' course.

Three elements predominate in the works of this period: the sceptical analysis; the nihilist conclusions, and the effort to see beyond them; and the evolving theory of will to power. We shall here consider the first and second, and reserve the third for the next chapter, when a connected account of the whole theory will be attempted.

The sceptical analysis occupies the major amount of space in the five books; but since much of what is most significant and characteristic is to be found already at the beginning of the first of them, it seems to me that a brief commentary on these earliest passages would be more profitable than to range over the whole field: such a commentary would demonstrate to what extent the essentials of Nietzsche's new outlook are present from the start – that they are to be discovered in the *first* exhibits that come to hand. It may also indicate the value to a study of Nietzsche of starting at the beginning. The following passages, then, constitute sections 1 to 5 of *Human, All Too Human*: with the exception of section 3 they are translated entire.

Chemistry of concepts and sensations   Almost all the problems of philosophy once again pose the same form of question as they did two thousand years ago: how can something originate in its opposite, for example rationality in irrationality, the sentient in the dead, logic in unlogic, disinterested contemplation in covetous desire, living for others in egoism, truth in errors? Metaphysical philosophy has hitherto surmounted this difficulty by denying that the one originates in the other and assuming for the more highly-valued thing a miraculous source in the very kernel and being of the 'thing in itself'. Historical philosophy, on the other hand, which can no longer be separated from natural science, the youngest of all philosophical methods, has discovered in individual cases (and this will probably be the result in every case) that there are no opposites, except in the customary exaggeration of popular or metaphysical interpretations, and that a mistake in reasoning lies at the bottom of this antithesis: according to this explanation there exists, strictly speaking, neither an unegoistic action nor completely disinterested contemplation; both are only sublimations, in which the basic element seems almost to have dispersed and reveals itself only under the most painstaking observation. All we require, and what can be given us only now the individual sciences have attained their present level, is a *chemistry* of the moral, religious and aesthetic conceptions and sensations, likewise of all the agitations we experience within ourselves in cultural and social intercourse, and indeed even when we are alone: what if this chemistry would end up by revealing that in this domain too the most glorious colours are derived from base, indeed from despised materials? Will there be many who desire to pursue such researches? Mankind likes to put questions of origin and beginnings out of its mind: must one not be almost inhuman to detect in oneself a contrary inclination? (*HA*, I)

Although *Human, All Too Human* is not organized systematically it is clearly not fortuitous that this 'aphorism' stands at the beginning, for a great deal of the later Nietzsche is encapsulated in it. It asserts that there are no opposites, and thus proclaims a monistic philosophy in opposition to the dualism which, it alleges, characterizes metaphysical philosophy; and it was the pursuit of a monistic principle which led eventually to the theory of a will to power. Denial of opposites is also basic to Nietzsche's ethics: 'beyond good and evil' means beyond simple antithesis and the substitution for moral opposites of a '*scale of values*'. *HA* I explains apparent antitheses by employing the concept of 'sublimation', which subsequently acquired the status of a key concept in Nietzsche's psychology. 'Historical philosophy' here means evolutionary philosophy, the consideration of things as they have *become*, and the repudiation of static conceptions and of 'being': it is equated with the scientific investigation of individual cases, which remained Nietzsche's 'method' until the end of his active life. The opening word is 'chemistry', and what is demanded is the 'chemical analysis' of things usually discussed in metaphysical terms, and especially of the things upon which the highest value is usually placed. I think 'chemistry' is here used metaphorically; what is probably meant is psychological investigation; but the employment of this particular word is symptomatic: Nietzsche wants to sound 'materialistic' in the most uncompromising sense. Subsequently, however, such scientific terms cease to be metaphorical, and if the present passage had appeared in, say, *Twilight of the Idols*, 'chemistry' would have meant chemistry. Nietzsche assumes that such a 'chemical analysis', however that term is to be interpreted, will degrade the thing analysed, and this is the first statement of an assumption basic to his whole philosophy. The interrogative form of the statement is rhetorical, and the earliest example of what became a fingerprint of his style: rhetorical questions of this type are posed throughout his subsequent works, the objective being dramatization. Mankind, he asserts, wants to ignore origins because the origin of everything is, from the point of view of prevailing taste, unpleasing and discreditable: but investigation of origins continued to be among his major preoccupations, and *On the Genealogy of Morals* is almost wholly devoted to it. To engage in such researches one has to be 'almost inhuman': again the first statement of a permanent position and again put into the form of a rhetorical question. Truth is ugly and painful, and one has to be almost inhuman to desire it.

Family failing of philosophers All philosophers have the common failing of starting out from man as he is now and thinking they can reach their goal through an analysis of him. They involuntarily think of 'man' as an *aeterna veritas*, as something that remains constant in the midst of all flux, as a sure measure of things. Everything the philosopher has declared about man is, however, at bottom no more than a testimony as to the man of a *very limited* period of time. Lack of historical sense is the family failing of all philosophers; many, without being aware of it, even take the most recent manifestation of man, such as has arisen under the impress of certain religions, even certain political events, as the fixed form from which one has to start out. They will not learn that man has become, that the faculty of cognition has become; while some of them would have it that the whole world is spun out of this faculty of cognition. Now, everything *essential* in the development of mankind took place in primeval times, long before the 4,000 years we more or less know about; during these years mankind may well not have altered very much. But the philosopher here sees 'instincts' in man as he now is and assumes that these belong to the unalterable facts of mankind and to that extent could provide a key to the understanding of the world in general: the whole of teleology is constructed by speaking of the man of the last four millennia as of an *eternal* man towards whom all things in the world have had a natural relationship from the time he began. But everything has become: there are *no eternal facts*, just as there are no absolute truths. Consequently what is needed from now on is *historical philosophizing*, and with it the virtue of modesty. (*HA*, 2)

'*Alles ist geworden*' is the key phrase, to be repeated almost endlessly in subsequent books: everything has become, 'being is an empty fiction' (*T*, III. 2). It is a direct transference of 'evolutionism' to the plane of philosophizing, and is what is meant by 'historical philoso- phizing'. If any single conception could be called basic to Nietzsche's philosophy it would be this. Its consequence, that there are no eternal facts or absolute truths, is one he went on to draw in every department of life. That man 'has become' is in itself a denial of the existence of 'human nature' and an objection to the idea that 'man' can be defined: this opens the road to a philosophy of conscious self-modification – there being no standard man but only man at this or that stage of his evolution – and thus to the 'superman' and to 'existentialism'.

Estimation of unpretentious truths   It is the mark of a higher culture to value the little unpretentious truths which have been discovered by means of rigorous method more highly than the errors handed down by metaphysical and artistic ages and men, which blind us and make us happy.' (*HA*, 3, opening sentence)

Nietzsche here states his new attitude towards 'truth': truth is to be discovered piecemeal by 'rigorous method', that is by science; meta- physics and art produce errors, not truths; errors make us happy, truths (by implication) do not.

Astrology and what is related to it   It is probable that the objects of the religious, moral and aesthetic sensations belong only to the surface of things, while man likes to believe that here at least he is in touch with the world's heart; the reason he deludes himself is that these things produce in him such profound happiness and unhappiness, and thus he exhibits here the same pride as in the case of astrology. For astrology believes the starry firmament revolves around the fate of man; the moral man, however, supposes that what he has essentially at heart must also constitute the essence and heart of things. (*HA*, 4)

This aphorism contains three implications, all of them significant for Nietzsche's future work. 1. Everything is 'appearance', there is no 'real world'; the distinction between reality and appearance is a false one. 2. Feelings of pleasure and displeasure are employed as criteria of truth, but this is impermissible: if a thing moves us deeply that is evidence that it moves us deeply and not evidence of anything else, e.g. that it is true, or 'profound', or 'real'. 3. Religion, morals and beauty are phenomena of the human world, not of any other: there is no 'moral world-order': the belief that good and evil are eternal, rooted in the essence of things, is on a par with the beliefs of astrology.

Misunderstanding of the dream The man of the ages of barbarous primordial culture believed that in the dream he was getting to know a *second real world*: here is the origin of all metaphysics. Without the dream one would have had no occasion to divide the world into two. The dissection into soul and body is also connected with the oldest idea of the dream, likewise the postulation of a life of the soul, thus the origin of all belief in spirits, and probably also of the belief in gods. 'The dead live on, *for* they appear to the living in dreams': that was the conclusion one formerly drew, throughout many millennia. (*HA*, 5)

Since Nietzsche's opinions conflicted with almost all commonly held opinions, he was constantly concerned to suggest how commonly held opinions could have originated; and again and again he retreats into prehistoric times – when 'everything *essential* in the development of mankind took place' – and seeks a solution there. His basic proposition is that primitive man stuck to the *first* idea that came into his head. The distinction between true and untrue did not exist; all that was understood was the need for an explanation; to require that an explanation be true is a very sophisticated demand which primitive man would not have understood. What he required was merely that the unaccountable be accounted for, and he thus had no motive for doubting the first explanation which occurred to him; and any explanation was better than none. This is how Nietzsche sought to account for the multitude of false, unwarranted, or even impossible opinions at large in the world. (He was also suggesting, of course, that most people still 'reason' as primitive man did.) The present aphorism is a first exercise in this method. Its abruptness is deliberate, and calculated to leave no doubt as to his position with respect to metaphysics, the 'real and apparent world', the existence of the 'soul', and the belief in spirits, gods and immortality: they are all primitive errors. The very far-reaching consequences of a single misunderstanding – the world of religion and metaphysics brought into existence simply by a failure to comprehend the nature of dreams – may seem *too* far-reaching: it may seem that far too much is being inferred from far too little. But, in the light of Nietzsche's later work, this 'too much' must also be seen as deliberate. As Darwin had to suppose a very long time span if his theory of the origin of species was to work, so Nietzsche had to suppose an extreme simplicity of mind in primitive man if his theory of the origin of common errors was to work. Every kind of second thought, every sort of hesitation or doubt, had to be excluded: it had to be allowed that primitive man really accepted the first explanation that occurred to him, and then really accepted everything that, along the simplest line of 'reasoning' possible, followed from it. But if this is granted, at least hypothetically, there is no limit whatever to the number or the far-reachingness of the false conclusions primitive man could draw.

I hope that the interconnectedness of Nietzsche's mature work, the amount he is able to say or imply in a brief passage, the 'tip of the iceberg' aspect of his 'aphorisms' and the destructive quality of his thought during this period will have come across in these brief comments.

The accumulation of insights into the questionable character of all values quickly produced a sense of the devaluation of existence: when life was subjected to scientific examination, the meaning went out of it. His consciousness that this was what was happening was expressed in various ways which, taken together, give these aphoristic books a moonscape quality which is often the first and sometimes the most lasting impression they make on the reader. An idea of this bleakness may be gathered from a few of the relevant passages.

From experience The irrationality of a thing is no argument against its existence, rather a condition of it. *Fundamental insight*

There is no pre-established harmony between the furtherance of truth and the wellbeing of mankind. *The human lot* He who considers more deeply knows that, whatever his acts and judgments may be, he is always wrong. *Truth as Circe* Error has transformed animals into men; could truth be capable of transforming man again into an animal? (*HA*, 515, 517, 518, 519)

A fable The Don Juan of knowledge: no philosopher or poet has yet discovered him. He does not love the things he knows, but he has spirit and appetite for and enjoyment of the chase and intrigues of knowledge – up to the highest and remotest stars of knowledge! – until at last there remains to him nothing of knowledge left to hunt down except the absolutely *detrimental*; he is like the drunkard who ends by drinking absinth and aqua fortis. Thus in the end he lusts after Hell – it is the last knowledge that *seduces* him. Perhaps it too proves a disillusionment, like all knowledge! And then he would have to stand to all eternity transfixed to disillusionment and himself become a stone guest, with a longing for a supper of knowledge which he will never get! – for the whole universe has not a single morsel left to give to this hungry man. (*D*, 327)

Let us beware! Let us beware of thinking the world is a living being. Whither should it spread itself? What should it nourish itself with? How could it grow and multiply? We know indeed more or less what the organic is: and shall we reinterpret the unspeakably derivative, late, rare, chance phenomena which we perceive only on the surface of the earth into the essential, universal, eternal, as they do who call the universe an organism? I find that disgusting. Let us likewise beware of believing the universe is a machine; it is certainly not constructed so as to perform some operation, we do it far too great honour with the word 'machine'. Let us beware of presupposing that something so orderly as the cyclical motions of our planetary neighbours are the general and universal case; even a glance at the Milky Way gives rise to doubt whether there may not there exist far more crude and contradictory motions, likewise stars with eternally straight trajectories and the like. The astral order in which we live is an exception; this order and the apparent permanence which is conditional upon it is in its turn made possible by the exception of exceptions: the formation of the organic. The total nature of the world is, on the other hand, to all eternity chaos, not in the sense that necessity is lacking but in that order, structure, form, beauty, wisdom, and whatever other human aesthetic notions we may have are lacking. Judged from the viewpoint of our reason, the unsuccessful cases are far and away the rule, the exceptions are not the secret objective, and the whole contraption repeats its theme, which can never be called a melody, over and over again to eternity – and ultimately even the term 'unsuccessful case' is already a humanization which contains a reproof. But how can we venture to reprove or praise the universe! Let us beware of attributing to it heartlessness and unreason or their opposites: it is neither perfect nor beautiful nor noble, and has no desire to become any of these; it is by no means striving to imitate mankind! It is quite impervious to all our aesthetic and moral judgments! It has likewise no impulse to self-preservation or impulses of any kind; neither does it know any laws. Let us beware of saying there are laws in nature. There are only necessities: there is no one to command, no one to obey, no one to transgress. When you realize that there are no goals or objectives, then you realize too that there is no chance: for only in a world of objectives does the word 'chance' have any meaning. Let us beware of saying that death is the opposite of life. The living being is only a species of the dead, and a very rare species . . .' (GS, 109)

The four errors Man has been reared by his errors: first he never saw himself other than imperfectly, second he attributed to himself imaginary qualities, third he felt himself in a false order of rank with animal and nature, fourth he continually invented new tables of values and for a time took each of them to be eternal and unconditional, so that now this, now that human drive and state took first place and was, as a consequence of this evaluation, ennobled. If one deducts the effect of these four errors, one has also deducted away humanity, humaneness and 'human dignity'. (GS, 115)

The madman Have you not heard of that madman who lit a lantern in the bright morning hours, ran to the market place and cried incessantly: 'I am looking for God! I am looking for God!' – As many of those who did not believe in God were standing together there he excited considerable laughter. Have you lost him then? said one. Did he lose his way like a child? said another. Or is he hiding? Is he afraid of us? Has he gone on a voyage? or emigrated? – thus they shouted and laughed. The madman sprang into their midst and pierced them with his glances. 'Where has God gone?' he cried. 'I shall tell you. *We have killed him* – you and I. We are all his murderers. But how have we done this? How were we able to drink up the sea? Who gave us the sponge to wipe away the entire horizon? What did we do when we unchained this earth from its sun? Whither is it moving now? Whither are we moving now? Away from all suns? Are we not perpetually falling? Backward, sideward, forward, in all directions? Is there any up or down left? Are we not straying as through an infinite nothing? Do we not feel the breath of empty space? Has it not become colder? Is more and more night not coming on all the time? Must not lanterns be lit in the morning? Do we not hear anything yet of the noise of the gravediggers who are burying God? Do we not smell anything yet of God's decomposition? – gods too decompose. God is dead. God remains dead. And we have killed him. How shall we, the murderers of all murderers, console ourselves? That which was holiest and mightiest of all that the world has yet possessed has bled to death under our knives – who will wipe this blood off us? With what water could we purify ourselves? What festivals of atonement, what sacred games shall we need to invent? Is not the greatness of this deed too great for us? Must not we ourselves become gods simply to seem worthy of it? There has never been a greater deed – and whoever shall be born after us, for the sake of this deed he shall be part of a higher history than all history hitherto.' Here the madman fell silent and again regarded his listeners; and they too were silent and stared at him in astonishment. At last he threw his lantern to the ground and it broke and went out. 'I come too early', he said then; 'my time has not yet come. This tremendous event is still on its way, still travelling – it has not yet reached the ears of men. Lightning and thunder require time, the light of the stars requires time, deeds require time after they have been done before they can be seen and heard. This deed is still more distant from them than the most distant stars – *and yet they have done it themselves*.' – It has been related further that on that same day the madman entered divers churches and there sang a *requiem aeternam deo*. Let out and quietened, he is said to have retorted each time: 'What are these churches now if they are not the tombs and sepulchres of God?' (*GS*, 125)

Ultimate scepticism   What then in the last resort are the truths of mankind? – They are the *irrefutable* errors of mankind. (*GS*, 265)

Against this we must set at once the *other* voice heard in these books: the strenuously optimistic voice which refuses to acquiesce in this nihilistic devaluation, and insists that the demolition going forward may be only the essential preparation for future construction.

We aeronauts of the spirit!   All those brave birds which fly out into the distance, into the farthest distance – it is certain! Somewhere or other they will be unable to go on and will perch down on a mast or a bare cliff-face – and they will even be thankful for this miserable accommodation! But who could venture to infer from that, that there was *not* an immense open space before them, that they had flown as far as one *could* fly! All our great teachers and predecessors have at last come to a stop . . . it will be the same with you and me! But what does that matter to you and me! *Other birds will fly farther!* This insight and faith of ours vies with them in flying up and away; it rises above our heads and above our impotence into the heights and from there surveys the distance and sees before it the flocks of birds which, far stronger than we, still strive whither we have striven, and where everything is sea, sea, sea! – And whither then would we go? Would we *cross* the sea? Whither does this mighty longing draw us, this longing that is worth more to us than any pleasure? Why just in this direction, thither where all the suns of humanity have hitherto *gone down*? Will it perhaps be said of us one day that we too, *steering westward hoped to reach an India* – but that it was our fate to be wrecked against infinity? Or, my brothers? Or? – (*D*, 575)

For the New Year   I am still living, I am still thinking: I have to go on living because I have to go on thinking. . . . Today everyone is permitted to express his desire and dearest thoughts: so I too would like to say what I have desired of myself today and what thought was the first to cross my heart this year – what thought shall be the basis, guarantee and sweetness of all my future life! I want to learn more and more to see what is necessary in things as the beautiful in them – thus I shall become one of those who make things beautiful. *Amor fati*: may that be my love from now on! I want to wage no war against the ugly. I do not want to accuse, I do not want even to accuse the accusers. May *looking away* be my only form of negation! And, all in all: I want to be at all times hereafter only an affirmer [*ein Ja-sagender*]! (GS, 276)

Preparatory men   I greet all the signs that a more manly, warlike age is coming, which will, above all, bring valour again into honour! For it has to prepare the way for a yet higher age, and assemble the force which that age will one day have need of – that age which will carry heroism into knowledge and *wage war* for the sake of ideas and their consequences. To that end many brave pioneers are needed now ... men who know how to be silent, solitary, resolute ... who have an innate disposition to seek in all things that which must be *overcome* in them: men to whom cheerfulness, patience, simplicity and contempt for the great vanities belong just as much as do generosity in victory and indulgence towards the little vanities of the defeated ... men with their own festivals, their own work-days, their own days of mourning, accustomed to and assured in command and equally ready to obey when necessary, equally proud in the one case as in the other, equally serving their own cause: men more imperilled, men more fruitful, happier men! For believe me! – the secret of realizing the greatest fruitfulness and the greatest enjoyment of existence is: to *live dangerously*! Build your cities on the slopes of Vesuvius! Send your ships out into uncharted seas! Live in conflict with your equals and with yourselves! Be robbers and ravagers as long as you cannot be rulers and owners, you men of knowledge! The time will soon be past when you could be content to live concealed in the woods like timid deer! (GS, 283)

Excelsior!   'You will never again pray, never again worship, never again repose in limitless trust – you deny it to yourself to remain halted before an ultimate wisdom, ultimate good, ultimate power, and there unharness your thoughts – you have no perpetual guardian and friend for your seven solitudes ... there is no longer for you any rewarder and recompenser, no final corrector – there is no longer any reason in what happens, no longer any love in what happens to you – there is no longer any resting-place open to your heart where it has only to find and no longer to seek, you resist any kind of ultimate peace, you want the eternal recurrence of war and peace – man of renunciation, will you renounce in all this? Who will give you the strength for it? No one has yet possessed this strength!' – There is a lake which one day denied it to itself to flow away and threw up a dam at the place where it formerly flowed away: since then this lake has risen higher and higher. Perhaps it is precisely that renunciation which will also lend us the strength by which the renunciation itself can be endured; perhaps man will rise higher and higher from that time when he no longer *flows out* into a God. (*GS*, 285)

If you compare these two sets of exhibits, and note that they are contemporaneous, you will see the extent to which this period is one of conflict between diametrically opposed emotions.

At this point we have to descend into biography, for the intensity of the crisis of January 1883 is only partly explicable in the terms already suggested.

Nietzsche was a solitary. For most of his adult life he lived alone, and as a rule he did not mind living alone: occasional complaints in his letters of the loneliness of his existence are usually (not invariably, of course) to be read as lamentations over his *essential* aloneness, his spiritual and intellectual isolation. One has to use a little commonsense when considering Nietzsche's way of life, and call in question the notion that his solitude was a voluntary renunciation in the service of some higher ideal. He was not, as he himself vehemently insisted he was not, a saint: his instincts were normal, he enjoyed what most men enjoy, he disliked what most men dislike. What distinguished him was, firstly, the intensity of his involvement with 'intellectual' problems, which thus became part of his normal waking life, and, secondly, the fact that he was more or less permanently ill. These two circumstances alone suffice to explain his 'solitude': he chose solitude because he preferred it, but his illness would in any case have made him very much alone; his illness compelled him to solitude, but his preoccupation with his own ideas would in any case have predisposed him to a love of being alone.

He did not marry, and he 'justified' his bachelorhood with the well-known remark, made with reference to Socrates, that a married philosopher belongs in comedy (*GM*, III. 7). In the days when he was taken for a latter-day prophet and self-denying ascetic – a view made possible by general ignorance of his real as opposed to fictional biography – this remark was taken in earnest, and people used to say that a philosopher ought not to marry because Nietzsche had said so. But one has only to think of Bertrand Russell to refute the idea that a married philosopher belongs in comedy, if that idea is intended to imply that a married philosopher is any more comic than any other married man. The fact of the matter is that Nietzsche would have made a very bad husband, and he knew it: his character was totally unsuited to the consideration for someone else and the modification of one's own preferences demanded by a marriage if it is to last as long as a week. Even more to the point is the delicate consideration of the nature of his 'illness'. It is virtually certain that he contracted syphilis while a student in Leipzig, and that his subsequent recurrent prostration and final collapse was a consequence of it. The treatment he received was of the kind then given to a person suffering from this incurable disease, that is to say it was not treatment at all in the modern sense; and although it is quite possible he was never told in so many words what it was he was suffering from, it is not reasonable to think he failed to realize he was a victim of syphilis, or that his male acquaintances did not realize it also. His symptoms – migraine, vomiting, sensitivity of the eyes, days-long incapacitation, above all the recurrence of these symptoms at regular intervals and their intractability to medication – are entirely typical; and it goes without saying that no man of honour who even suspected he might be suffering from syphilis would seriously have entertained the idea of marriage.

But in April 1882 Nietzsche for the first time in his life did precisely that. During earlier years he had been formally 'looking for a wife', and on one occasion he got as far as a written proposal of marriage: but the way he conducted himself, the casualness of his approach, are evidence, to me at any rate, that 'in his heart' he knew he was not and could not be serious. But the 'affair' with Lou Salomé was of a different order of things: he pursued her with total earnestness and, when his frank avowals failed to achieve their object, with cunning and desperation. He was in his thirty-eighth year, Lou was twenty-one and he 'wanted' her in the most ordinary human fashion. A man of thirty-eight no doubt regarded himself in the 1880s as middle-aged, or at least as on the brink of middle age, and there is a 'last chance' tenseness and extremism in Nietzsche's conduct. His meeting with her had clearly brought to a head, suddenly and with great force, his consciousness of how much in life he was missing and how close he was to having missed it altogether: for the first and only time he found his mode of living truly unbearable, and he wanted to put an end to it. He would have agreed to a celibate marriage, and since Lou's subsequent marriage *was* celibate this idea was, with regard to this particular woman, not eccentric but quite an astute reading of her character. He would, indeed, have agreed to almost anything. But it was all in vain: she would not marry him, she would not marry anybody, she wanted independence and she went off under circumstances which led him to suspect he had been making himself ridiculous.

His behaviour during this unsuccessful courtship had already been very uncharacteristic, but now he went right off the rails. This crisis was far worse than those we have glanced at previously: he was at the end of his rope in all respects. 'I have suffered from the disgraceful and anguishing recollections of this past summer [i.e. that of 1882] as from a kind of madness,' he wrote:

They involve a conflict of contrary emotions which I am not equal to ... If only I could sleep! But the strongest sleeping-draughts help as little as do the six to eight hour walks I take. If I cannot find the magic formula to turn all this – muck to *gold*, I am lost ... I now mistrust everybody: I sense in everything I hear contempt towards me ... Sometimes I think of renting a small room in Basel, visiting you now and then and attending lectures. Sometimes I think of doing the opposite: of driving my solitude and resignation to the ultimate limit and —' (letter to Franz Overbeck, undated, posted Christmas Day 1882)

In the event, he neither retired to Basel nor committed suicide: he wrote *Thus Spoke Zarathustra* instead. That it was under these circumstances that the book originated – that it was at bottom the product of an absolute unwillingness to go under – accounts for many of its unusual features, and especially for its relentless exuberance. It represents a flight to an opposite extreme; and one can easily believe that the account given in *Ecce Homo* of the state its author was in during the days of January 1883 when the first part was written is an accurate and unvarnished recollection:

Has anyone at the end of the nineteenth century a distinct conception of what poets of strong ages called inspiration? If not,

I will describe it. – If one had the slightest residue of superstition left in one, one would hardly be able to set aside the idea that one is merely incarnation, merely mouthpiece, merely medium of overwhelming forces. The concept revelation, in the sense that something suddenly, with unspeakable certainty and subtlety, becomes *visible*, audible, something that shakes and overturns one to the depths, simply describes the fact. One hears, one does not seek; one takes, one does not ask who gives; a thought flashes up like lightning, with necessity, unfalteringly formed – I have never had any choice. An ecstasy whose tremendous tension sometimes discharges itself in a flood of tears, while one's steps now involuntarily rush along, now involuntarily lag . . . a depth of happiness in which the most painful and gloomy things appear, not as an antithesis, but as conditioned, demanded, as a *necessary* colour within such a superfluity of light . . . Everything is in the highest degree involuntary but takes place as in a tempest of a feeling of freedom, of absoluteness, of power, of divinity . . . this is *my* experience of inspiration; I do not doubt that one has to go back thousands of years to find anyone who could say to me 'it is mine also'. (section on *Z*, 3)

V: 1883 to 1889

Nietzsche had a special relationship with his *Zarathustra*, and in the end – in the latter half of 1888, when he had let all inhibitions go – he came to regard it not only as *his* best book but as *the* best book. 'I have given mankind the profoundest book it possesses, my *Zarathustra*,' he wrote (*T*, IX. 51); and in *Ecce Homo* he said of it:

This work stands altogether alone. Let us leave the poets aside: perhaps nothing at all has ever been done out of a like superfluity of strength . . . That a Goethe, a Shakespeare would not for a moment have known how to breathe in this tremendous passion and altitude, that Dante is, compared with Zarathustra, merely a believer and not one who first *creates* truth, a *world-ruling* spirit, a destiny – that the poets of the Veda are priests and not even worthy to unloose the latchet of the shoes of a Zarathustra – all this is the least of it, and gives no idea of the distance, of the *azure* solitude, in which this work lives . . . Reckon into a single sum the spirit and goodness of all great souls: all of them together would not be capable of producing one of Zarathustra's discourses . . . There is not one moment in this revelation of truth which would have been anticipated or divined by even *one* of the greatest. There is no wisdom, no psychology, no art of speech before Zarathustra . . .' (section on Z, 6)

These and similar ravings are of course a foretaste of madness, and they are the more deplorable in that *Zarathustra* is not even Nietzsche's 'best book', though certainly it is his most famous. The ideas epitomized in it are often expressed so laconically that the book has acquired the reputation of being 'difficult', which it is not to anyone who knows his other books. In point of style, too, *Zarathustra* is an acquired taste: the prophet-tone and the far-fetched, sometimes impossible imagery are not unexampled elsewhere, but here they are all-pervading; there are passages of great beauty and intensity, and many memorable 'aphorisms', but the fact remains that when one recommends Nietzsche as a master of German prose it is not *Zarathustra* one has in mind. On the other hand, it has to be conceded that a writer's most popular work does not attain that status accidentally, or because of some mistake on the part of the public, or because its author has published extravagant claims on its behalf: it does so because it possesses certain real and attractive qualities which his other works perhaps lack or do not possess to so marked a degree. *Zarathustra* is, all its faults notwithstanding, a liberating book: it can perform for the reader what its writing performed for its author. If the circumstances under which you read it are right it can make as powerful and lasting an impression on you as any book in world literature. There is something of the inspirational tract in it; and its reputation as a sort of atheists' Bible is not altogether undeserved: but there must be many thousands of people who first discovered from its pages that conventional beliefs can without any difficulty be systematically inverted – that moral and spiritual values are not 'obvious'. It contains dozens of phrases that have become familiar, many of them of the 'outrageous' or 'provocative' sort (e.g. 'War and courage have done more great things than charity'; 'Man should be trained for war and woman for the recreation of the warrior: all else is folly'; 'Are you visiting a woman? Do not forget your whip!'; 'Life is a fountain of delight; but where the rabble drinks too, all wells are poisoned'). Above all, it is for the great majority of readers the vehicle of the 'gospel of the superman' – a conception which has stepped out of its pages and gone on to live a life of its own independently of its author's intentions.

The beginning of *Zarathustra* repeats almost literally the closing section (342) of *The Gay Science* in its original form; the following work, *Beyond Good and Evil*, was intended to elucidate in other terms the ideas set down in *Zarathustra*; the *Genealogy of Morals* is described as a supplement to and clarification of *Beyond Good and Evil*; and the short books of 1888 are a summation: the whole series from *Human, All Too Human* onwards is now consciously intended as a single evolving work. *Zarathustra* introduces the will to power, the superman, and the eternal recurrence of the same events. *Beyond Good and Evil* surveys the entire field of Nietzsche's philosophical and cultural interests, and introduces 'master morality and slave morality'. *On the Genealogy of Morals* is an inquiry into the origins of morality, elaborates the concept of sublimation, and introduces the psychology of '*ressentiment*'. At the same time the sceptical analysis of current values is not abandoned, but pursued with, if anything, greater vigour and subtlety: yet there is no longer any feeling of conflict between this nihilism and a desire to go beyond it, for Nietzsche is now convinced of the inevitability of nihilism and that it is only out of this state that a new transcendence can arise. The harsh juxtaposition of 'moonscape' passages and passages of determined optimism such as we found in the works before *Zarathustra* is now softened into the kind of contrast represented by the two following exhibits:

The Olympian vice In spite of that philosopher who, being a real Englishman, sought to bring laughter into disrepute among all thinking minds – 'laughter is a bad infirmity of human nature which every thinking man will endeavour to overcome' (Hobbes) – I would go so far as to venture an order of rank among philosophers according to the rank of their laughter – rising to those capable of *golden* laughter. And if gods too philosophize, as many an inference has driven me to suppose – I do not doubt that while doing so they also know how to laugh in a new and superhuman way – and at the expense of all serious things! Gods are fond of mockery: it seems they cannot refrain from laughter even when sacraments are in progress. (*BGE*, 294)

Alas, and yet what *are* you, my written and painted thoughts! It is not long ago that you were still so many-coloured, young and malicious, so full of thorns and hidden spices you made me sneeze

and laugh – and now? You have already taken off your novelty
and some of you, I fear, are on the point of becoming truths ...
And has it ever been otherwise? For what things do we write
and paint, we mandarins with Chinese brushes, we immortalizers
of things which *let* themselves be written, what alone are we
capable of painting? Alas, only that which is about to wither and
is beginning to lose its fragrance! Alas, only storms departing
exhausted and feelings grown old and yellow! Alas, only birds
strayed and grown weary in flight who now let themselves be
caught in the hand – in *our* hand! We immortalize that which
cannot live and fly much longer, weary and mellow things alone!
(*BGE*, 296)

Whether his 'development' was finished by the end of 1888 it is
impossible to say. When Nietzsche finally, and literally, collapsed on 3
January 1889 his intellect was wiped away as if with a sponge, and the
brief letters he wrote afterwards show that he no longer knew who he
was. The course of his career came to as sudden and definitive an end
as it would have if he had fallen dead.

4

Philosophy of Power

To grasp Nietzsche's theory of will to power and its ramifications one cannot do better than trace the idea as it appears at this or that place in his works and see how it formed itself into a hypothesis which was then consciously employed, consistently yet still experimentally, as an explanatory principle. But perhaps it would help to provide a sense of direction to look first at the end result and the final formulation. Near the beginning of *The Anti-Christ* we find the following series of questions and answers:

'What is good? – All that heightens the feeling of power, the will to power, power itself in man. What is bad? – All that proceeds from weakness. What is happiness? – The feeling that power *increases* – that a resistance is overcome' (*A, 2*).

The abruptness and uncompromisingness of these assertions are characteristic of the works of 1888: they are a condensation of the sense and purpose of the whole 'philosophy of power' as it has been built up during the course of years. 'Goodness' and 'happiness' are identified: what is good is what heightens the feeling of power, happiness is this feeling itself, which can be experienced only in the form of the feeling of *more* power. This final conception is one we ought to try to keep in mind throughout the following account.

II

Human, All Too Human includes many attempts to understand human behaviour in terms of a desire for the preservation or enhancement of power. For example:

Gratitude and revenge   The reason the powerful man is grateful is as follows. His benefactor has, through the help he has given him, as it were laid hands on the sphere of the powerful man and intruded into it: now, by way of requittal, the powerful man in turn lays hands on the sphere of his benefactor through the act of gratitude. It is a milder form of revenge. If he did not have the compensation of gratitude, the powerful man would have appeared unpowerful, and henceforth counted as such. That is why every community of the good – which is to say, originally of the powerful – places gratitude among its first duties. (*HA*, 44)

This observation is followed immediately by a first attempt at a 'prehistory of good and evil' in which the decisive element is the power position of the moral legislator. In the case of the

ruling tribes and castes . . . he who possesses the power to requite good with good and evil with evil, and also actually practises requittal, and is thus grateful and revengeful, is called good; he who is unpowerful and cannot requite counts as bad . . . Good and bad is for a long time the same thing as noble and base, master and slave. On the other hand, one does not regard the enemy as evil: he can requite. In Homer, the Trojan and the Greek are both good. (*HA*, 45)

Among the means employed by those with little power to give themselves the feeling of possessing power is, it is next suggested, the arousal of pity:

Observe children who weep and wail *in order that* they shall be pitied . . . live among invalids and the mentally afflicted and ask yourself whether their eloquent moaning and complaining, their displaying of misfortune, does not fundamentally have the objective of *hurting* those who are with them: the pity which these then express is a consolation for the weak and suffering, inasmuch as it shows them that, all their weakness notwithstanding, they possess at any rate *one power*: the *power to hurt*. In this feeling of superiority of which the demonstration of pity makes him conscious, the unfortunate man gains a sort of pleasure; in the conceit of his imagination he is still of sufficient importance to cause affliction in the world. (*HA*, 50)

'*Luke 18: 14 improved*   He that humbleth himself wants to be exalted' (*HA*, 87), interprets an apparently antithetical act as in reality a move for obtaining greater power, and does so by changing, in the original, only one word (*will* instead of *soll*).

One of the theses advanced in *Human, All Too Human* is that the wicked element in wickedness is conventionally much exaggerated: '"Procuring pain in the abstract" *does not exist*, except in the minds of philosophers, just as "procuring pleasure in the abstract" does not exist' (*HA*, 99); and in the course of one of his arguments in support of this thesis, Nietzsche declares that 'wickedness does not have the suffering of another as such as its objective, but only your own enjoyment, for example the enjoyment of the feeling of revenge or of a powerful excitation of the nerves. Even teasing demonstrates what pleasure it gives to vent our power on others and produces in ourselves the pleasurable feeling of ascendancy (*HA*, 103). What is suggested here is that 'wicked' actions are prompted solely by the desire to feel subjective sensations, among which is the 'pleasurable feeling of ascendancy', and are directed only to that end: later he will suggest that all actions are prompted by the desire for the subjective sensation of increased power, and that the distinction between 'good' and 'wicked' acts, whatever it may be, is therefore not a difference of motive and intention.

The 'pleasurable feeling' associated with the acquisition of knowledge is accounted for on similar lines:

> Why is knowledge, the element of the scholar and philosopher, associated with pleasure? Firstly and above all, because one here becomes conscious of one's strength ... Secondly, because in the course of acquiring knowledge, one goes beyond former conceptions and their advocates and is victor over them, or at least believes oneself to be. Thirdly, because through a new piece of knowledge, however small, we become superior to *all* and feel ourselves as the only one who in this matter knows aright. These three causes of pleasure are the most important. (*HA*, 252)

The idea behind this passage is of course that, to put it at its broadest, life is a contest, and that the agonistic character of human existence extends into fields where one would not necessarily expect to find it. That the *agon* was the model for all human activity had already suggested itself to Nietzsche during his studies of Greek culture and civilization, where it seemed to him to stand out clearly as a fact. His conclusions had been summarized in 'Homer's Contest', the fifth of the *Five Prefaces to Five Unwritten Books* (1872), where he drew

78

attention to the opening of Hesiod's *Works and Days* – the passage in which Hesiod says there are *two* Eris-goddesses on earth, one the promoter of war, the other 'much better one' the promoter of competition – and commented: 'The whole of Greek antiquity thinks of spite and envy otherwise than we do, and judges as does Hesiod, who first designates as evil that Eris who leads men against one another to a war of extermination, and then praises another Eris as good who, as jealousy, spite, envy, rouses men to deeds, but not to deeds of war but to deeds of *contest*.' The conception thus summarized in an unpublished manuscript achieved publication in *Human, All Too Human* in the form: 'The Greek artists, the tragedians for example, poetized in order to conquer; their entire art is inconceivable without contest: Hesiod's good Eris, ambition, gave their genius its wings' (*HA*, 170).

This agonistic interpretation of culture is extended, naturally enough, to include the realm of philosophy, and it is done so in a very wholehearted and comprehensive way: the Greek philosophers, Nietzsche writes, 'had a sturdy faith in themselves and their "truth" and with it they overthrew all their contemporaries and predecessors; every one of them was a violent and warlike *tyrant*'. Perhaps, he suggests, Solon constitutes an exception, for Solon said specifically that he had rejected the opportunity of personal rule. 'But he did it out of love of his work, of his lawgiving, and to be a lawgiver is a more sublimated form of tyranny.' Parmenides, too, was a lawgiver, and so probably were Pythagoras and Empedocles; Anaximander founded a city. As for Plato, he 'was the incarnate desire to become the supreme philosophical lawgiver and founder of states; he appears to have suffered dreadfully from the non-fulfilment of his nature, and towards his end his soul became full of the blackest gall' – a fate which overtook all Hellenic philosophers as philosophy lost the power to influence events (*HA*, 261).

The suggestion that justice originated in an arrangement between approximately equal powers has already been quoted (p. 8).

Here, then, we see, even in these few extracts, a large range of effects which it is suggested proceed from a single cause: gratitude, moral evaluations, the desire to arouse pity, humility, teasing, love of knowledge, production of works of art, philosophizing, lawgiving, the idea of justice, all taking their origin from some aspect of the possession of, or the drive to preserve, or the desire to enhance power. And there is also a further suggestion of a different kind which will turn out to be more fruitful in consequences than any of the others:

> There is a *defiance of oneself* of which many forms of asceticism are among the most sublimated expressions. For certain men feel so great a need to exercise their strength and lust for power that, in default of other objects or because their efforts in other directions have always miscarried, they at last hit upon the idea of tyrannizing over certain parts of their own nature, over as it were segments or stages of themselves. (*HA*, 137)

Asceticism, or at least many forms of it, is here explained as an outcome of the redirection of the tyrannical drive back on to oneself, which drive is then said to have been 'sublimated'. In Nietzsche's subsequent discussions of it, asceticism acquires a very wide connotation, sometimes being virtually equated with self-control: the 'problem of the ascetic' was for him at bottom the problem of how self-control is possible; and in linking this phenomenon with a sublimated form of the thirst to tyrannize he was taking the first step towards a theory of 'will to power' as a monistic principle by which all activity might be understood.

III

Daybreak and *The Gay Science* take the conception of the dominant role of the desire for power a good deal further. (*Daybreak* also offers a number of interpretations of human behaviour in terms of fear – in, for example, sections 26, 104, 142, 173, 174, 220, 250, 309 and 310 – but the idea does not, in the present context, need extended discussion, since it was soon abandoned in favour of regarding the emotion of fear as a negative aspect of the drive to power, i.e. as the feeling of lack of power.)

The term 'recipes for the feeling of power' is employed in a passage which asserts that there is one order of them for those 'who can control themselves and who are thereby already accustomed to a feeling of power' and another for those 'in whom precisely this is lacking': men of the former sort are catered for by Brahmanism, those of the latter sort by Christianity (*D*, 65). A recipe of Nietzsche's own is given in the one-line aphorism: '*Field dispensary of the soul.* – What is the strongest remedy? – Victory.' (*D*, 571).

Victory restores or confirms our sense of power; if victory eludes us, however, we try to achieve this by a different recipe:

> If a war proves unsuccessful, one always asks who was 'to blame' for it . . . Guilt is everywhere sought in cases of failure; for failure

brings with it a depression of spirits the sole remedy for which is instinctively applied: a new arousal of the *feeling of power* – and this is to be found in the *condemnation* of the 'guilty party'. This guilty one is not a scapegoat for the guilt of others: he is a sacrifice to the weak, humiliated and depressed, who want to demonstrate to themselves on something that they still have some strength left. To condemn oneself can also be a means towards restoring the feeling of strength after a defeat. (*D*, 140)

These are fairly direct methods of enjoying the feeling of power, but it is the indirect and 'masked' methods which exercise a greater fascination on the psychological investigator. It is observed that 'a person of aristocratic habits, man or woman, does not like to fall into a chair as if utterly exhausted; where everybody makes himself comfortable, when travelling on the railway for example, he avoids leaning against his back': these and similar practices 'are an expression of the fact that the consciousness of power is constantly playing its charming game in his limbs' (*D*, 201). The habits of the capitalist class are, however, traceable to a comparable origin: if a man perpetrates petty crimes with the object of acquiring more money,

> if three-quarters of the upper classes indulge in permitted fraud and have the stock exchange and speculations on their conscience: what drives them? Not actual need, for they are not so badly off . . . they are afflicted day and night by a fearful impatience at the slow way in which their money is accumulating and by an equally fearful pleasure in and love of accumulated money. In this impatience and this love, however, there turns up again that fanaticism of the *lust for power* which was in former times inflamed by the belief one was in possession of the truth and which bore such beautiful names that one could thenceforward venture to be inhuman *with a good conscience* (to burn Jews, heretics and good books and exterminate entire higher cultures, such as those of Peru and Mexico). (*D*, 204)

The 'means employed by the lust for power' have changed, but only the means: 'what one formerly did "for the sake of God" one now does for the sake of money, that is to say, for the sake of that which *now* gives the highest feeling of power and a good conscience.'

The 'improved' version of Luke 18:14 now receives an explicit exegesis in the form of a contrast between the 'unegoistic morality' of self-sacrifice and the 'egoistic morality' of self-control.

> 'Enthusiastic devotion', 'sacrifice of oneself' – these are the catchwords of your morality, and I can readily believe that you are, as you say, 'in earnest about it' . . . From the heights of this morality you look down on that other sober morality which demands self-control, severity, obedience, and even call it egoistic. And, to be sure . . . you *must* find it disagreeable! For by devoting yourselves with enthusiasm and making a sacrifice of yourselves you enjoy the ecstatic thought of henceforth being at one with the powerful being, whether a god or a man, to whom you dedicate yourselves: you revel in the feeling of his power, to which your very sacrifice is an additional witness. The truth of the matter is that you only *seem* to sacrifice yourselves: in reality you transform yourselves in thought into gods and enjoy yourselves as such . . . how poor and weak seems to you that 'egoistic' morality of obedience, duty, rationality: it is disagreeable to you because in this case real sacrifice and devotion are demanded *without* the sacrificer supposing himself transformed into a god.
> (*D*, 215)

In the political arena, whether domestic or international, the determining factor is seen as the desire for the feeling of power, together with a good conscience in possessing this feeling. 'Not necessity, not desire – no, the love of power is the demon of men. Let them have everything – health, food, a place to live, entertainment – they are and remain unhappy and low-spirited: for the demon waits and waits and will be satisfied. Take everything from them and satisfy this, and they are almost happy – as happy as men and demons can be.' But all this has already been said by Luther in the lines 'Let them take from us our body, goods, honour, children, wife: let it all go – the empire [*Reich*] must yet remain to us!' and Nietzsche comments: 'Yes! Yes! The "*Reich*"!' (*D*, 262). Luther's *Reich*, the kingdom of God, is a promise of power, and so is the earthly *Reich* recently re-established in the middle of Europe: the means are different but the end is the same.

In 'grand politics' the strongest tide is 'the need for the feeling of power, which, not only in the souls of the princes and the powerful, but not least in the lower orders of the people, bursts forth from time to time out of inexhaustible wells.' Again and again there comes the hour 'when the masses *are ready* to risk their lives, their goods, their consciences, their virtues, in order to procure that supremest of enjoyments and as a victorious, tyrannical, capricious nation to rule over other nations (or to imagine it rules).' This tyranny is not something that offends the conscience of the tyrant, though it does that of the nation tyrannized over: 'when man possesses the feeling of power he feels and calls himself good: and precisely then the others upon whom he has to *discharge* his power feel and call him *evil*' (D, 189).

An aphorism called 'The state as a product of the anarchists' attributes to pleasure in a feeling of power a phenomenon which has since become more familiar than it was in the 1880s:

> In the lands where man is restrained and subdued there are still
> plenty of backsliding and unsubdued men: at the present moment
> they collect in the socialist camps more than anywhere else. If it
> should happen that they should one day lay down *laws*, then you
> can be sure they will put themselves in iron chains and practice a
> fearful discipline: *they know themselves!* And they will endure
> these laws in the consciousness of having imposed them on
> themselves – the feeling of power, and of *this* power, is too new
> and delightful for them not to suffer anything for its sake. (D, 184)

Nietzsche's tendency is at this date to set aside all other affects as subsidiary and retain only the affect of increased power as the sensation towards the production of which all activity is directed. '"Procuring pain in the abstract" *does not exist* . . . just as "procuring pleasure in the abstract" does not exist' is now rephrased as 'In doing good and doing harm one exercises one's power on others – that is all one desires to do!' Even if we 'make sacrifices in doing good or doing harm', that does not alter

> the ultimate value of our action; even if we stake our life, as a
> martyr does for the sake of his church – it is a sacrifice to *our*
> longing for power or in order to preserve our feeling of power.
> He who then feels 'I am in possession of the truth', how many
> possessions does he not let go in order to retain this sensation!
> What does he not throw overboard in order to keep himself 'on
> high' – that is to say *above* the others who lack the 'truth'! (GS, 13)

A 'common basic drive' now unites the most diverse activities: 'The first effect of happiness is the *feeling of power*: this wants to *express itself*, either to us ourselves, or to other men, or to ideas or imaginary beings. The most usual modes of expression are: to give, to mock, to destroy – all three out of a common basic drive' (D, 356). And when Nietzsche turns again to the ascetic – to the man who practises that 'defiance of oneself' – he is now able to extrapolate the drive which finds expression in him to the whole world of human culture. In spite of its length the passage is worth quoting almost in full, for it demonstrates more convincingly than any second-hand account could to how great a degree the conception of the primacy of the power-demand had taken possession of his mind and how central it had become to his thinking about the origins of human behaviour:

> *The striving for distinction* The striving for distinction keeps a
> constant eye on the next man and wants to know what his
> feelings are: but the empathy which this drive requires for its
> gratification is far from being harmless or sympathetic or kind.
> We want, rather, to perceive or divine how the next man
> outwardly or inwardly *suffers* from us, how he loses control over
> himself and surrenders to the impressions our hand or even merely
> the sight of us make upon him; and even when he who strives
> after distinction makes and wants to make a joyful, elevating, or
> cheering impression, he none the less enjoys this success not
> inasmuch as he has given joy to the next man or elevated or
> cheered him, but inasmuch as he has *impressed* himself on the soul
> of the other, changed its shape and ruled over it at his own sweet
> will. The striving for distinction is the striving for domination
> over the next man, though it be a very indirect domination and
> only felt or even dreamed. There is a long scale of degrees of this
> secretly desired domination, and a complete catalogue of them
> would be almost the same thing as a history of culture, from the
> earliest, still grotesque barbarism up to the grotesqueries of
> over-refinement and morbid idealism. The striving for distinction
> brings with it *for the next man* – to name only a few steps on this
> long ladder: torment, then blows, then terror, then fearful
> astonishment, then wonderment, then envy, then admiration,
> then elevation, then joy, then cheerfulness, then laughter, then
> derision, then mockery, then ridicule, then giving blows, then
> imposing torment: – here at the end of the ladder stands the
> *ascetic* and martyr, who feels the highest enjoyment by himself
> enduring, as a consequence of his drive for distinction, precisely
> that which, on the first step of the ladder, his counterpart the

barbarian imposes on others on whom and before whom he wants
to distinguish himself. The triumph of the ascetic over himself . . .
this final tragedy of the drive for distinction in which there is
only one character burning and consuming himself – this is a
worthy conclusion and one appropriate to the commencement:
in both cases an unspeakable happiness at the *sight of torment*!
Indeed, happiness, conceived of as the liveliest feeling of power,
has perhaps been nowhere greater on earth than in the souls of
superstitious ascetics. This is expressed by the Brahmins in the
story of King Vicvamitra, who derived such strength from a
thousand-year *penance* that he undertook to build a new *Heaven*.
I believe that in this whole species of inner experience we are now
incompetent novices groping after the solution of riddles: they
knew more about these infamous refinements of self-enjoyment
four thousand years ago. The creation of the world: perhaps it
was then thought of by some Indian dreamer as an ascetic
operation on the part of a god! Perhaps the god wanted to banish
himself into active and moving nature as into an instrument of
torture, in order thereby to feel his bliss and power doubled!
And supposing it was a god of love: what enjoyment for such a
god to create *suffering* men, to suffer divinely and superhumanly
from the ceaseless torment of the sight of them, and thus to
tyrannize over himself! And even supposing it was not only a god
of love, but also a god of holiness and sinlessness: what deliriums
of the divine ascetic can be imagined when he creates sin and
sinners and eternal damnation and a vast abode of eternal
affliction and eternal groaning and sighing! – It is not altogether
impossible that the souls of Dante, Paul, Calvin and their like
may also once have penetrated the gruesome secrets of such
voluptuousness of power – and in face of such souls one can ask:
is the circle of striving for distinction really at an end with the
ascetic? Could this circle not be run through again from the
beginning . . . doing hurt to others in order thereby to hurt
oneself, in order then to triumph over oneself and one's pity and to
revel in an extremity of power! – Excuse these extravagant
reflexions on all that may have been possible on earth through the
psychical extravagance of the lust for power! (*D*, 113)

IV

Such a passage as this invites elucidation in *psychological* terms, and the invitation has been accepted by many commentators from Lou Salomé onwards: the ideas in it are explained as a product of neurotic tensions within the author, and the exegetical principle thus established is employed to account for the existence of his entire work. The main effect of such a procedure, it goes without saying, is to devalue the work: it is reduced to a psychiatric case history. The fault in this approach is not that its findings are wrong – for it does seem evident, indeed almost palpably evident, that many of Nietzsche's 'intuitions' are a product of neurotic tensions – but that the premise from which it starts is wrong. That it should occur to anyone to undertake a posthumous psychiatric examination of Nietzsche is already and in itself proof that his works are not reducible to a psychiatric case history: for if they were really no more than that, nobody would ever have heard of him. It is the independent existence of his 'ideas' as ideas, the interest they have aroused, and the influence they have exercised, which really constitutes 'Nietzsche' as a cultural phenomenon: the human being struggling with neurotic tension is 'Nietzsche' only in a very narrow sense. To employ an analogy: if someone undertook to show that the compositions of Verdi were in some sense a product of neurotic tension he would have plenty of evidence to draw on and his investigations would be interesting: but if he concluded that *Il Trovatore* was no more than an item in a psychiatric case history he would be no longer interesting but wrong. *Il Trovatore* is a cultural fact of the first order: and in relation to it 'Verdi' is in the last resort no more than a postulate necessitated by the fact that works of art do not produce themselves. To assess the quality of *Il Trovatore* by assessing the quality of Verdi is (obviously in this case) to stand the matter on its head: but the same is true in the case of Nietzsche. The false premise of the psychologizing approach is that the phenomenon to be explained and assessed is Professor Dr Nietzsche: but he is of interest only because he was, one understands, the author of *Beyond Good and Evil* and the other 'works of Nietzsche' – he derives his interest, importance and quality from them, and *they* are the phenomena to be assessed. The psychiatric approach is from the wrong direction. It says: 'The author of these ideas was neurotic: it is in this light that we should judge them.' It should say: 'These ideas are a cultural fact of the first order: it is in this light that we should judge their author.'

86

A different consideration brought into prominence by such a passage as D 113 is whether Nietzsche's reputation as an *advocate* of 'power' can possibly be justified. What he appears to say is that the drive to enhanced power is, as a matter of fact, the basic drive in man, and the feeling of enhanced power the becoming-conscious of the successful operation of this drive: mankind desires only greater power and is consequently happy when, and only when, this desire is satisfied. This assertion, whether it be true or false, is in itself neutral with respect to 'approval' or 'disapproval'; but the discovery of the power-drive behind a multitude of human activities has the effect of 'unmasking' them, and that in turn produces a discrediting effect: it tends to *show up* the valued qualities of man as being of base origin. There are, moreover, many instances in which he clearly does disapprove of the manifestations of the drive to power which he discusses.

Part of the answer to this question is that Nietzsche was evidently *not* an advocate of 'power' in the sense in which he is often understood to be. Ultimately he will have no choice but to say that 'power itself' is 'good' (*A*, 2), but that does not mean he will have to accord blanket approval to every form of activity prompted by the power-drive. Certainly he is not logically compelled to. To take another analogy: Freud, if he had been given to expressing himself in this fashion, would have had to describe 'sexuality itself' as good; but that would not have committed him to advocating rape.

V

In what way Nietzsche must, however, be called an advocate of power will begin to become clear if we consider some of the manifestations of the power-drive of which he does evidently approve. In an aphorism called 'Subtlety of the feeling of power' he discusses the tortuous way in which, he maintains, Napoleon dealt with his inability to speak well:

> Napoleon was annoyed at his inability to speak well ... but his lust for domination, which neglected no opportunity and was subtler than his subtle intellect, persuaded him into speaking worse *than he could*. Thus he revenged himself on his own annoyance (he was jealous of all his affects because they possessed *power*) and felt the enjoyment of exercising his autocratic *pleasure*. (*D*, 245)

This is a form of 'defiance of oneself' from the contemplation of which Nietzsche appears to derive satisfaction: it is a sort of active contempt for some defect in oneself. But its effect is still something relatively trivial, and amounts to hardly more than a personal quirk: of greater significance for a more general appreciation of what might be positively valuable in the exercise of the power-drive against oneself is the following passage on punishment and self-punishment:

> Is a state of affairs unthinkable in which the malefactor calls himself to account and publicly dictates his own punishment, in the proud feeling that he is thus honoring the law which he himself has made, that by punishing himself he is exercising his power, the power of the lawgiver? . . . Such would be the criminal of a possible future, who, to be sure, also presupposes a future lawgiving – one founded on the idea 'I submit only to the law which I myself have given, in great things and in small.' (D, 187)

What is recommended here is not the exercise of that sublimated form of tyranny 'lawgiving', but its exercise against oneself: and that in turn is only one aspect of what soon becomes a recommendation to a sort of total tyranny over oneself. In *The Gay Science*, Nietzsche calls this self-tyranny '"giving style" to one's character', and says that he exercises it 'who surveys all that his nature presents in strength and weakness and then moulds it to an artistic plan until everything appears as art and reason, and even the weaknesses delight the eye.' The operation is described metaphorically in terms of landscape gardening: 'Here a large amount of second nature has been added, here a piece of original nature removed – in both instances with protracted practice and daily labour. Here that which is ugly but cannot be removed is concealed, there reinterpreted into the sublime', and so on: and Nietzsche asserts that 'it will be the strong, imperious natures which experience their subtlest joy in exercising such control, in such constraint and perfecting under their own law' (GS, 290).

Let us at once, as a gloss on this passage, reproduce another in which the process described is related without metaphor:

> If we consider all that has hitherto been reverenced as 'superhuman mind', as 'genius', we come to the sad conclusion that the intellectuality of mankind must on the whole have been something very low and paltry: it has hitherto required so little mind to feel at once considerably superior to it! . . . We are still

on our knees before *strength* . . . and yet when the degree of *worthiness to be reverenced* is fixed, only the *degree of rationality in strength* is decisive: we must measure to what extent precisely strength has been overcome by something higher, in the service of which it now stands as means and instrument! . . . perhaps the most beautiful still appears only in the dark, and sinks, scarcely born, into eternal night – I mean the spectacle of that strength which employs genius *not for works* but *for itself as a work*; that is, for its own constraint, for the purification of its imagination, for the imposition of order and choice upon the influx of tasks and impressions. (D, 548)

In both passages the urge to overcome, the drive to enhanced power is exercised, not on others, but on oneself: it is directed back and becomes inward. This is not yet a 'theory of will to power', but it might become one by the addition of a single hypothesis: that the operation ascribed to 'genius' is in fact universal. If the formation of people, nations, and ultimately mankind itself could be seen as the expulsion of 'a piece of first nature' and the importation in its place of 'a great mass of second nature', the exercise of strength for 'its own constraint, . . . for the imposition of order and choice upon the influx of tasks and impressions', so that mankind itself would be that 'genius' which employs its strength '*not for works* but *for itself as a work*' – then the drive to power of which this self-control and self-modification is an aspect would appear in an entirely new light: it would be, not only a beneficent force, but actually the basic instinct behind all distinctively human activity and perhaps behind all activity, behind the phenomenon 'life' itself. The mass of suggestions regarding the existence of the power-drive behind all kinds of actions not obviously deriving from it would then fall into perspective: these actions would be relatively trivial manifestations of the drive to which, on the grandest scale, mankind itself owes its existence.

VI

It was this line of reasoning, or something similar to it, which transformed the essentially destructive analysis of human actions as expressions of the desire for a feeling of enhanced power into the idea expressed for the first time in the first part of *Thus Spoke Zarathustra*:

'A table of values hangs over every people. Behold, it is the table of its overcomings; behold, it is the voice of its will to power' (*Z*, I. 15).

The term 'overcomings' is immediately glossed: 'What it accounts hard it calls praiseworthy; what it accounts indispensable and hard it calls good; and that which relieves the greatest need, the rare, the hardest of all – it glorifies as holy.' And further: 'Whatever causes it to rule and conquer and glitter, to the dread and envy of its neighbour, that it accounts the sublimest, the paramount, the evaluation and meaning of all things.' If, Zarathustra goes on, you could know 'a people's need and land and sky and neighbour', you would then be able to divine 'the law of its overcomings, and why it is upon this ladder that it mounts towards its hope.' He then gives some examples. 'You should always be the first and outrival all others: your jealous soul should love no one except it be your friend': it was this command which 'made the soul of a Greek tremble: in following it he followed his path of greatness.' 'To speak the truth and know well how to handle bow and arrow' is the command which the Persian set over himself. 'To honour father and mother and to do their will even from the roots of the soul': it was this 'table of overcoming' which 'another people hung over itself and became mighty and eternal with it' – plainly the Jewish nation is meant. 'To practice loyalty [*Treue*] and for the sake of loyalty to risk honour and blood even in evil and dangerous causes': the self-overcoming of the Germans.

The conclusion he draws is that 'men have given themselves all their good and evil ... they did not take it, they did not find it, it did not descend to them as a voice from Heaven' (*Z*, I. 15). The question 'what is good?' – understood in the meta-ethical sense of 'when people say a thing is good what does "good" mean?' – is here answered: good means that which is hard but possible, which is attained by 'self-overcoming', and the attainment of which is attended by the feeling of enhanced power: power over others, power also over oneself. But since it is the drive to enhanced power turned inward which is the agent of 'self-overcoming'; since it is that same 'defiance of oneself' through which the ascetic enjoys a sense of power which here, on a grander scale, affects an entire people – this definition of what is good already comes close to the simple assertion 'power itself is good'.

As this theory had at first been developed from contemplation of the single individual, so, in the second part of *Zarathustra*, it is transferred back to him. In the chapter called 'Of Self-Overcoming' (*Z*, II. 12), Zarathustra says that what is called 'will to truth' is in reality 'will to the conceivability of all being', and explains this expression as the desire that 'all being ... shall bend and accommodate itself to you'. Thus 'will to truth' is 'will to power' over all things, and it remains this 'even when you talk of good and evil and of the assessment of values.' Will to power, however, is the fundamental fact of life. Every living thing 'is an obeying thing': and even that which commands itself is still obedient, inasmuch as it obeys its own commands: 'It must become judge and avenger and victim of its own law.' But how has this come about? 'What persuades the living creature to obey and command and to practise obedience even in commanding?' The answer is that 'where I found a living creature, there I found will to power.' Even in the will of the servant there is will to be master: the weaker serves the stronger so that it may be master over those weaker still; and the strongest of all 'for the sake of power stakes – life'. Zarathustra then repeats what 'life itself' has told him: 'I am that *which must overcome itself again and again* ... you call it will to procreation or impulse towards a goal, towards the higher, more distant, more manifold: but all this is one and *one* secret ... Whatever I create and however much I love it – soon I have to oppose it and my love: thus will my will have it. And you too, enlightened man, are only a path and footstep of my will: truly, my will to power walks with the feet of your will to truth! ... The living creature values many things higher than life itself; yet out of this evaluation itself speaks – the will to power!'

The 'self-overcoming' of a nation for the sake of power is now seen as a general characteristic of life itself, to which the continuance of life itself is subordinate: the 'living creature' wants power – power over others and power over itself ('self-overcoming') – *more* than it wants mere existence. If this proposition is not quite self-evident, it is only because of the appearance in it of the concept of 'power': for all history and all private experience provides evidence that there is at any rate *something* men, women and animals desire more than they desire the simple continuance of life, and for the sake of which they are willing to risk life. Nietzsche's innovation is to suggest that this something – which unquestionably exists – is the feeling of enhanced power: and he ventures the generalization that it is the drive to attain this feeling which lies behind all activity.

VII

That an individual's will to power can act on the individual himself – a process called in *Zarathustra* 'self-overcoming' and elsewhere 'sublimation' – is the presupposition behind the '*Übermensch*', who will be discussed in a moment. In the works which succeeded *Zarathustra*, Nietzsche expanded on the theory of will to power in other directions and expatiated on its consequences.

He suggests that, granted 'nothing is "given" as real except our world of desires and passions', granted 'we can rise or sink to no other "reality" than the reality of our drives – for thinking is only the relationship of these drives to one another', we ought to see whether this which is given does not suffice to explain the rest of the world – 'the so-called mechanical (or "material") world' – also, and then whether 'our world of desires and passions' cannot be explained as 'the development and ramification of *one* basic form of will – as will to power, as is *my* theory.' Supposing this were done, 'one would have acquired the right to define *all* efficient force unequivocally as: *will to power*. The world seen from within, the world described and defined according to its "intelligible character" – it would be "will to power" and nothing else' (*BGE*, 36). This line of inquiry does not seem very promising and is not pursued except in unpublished notes, where, as previously remarked, an effort is made to reduce 'power' to 'force', and the uncomfortable word 'will' is sometimes avoided. The ineradicable teleology of a 'drive to power', whatever form of words is used to describe it, continued however to constitute an insurmountable obstacle to its impersonalization.

A more satisfactory development lay in the direction of employing the asserted ubiquity of the power drive to account for those conventionally condemned – or, as Nietzsche puts it, 'slandered' – phenomena which Schopenhauer had attributed to an uncompromising 'will to live'. Nietzsche again and again insists that 'life' *is* contest, conflict, 'injustice'. 'To refrain from mutual injury, mutual violence, mutual exploitation,' he writes in *Beyond Good and Evil*,

> may in a certain rough sense become good manners between individuals if the conditions for it are present (namely if their strength and value standards are in fact similar and they both belong to *one* body). As soon as there is a desire to take this

principle further, however, and if possible even as the *fundamental principle of society*, it at once reveals itself for what it is: as the will to *denial* of life ... Life itself is *essentially* appropriation, injury, overpowering of the strange and weaker, suppression, severity, imposition of one's own forms, incorporation and, at the least and mildest, exploitation ... 'Exploitation' does not pertain to a corrupt or imperfect and primitive society: it pertains to the *essence* of the living thing as a fundamental organic function, it is a consequence of the intrinsic will to power which is precisely the will of life. (*BGE*, 259)

I call such an idea more satisfactory because it faces certain facts about life which many today would like to deny, although they are as palpable now as they ever were. The nineteenth-century 'Darwinist' doctrine that life is a war of all against all was unquestionably onesided: it ignored the immense amount of co-operation or at least peaceful coexistence which obtains even in the animal kingdom. At present the onesidedness is probably reversed: the life of society, even the day-to-day life of the individual, is informed with conflicts of all kind, but we like to think they could all, in theory at least, be avoided. Nietzsche's view was that conflict is a general condition of life, to be accounted for through the ubiquity of the 'will to power'; that it is through conflict that 'progress' in any sense is possible; and that a condition in which conflict is absent, or even the desire for such a condition, is an end-condition, a state of stagnation.

This attitude of mind colours a great deal of his later writing, and gives it its characteristic pathos; and it is something about which the reader of Nietzsche has sooner or later to make up his mind. It is largely a question of deciding how far you can follow him when he spins out the consequences of his thesis that that which enhances the feeling of power is, in the last resort, to be accorded approval. One is, for instance, unlikely to experience very much *emotional* reaction from the reading of such a passage as this, from the later, fifth book of *The Gay Science*:

To want to preserve oneself is the expression of a state of distress, of a limitation of the true basic drive of life, which aims at *extension of power* and with this in view often enough calls in question self-preservation and sacrifices it ... in nature, the *rule* is not a state of distress but one of superfluity and prodigality, even to the point of absurdity. The struggle for existence is only

93

an *exception*, a temporary restriction of the basic will of life; the struggle, great and small, turns everywhere on ascendancy, on growth and extension, on power, in accordance with the will to power, which is precisely the will of life. (*GS*, 349)

The criticism of Darwin involved here – the question whether the conflict which, it is asserted, determines the course of existence arises from need or from a drive to power – is likely to seem an academic and theoretical one; and the simplified formulation in *Beyond Good and Evil* – 'Physiologists should think again before positing the drive to self-preservation as the cardinal drive in an organic being. A living thing wants above all to *vent* its strength – life itself is will to power –: self-preservation is only one of the indirect and most frequent consequences of it' (*BGE*, 13) – may even appear to be nothing more than a difference over what terms to employ.

It is when certain other consequences are drawn that the reader cannot remain quite so indifferent: as, for example, they are in this extract from a lengthy argument in the *Genealogy of Morals*:

> Even a partial *becoming useless*, an atrophying and degeneration, a loss of meaning and purposiveness, in short death, is among the conditions of actual *progressus*; and this always appears in the form of a will and way to *greater power*, and is always carried through at the expense of numerous smaller powers. The magnitude of an 'advance' is even to be *measured* by the mass of things that had to be sacrificed to it; mankind in the mass sacrificed to the prosperity of a single *stronger* species of man—that *would* be an advance ... (*GM*, II. 12)

Everyone who elects to concern himself with Nietzsche and his philosophy will have to decide for and by himself what he is to make of such assertions. He will need to remember that they are consistent with Nietzsche's later philosophical position that what increases 'power in man' is good; he will also need to remember what happened when a movement dedicated itself, in some of its more intellectual members at any rate, to a programme of sacrificing mankind in the mass to an ideal of progress; and he will need to remember, thirdly, that the nature and deeds of this movement do not constitute a proof that 'mankind in the mass sacrificed to the prosperity of a single *stronger* species of man' would *not* constitute real progress: the question would be what constituted a 'stronger' species of man, what the 'sacrifice' of the mass of mankind entailed, and what was meant by 'progress'.

It does not, however, require much insight to see that by 'species' Nietzsche does not mean primarily a particular nation or race, but a kind of man, a strong and powerful *type*: an individual whose 'victory' would not be the victory of Tweedledum over Tweedledee. In this direction, though, there also lie very uncomfortable assertions: such as this unpublished one regarding the higher type represented by Napoleon:

> The Revolution made Napoleon possible: that is its justification.
> For the sake of a similar prize one would have to desire the
> anarchic collapse of our entire civilization ... the value of a human
> being ... does not reside in his usefulness: for it would continue
> to exist even if there were nobody to whom he could be useful.
> And why could the human being from whom the most deleterious
> effects proceeded not be the summit of the entire species man: so
> elevated, so superior that everything perished from envy of him?
> (*WP*, 877)

This, it must be emphasized, is not Nietzsche's last considered view of Napoleon; but the second part of it is certainly an entirely consistent, if paradoxically phrased, additional statement of what is already said and implied in his published works with regard to the 'great human being' who constitutes in himself a 'stronger species of man'; that his 'value' lies in himself and in what he is, and not in the 'use' to which he can be put.

In this direction the consequences following from the theory of will to power are, in fact, not social at all, and have nothing to do with the 'struggle for survival' or the domination of one species by another, one nation by another, one individual by another: they are concerned with what takes place within a single 'soul'.

VIII

That the central significance of the theory of will to power lies in its providing a means of individual self-transcendence has already been indicated in those passages in which Nietzsche describes effects of the drive to power of which he seems to approve: the 'spectacle of that strength which employs genius *not for works* but *for itself as a work*', for example, and the process described as '"giving style" to one's

95

character'. Similar thoughts are expressed in different ways in the passage headed '*Excelsior!*' (quoted on p. 68), and in such aphorisms as these following:

> *What we are at liberty to do* One can dispose of one's drives like a gardener and, though few know it, cultivate the shoots of anger, pity, curiosity, vanity as productively and profitably as a beautiful fruit tree on a trellis; one can do it with the good or bad taste of a gardener, and as it were in the French or English or Dutch or Chinese fashion; one can also let nature rule and only attend to a little embellishment and tidying-up here and there; one can, finally, without paying any attention to them at all, let the plants grow up according to their natural advantages and impediments and fight their fight out among themselves – indeed, one can take delight in such a wilderness and desire precisely this delight, though it gives one some trouble too. All this we are at liberty to do: but how many know we are at liberty to do it? Do the majority not *believe* in *themselves* as in complete *fully developed facts*? Have the great philosophers not put their seal on this prejudice with the doctrine of the unchangeability of character? (*D*, 560)

'Let us *limit* ourselves ... to the purification of our opinions and evaluations and to the *creation of our own new tables of values ... we ... want to become them who we are* – the new, the unique, the incomparable, those who give themselves their own laws, those who create themselves' (*GS*, 335).

The italicized phrase 'we ... *want to become them who we are*' has a history of its own in Nietzsche's writings which is not irrelevant to our discussion. It comes from Pindar, and Nietzsche first quoted it in 1868 as the motto of the first part of his prize essay on Diogenes Laertius (*De Laertii Diogenis fontibus*, 1868–9): 'Become him who you are!' It is repeated twice in *The Gay Science*, the first time as the answer to one of the eight questions which stand at the end of the second book: 'What does your conscience say? – "You should become him who you are"' (*GS*, 270). In the meantime it had received an explanatory gloss in *Schopenhauer as Educator*: 'The man who does not want to belong to the mass needs only to cease taking himself easily and to follow his conscience, which calls to him: "Be yourself! All you are now doing, thinking, desiring, is not you yourself" ... for your real nature lies ... immeasurably high above you, or at least above that which you usually take for yourself' (*UIII*, 1). Finally, in the last quarter of his active life, the phrase is accorded the greatest prominence as the subtitle of his autobiography: *Ecce Homo. How One Becomes What One Is.*

Even in the *Untimely Meditations* there is a clear, though as yet not explicit connection between the idea of 'becoming him who you are' and an insistence, firstly on the supreme value of the individual, then on the notion that this individual has to be *formed*. The *Meditation* on history asserts that 'the *goal of humanity* cannot lie in the end but only *in its highest specimens*' (*UII*, 9), and suggests that the formation of individuals is a process analogous to that by which Greek civilization was created:

> There were centuries during which the Greeks found themselves
> faced by a danger similar to that which faces us: the danger of
> being overwhelmed by what was past and foreign ... their
> culture was for a long time a chaos of foreign, Semitic,
> Babylonian, Lydian, Egyptian forms and ideas, and their religion
> a battle of all the gods of the East ... The Greeks gradually
> learned to *organize the chaos* by ... thinking back to themselves,
> that is to their real needs ... Thus they again took possession of
> themselves ... This is a parable for each of us: he must organize
> the chaos within him by thinking back to his real needs ... Thus
> there will be revealed to him the Greek idea of culture ... as a
> new and improved *physis*' (*UII*, 10)

The proposition that you should become him who you are, illumined by this account of what the process might entail and by the assertion that 'your real nature lies ... immeasurably high above you', is then generalized into the proposition that becoming him who you are is something all mankind, indeed all nature, is engaged upon: 'As long as anyone desires life as a pleasure he has not raised his eyes above the horizon of the animal ... But that is what we all do for the greater part of our lives: we do not usually get beyond animality ... But there are moments *when we realize this* ... we see that, in common with all nature, we are pushing towards man [*Mensch*] as towards something that stands high above [*über*] us' (*UIII*, 5).

IX

This background alone, it seems to me, almost suffices to make clear what is meant by the word *Übermensch* when Zarathustra employs it: 'I teach you the *Übermensch*. Man is something that should be overcome'

(Z, Prologue, 3); and when he goes on: 'All creatures hitherto have created something beyond themselves: and do you want to be the ebb of this great tide, and return to the animals rather than overcome man?' It almost suffices to explain what he means by the assertion: 'Man is a rope, fastened between animal and superman ... What is great in man is that he is a bridge and not a goal' (ibid., 4); and by the saying, 'Uncanny is human existence and still without meaning ... I want to teach men the meaning of their existence: which is the superman, the lightning from the dark cloud man' (ibid., 7). These are 'poetical' expressions of the by now familiar idea that 'man' is something which as yet lies high 'over' mankind, and that mankind's task is to form and cultivate him.

The 'superman' is a certain type of *man*, and not – as Zarathustra's rhapsodies sometimes give the impression he is – a form of life destined to supercede man. It must have been a consciousness that he succeeded in conveying this mistaken and rather absurd idea that prompted Nietzsche to the more explicit account given in *The Anti-Christ*: 'The problem I raise here is not what ought to succeed mankind in the sequence of species (the human being is an *end*): but what type of human being one ought to *breed*, ought to *will*, as more valuable, more worthy of life, more certain of the future. This more valuable type has existed often enough already: but as a lucky accident, as an exception, never as *willed*' (A, 3). And again: 'Mankind does *not* represent a development of the better or the stronger or the higher in the way that is believed today ... onward development is not by *any* means, by any necessity the same thing as elevation, advance, strengthening. In another sense there are cases of individual success constantly appearing in the most various parts of the earth and from the most various cultures in which a *higher type* does manifest itself: something which in relation to collective mankind is a sort of superman' (A, 4). The superman is not man's successor, but rather God's. Immediately before his speech on the superman, Zarathustra announces that 'God is dead' (Prologue, 2), and the death of God is referred to in the course of the same speech. But God had hitherto been the 'meaning of ... being': now the superman is to fill this office. 'Once you said "God" when you gazed upon distant seas', he says later on; 'but now I have taught you to say "superman". God is a supposition; but I want your supposing to reach no further than your creating will. Could you *create* a god? – So be silent about all gods. But you could surely create the superman' (Z, II. 2).

The reader may remember what I wrote earlier about the superman as a 'cipher' (see p. 12): in this sense the conception is to be understood as an image of the kind of man in whose person the nihilism of the world-outlook Nietzsche had been evolving would be overcome; and note that here too, as in the passages from *The Anti-Christ*, this kind of man is not envisaged as belonging to some remote or perhaps impossible future, but is described as having already existed. The *Übermensch*, in fact, is to some extent a compendium of all that Nietzsche regards as desirable in man: compare, as a single instance, the character of the 'criminal of a possible future' who submits 'only to the law which I have given myself' with Zarathustra's admonition to the man who wants to seek 'the way to himself': 'can you furnish yourself with your own good and evil and hang up your own will above yourself as a law? Can you be judge of yourself and avenger of your law?' (*Z*, I. 17).

This 'cipher' of the man who is a '*Typhus höchster Wohlgeratenheit*' – a type who has turned out supremely well – is described many times, but perhaps nowhere better than in two notes dating from the *Zarathustra* period (1885 and 1884 respectively):

> In the main I am more in accord with the artists than with any of the philosophers hitherto: they have not lost the great scent of life, they have loved the things of 'this world' – they have loved their senses. To strive for 'desensualization': that seems to me a misunderstanding or a sickness, or a cure, where it is not mere hypocrisy or self-deception. I wish for myself and for all those who live – who *may* live – without the anguish of a puritan conscience an ever-greater spiritualization and multiplication of their senses; let us, indeed, be grateful to the senses for their subtlety, plenitude and strength and offer them in exchange the best we have of spirit. What are priestly and metaphysical calumnies of the senses to us! We no longer require this calumny: it is a sign of having turned out well [*Wohlgeratenheit*] when, like Goethe, a man clings with ever-greater joy and cordiality to the 'things of the world' – for in this way he adheres to the great conception of man that man becomes *the transfigurer of existence* when he learns to transfigure himself. (*WP*, 820)

> I teach: that there are higher and lower men, and that a single individual can under certain circumstances justify the existence of entire millennia – that is to say, a full, rich, great, whole man in regard to countless incomplete fragmentary men. (*WP*, 997)

X

The *psychological* content of the superman is that he is the embodiment of sublimated will to power. The process of 'sublimation' – the basic idea behind which is that activities of a distinctively human sort are made possible by the transformation in man of the drives he shares with the animals, and that these drives are capable of an almost limitless *degree* of transformation – is described very many times. The earlier accounts refer to the transformation of 'drives' and 'passions', with sexuality well to the fore – as might be expected in a student of Schopenhauer, to whom sexuality was the strongest, indeed the focal point of the 'will to live'; later, all drives and passions are subsumed under the rubric 'will to power', and it is this the transformation of which is discussed. For our present purpose we need go no further back than the essay 'Homer's Contest' (*Five Prefaces to Five Unwritten Books*, 1872), the opening paragraph of which reads:

> When one speaks of *humanity*, there lies behind it the idea that humanity is that which *separates* and distinguishes mankind from nature. But in reality there is no such separation: the 'natural' qualities and those called specifically 'human' are inextricably entwined together. Man is in his highest and noblest powers entirely nature and bears in him nature's uncanny dual character. Those capacities which are dreadful and accounted inhuman are, indeed, perhaps the fruitful soil out of which alone all humanity in impulse, act and deed can grow.

Mankind's 'highest and noblest powers' – those qualities which are human as distinct from animal – are not to be separated from the 'dreadful and inhuman' capacities. Perhaps the former would not even exist at all if they had not evolved from the latter.

The 'perhaps' is soon dropped: if the human qualities have *not* evolved from the animalic, Nietzsche cannot see where they can possibly have come from. But that means that the 'inhumanity' in man must be accorded its rights: it is not something which it would be desirable to abolish. The 'passions' must not be destroyed or 'slandered': 'let us rather work honestly together at the task of transforming the passions [*Leidenschaften*] of mankind one and all into joys [*Freudenschaften*]' (*WS*, 37). The passions are silently equated with what psycho-analysis would later call 'libido', and in an aphorism called

'Overcoming of the passions' Nietzsche asserts that 'The man who has overcome his passions has come into possession of the most fruitful of all soil; he is like the colonist who has mastered the forests and swamps' (*WS*, 53). In *Zarathustra* the transformation of the passions into virtues is described 'poetically', yet still in very much the same language as that used in *The Wanderer and his Shadow*: the chapter 'Of Joys and Passions' (*Von den Freuden-und Leidenschaften*) is wholly devoted to this phenomenon:

> Once you had passions and called them evil. But now you have
> only your virtues: they grew from out your passions. You laid
> your highest aim in the heart of these passions: then they become
> your virtues and joys. And though you came from the race of the
> hot-tempered or of the lustful or of the fanatical or of the
> revengeful: at last all your passions have become virtues and all
> your devils angels. Once you had fierce dogs in your cellar: but
> they changed at last into birds and sweet singers. From your
> poison you brewed your balm; you milked your cow affliction –
> now you drink the sweet milk of her udder. (*Z*, I. 5)

The conceptual content of all this is no more than what is stated in fewer words in 'Homer's Contest', namely that the human 'capacities which are dreadful and accounted inhuman' are 'the fruitful soil out of which alone all humanity in impulse, act and deed can grow'.

The employment of the 'passions', consequently *not* their extirpation: this is from now on Nietzsche's constant theme. '"Man is evil" – all the wisest men have told me that to comfort me. Ah, if only it be true today! For evil is man's best strength. "Man must grow better and more evil" – thus do *I* teach. The most evil is necessary for the super-man's best. . . . It does not suffice me that the lightning no longer does harm. I do not want to conduct it away: it shall learn – to work for *me*' (*Z*, IV. 13:5, 7). This 'provocative' formulation of 1885 – only one of many – says in essence what is said more soberly in this note of 1887 (again only one of many): 'To *press into service* everything dreadful . . . this is what the task of culture demands. . . . *Thesis*: everything good is something evil of former days made serviceable. *Standard*: the greater and more dreadful the passions are which an age, a people, an individual can permit themselves – because they are capable of employ-ing them *as means – the higher stands their culture*' (*WP*, 1025).

XI

Many difficulties about the 'superman' and what he is disappear if you grasp that Nietzsche is not trying to invert our moral judgments, but seeking a solution to the 'problem of evil'. It is wrong, for instance, to think that he 'is fond of expressing himself paradoxically' and 'does this by employing the words "good" and "evil" with their ordinary connotations, and then saying that he prefers "evil" to "good"', his real aim being to change 'the reader's opinion of what is good and what is evil' (Russell, *History of Western Philosophy*, p. 790). Nietzsche does, certainly, want to change the reader's attitude towards 'good and evil', but not in the sense of urging him to adopt a new code of morals antithetical to the old. To get beyond such simple antithesis is one of the main objectives of his moral philosophy, and is actually the meaning of 'beyond good and evil', the title of the book to which Russell is specifically referring in the passage from which the above sentences are taken. Russell believes that Nietzsche approves as 'good' that which he, Russell, regards as 'evil', but this is not the case. Nietzsche's critique of morality, in which he seeks to discover what 'good and evil' really are, will be considered later: but, quite aside from this, unless you understand that, when he uses the words good and evil 'with their ordinary connotations', he is not ushering in a paradox – that he, too, approves of 'good' and dislikes 'evil' – literally hundreds of passages in his works will make no sense. The point is crucial and we should therefore consider some examples.

Take, firstly, the passage already quoted from 'Homer's Contest': the assertion that 'all humanity in impulse, act and deed' can perhaps originate only out of 'those capacities which are dreadful and accounted inhuman'. If Russell's view of him were correct, Nietzsche would probably dislike the former qualities and approve of the latter: but can the passage possibly mean that? What it obviously means is that he approves of 'humanity', but suggests that it would not be possible without the existence of 'inhumanity', of which as such he disapproves. The same thought, persisting unchanged through the years, lies behind this note of 1887: 'Man is beast [*Untier*] and superbeast [*Übertier*]; the higher man is monster [*Unmensch*] and superman [*Übermensch*]: these things belong together. With every growth of man in greatness and height there is also a growth in depth and dreadfulness' (*WP*, 1027). Such a remark as this would be meaningless if Nietzsche regarded 'depth and dreadfulness' as good in the ordinary connotation of the word.

From *Human, All Too Human*:

> When we behold those deeply-furrowed hollows in which glaciers have lain, we think it hardly possible that a time will come when a wooded, grassy valley, watered by streams, will spread itself out upon the same spot. So it is too in the history of mankind: the most savage forces beat a path, and are mainly destructive; but their work was none the less necessary, in order that later a gentler civilization might raise its house. The frightful energies – those which are called evil – are the cyclopean architects and road-makers of humanity. (246)

What attitude towards 'the frightful energies – those which are called evil' is implied in this passage? That they are really 'good'? Obviously not: such an interpretation would, again, render the passage meaningless. Civilization is the desideratum, but it cannot be achieved without the preliminary work of the uncivilized forces 'called evil': that, surely, is the plain sense of it.

From *The Gay Science*:

> *Evil*   Examine the lives of the best and most fruitful men and peoples, and ask yourselves whether a tree, if it is to grow proudly into the sky, can do without bad weather and storms: whether unkindness and opposition from without, whether some sort of hatred, envy, obstinacy, mistrust, severity, greed and violence do not belong to the *favouring* circumstances without which a great increase even in virtue is hardly possible. (19)

Nietzsche is here urging us to change our attitude towards 'evil', but not in the sense of calling it 'good'. If 'bad weather and storms' were not evil and a tree growing 'proudly into the sky' not good; if 'hatred, envy, obstinacy, mistrust, severity, greed and violence' were not evil and 'a great increase . . . in virtue' not good – good and evil here used with their ordinary connotations – then the passage would, for a fourth time, make no sense. The (conventionally) good things are desired, but the (conventionally) evil things are held to be indispensable for their attainment.

From *Beyond Good and Evil*:

> Almost everything we call 'higher culture' is based on the

spiritualization and intensification of *cruelty* . . . That which constitutes the painful voluptuousness of tragedy is cruelty; that which produces a pleasing effect in so-called tragic pity, indeed fundamentally in everything sublime up to the highest and most refined thrills of metaphysics, derives its sweetness solely from the ingredient of cruelty mixed in with it. What the Roman in the arena, the Christian in the ecstasies of the Cross, the Spaniard watching burnings or bullfight, the Japanese of today crowding into the tragedy, the Parisian suburban workman who has a nostalgia for bloody revolutions, the Wagnerienne who, with will suspended, 'experiences' *Tristan und Isolde* – what all of these enjoy and look with secret ardour to imbibe is the spicy potion of the great Circe 'cruelty'. Here, to be sure, we must put aside the thick-witted psychology of former times which had to teach of cruelty only that it had its origin in the sight of the sufferings of *others*: there is also an abundant, over-abundant enjoyment of one's own suffering, of making oneself suffer – and wherever man allows himself to be persuaded to self-denial in the *religious* sense, or to self-mutilation . . . or in general to desensualization, decarnalization, contrition, to puritanical spasms of repentance, to conscience-vivisection and to a Pascalian *sacrifizio dell'intelletto*, he is secretly lured and urged onward by his cruelty, by the dangerous thrills of cruelty directed *against himself.* Consider, finally, how even the man of knowledge, when he compels his spirit to knowledge which is *counter* to the inclination of his spirit and frequently also to the desires of his heart – by saying No, that is, when he would like to affirm, love, worship – disposes as an artist in and transfigurer of cruelty . . . in all desire to know there is already a drop of cruelty. (229)

This is a description of phenomena which, it is asserted, are or contain sublimated cruelty, and an attempt to account for the existence of these phenomena at all: its author wants to persuade the reader to change his view of cruelty, so as to see it as a part of the total psychical economy of man the eradication of which would not be the wholly desirable thing many people might think. It is not the *plaidoyer* of a cruel man seeking to prove that cruelty is 'good'.

From *Twilight of the Idols*: 'The spiritualization of sensuality is called *love*: it is a great triumph over Christianity. Another triumph is our spiritualization of *enmity*' (V. 3). 'Spiritualization' (*Vergeistigung*) is one of Nietzsche's terms for sublimation. 'There is a time with all passions', he says, 'when they are merely fatalities, when they drag their victim down with the weight of their folly – and a later, very much later time when they are wedded with the spirit, when they are "spiritualized".' Formerly one desired to destroy the passions on account of the 'folly' inherent in them: 'the most famous formula for doing this is contained in the New Testament, in the Sermon on the Mount, where . . . for example it is said, with reference to sexuality, "if thy eye offend thee, pluck it out"'; today, however, 'to *exterminate* the passions and desires merely in order to do away with their folly and its unpleasant consequences seems to us merely an acute form of folly'. The church combats the passions 'with excision in every sense: its practice, its "cure" is *castration*. It never asks: "How can one spiritualize, beautify, deify a desire?" . . . But to attack the passions at their roots means to attack life at its roots: the practice of the church is *hostile to life*' (V. 1). The passions specifically referred to are 'sensuality, pride, lust for power, avarice, revengefulness': and sensuality 'spiritualized, beautified, deified', in short sublimated, is *love*. The nature of sublimated enmity and lust for power has been described often enough already; and the reader might care to infer for himself what sublimated pride, avarice and revengefulness might be. Is Nietzsche urging us to call these 'passions', normally regarded as bad, good? Is the sense of the argument not rather that what is good is their *Vergeistigung*? And does that not imply that in themselves they are not good? There is really no paradox at all in any of this, but the plain statement of a plain meaning: the good, humane qualities evolve from the evil, animal qualities – good and evil here bearing their ordinary meaning – because they cannot come from anywhere else; they are desirable, therefore that out of which they evolve must not be eradicated.

XII

Very many of the unpublished notes of the 1880s reinforce the argument that the 'bad' passions must not be rooted out but cultivated into 'good' ones. A brief note asks whether the aim should be 'overcoming of the affects' and replies 'No, if what is meant is their weakening and extirpation. *But to press them into service*: which may involve submitting them to protracted tyranny' (*WP*, 384). 'Moral intolerance' is interpreted as 'an expression of a man's *weakness*: he is afraid of his "immorality", he has to *deny* his strongest drives because he does not yet know how to employ them' (*WP*, 385). It is the employment – that is to say the sublimation – of the 'immoral' drives which is insisted upon at all times; but equally the necessity of allowing them to continue to exist and to remain strong: 'There are very naive peoples and individuals who believe that constant fine weather is something desirable: even today they believe *in rebus moralibus* that the "good man" alone, and nothing but the "good man" is something desirable'; but that is an 'uneconomic' thought: one ought to desire 'precisely the contrary: the greater and greater *dominion of evil*, the growing emancipation of man from narrow and fear-ridden moral bondage, the enhancement of strength, in order to be able to press the mightiest natural forces – the affects – into service' (*WP*, 386: a section constructed, reasonably enough, out of two separate notes).

It is plenitude of affects, '*richness of personality*, abundance in oneself, overflowing and bestowing, instinctive wellbeing and affirmation of oneself', which produces 'great sacrifice and great love'; and these affects grow out of 'strong and godlike selfhood ... if one is not firm and valiant within oneself, one has nothing to bestow, one cannot extend one's hand, one cannot be shield and staff' (*WP*, 388). Notice – to remark on it once more and for the last time – that if Nietzsche did not agree in regarding the conventionally good act 'sacrifice' and the conventionally good affect 'love' as desirable, this is another passage that would make no sense.

XIII

The *Übermensch* as the product of certain possibilities of human psychology is envisaged not only as a future goal but also as a present and past actuality. *Zarathustra* places all its emphasis on the future, and even declares: 'There has never yet been a superman. I have seen them both naked, the greatest and the smallest men: they are still all too similar to one another. Truly, I found even the greatest man – all too human!' (*Z*, II. 4). But this is part of the 'prophetic' tone and aspect of this particular book: everything has to be presented as a 'goal', as something mankind is to strive after. In subsequent works a more realistic, if also somewhat more mundane, picture is drawn of the conditions under which the 'superior type' of man who is 'a sort of *Übermensch*' (*A*, 4) has actually been produced or has produced himself. In the description of Goethe already quoted (p. 12) the positive qualities are thrown into relief; but the negative, or 'immoral' qualities also receive their due:

the emphasis on 'pressing into service' is balanced by an emphasis on that which is pressed into service. This emphasis is to be found in those passages in which the 'higher man' is depicted as *not moral* in the sense of what Nietzsche asserts to be Christian morality.

According to Nietzsche, as we have already seen, Christian morality demands the extirpation of the passions: a note of 1888 with the title 'Religious morality' reduces this conception to a simple direct statement:

> The affect, great desire, the passion for power, love, revenge, possession – moralists want to extinguish and tear them out, to 'purify' the soul of them. The logic is: the desires often do great mischief – consequently they are evil, reprehensible. A man must get free of them: before he has done that he cannot be a *good* man ... The great sources of strength, those gushing and overwhelming torrents of the soul which are often so dangerous: instead of pressing their power into service and *economizing* it, this most shortsighted and ruinous mode of thought, the moral mode of thought, wants to make it *dry up*. (*WP*, 383)

Against this demand he sets his own demand: 'I assess a man by the *quantum of power and abundance of his will*: *not* by its weakening and extinction ... I assess the *power* of a *will* by how much resistance, pain, torture it endures and knows how to transform to its advantage'; and he adds, with complete consistency, that 'I do not account the evil and painful character of existence a reproach to it, but harbour the hope that it will one day be more evil and painful than hitherto ...' (*WP*, 382).

This insistence on the value of the negative, 'bad' aspects of life is a major theme repeated many times, but never more forcefully than in a passage in *Beyond Good and Evil* in which those who 'want if possible – and there is no madder "if possible" – *to abolish suffering*' are answered with:

> The discipline of suffering, of *great* suffering – do you not know that it is *this* discipline alone which has created every elevation of mankind hitherto? That tension of the soul in misfortune which cultivates its strength, its terror at the sight of great destruction, its inventiveness and bravery in undergoing, enduring, interpreting, exploiting misfortune, and whatever of depth, mystery, mask, spirit, cunning and greatness has been bestowed

upon it – has it not been bestowed through suffering, through the discipline of great suffering? In man, *creature* and *creator* are united: in man there is matter, fragment, excess, clay, mud, madness, chaos; but in man there is also creator, sculptor, the hardness of the hammer, the divine spectator and the seventh day – do you understand this antithesis? And that *your* pity is for the 'creature in man', for that which has to be formed, broken, forged, torn, burned, annealed, refined – that which has to *suffer* and *should* suffer? (*BGE*, 225)

It is the power to transform which is taken away when the conditions for the retention and enhancement of such power are taken away: therefore they must not be taken away. Historically there have been periods when the ruling morality was one which permitted the 'passions' to remain strong, and the results are generally admired: but one has to understand what it was that produced these results, and if one wants them to be possible again one has to want the circumstances which made them possible: 'One recognizes the *superiority* of Greek man, of Renaissance man – but one would like to have him without his causes and conditions' (*WP*, 882). This 'superiority' has been *achieved*: that is the point of this observation; and it has been achieved by overcoming that which opposed it. It is the act of overcoming which produces the 'superiority', and for that act to be possible there has to exist that which is overcome. 'How is freedom measured, in individuals as in nations?' Nietzsche asks, and answers:

By the resistance which has to be overcome, by the effort it costs to stay *aloft*. One would have to seek the highest type of free man where the greatest resistance is constantly being overcome: five steps from tyranny, near the threshold of the danger of servitude. This is true psychologically when one understands by 'tyrants' pitiless and dreadful instincts, to combat which demands the maximum of authority and discipline towards oneself . . . it is also true politically . . . The nations which were worth something, which *became* worth something, never became so under liberal institutions: it was *great danger* which made of them something deserving reverence, danger which first teaches us to know our resources, our virtues, our shield and spear, our *spirit* – which *compels* us to be strong . . . *First* principle: one must need strength, otherwise one will never have it. (*T*, IX. 38)

XIV

A state of conflict, external and internal, is the pre-condition for 'growth', 'enhancement', in short for *Übermensch*: this dictum is re-iterated in a hundred different ways and at all periods of Nietzsche's life. 'Strife is the perpetual food of the soul', he wrote in 1862, at the age of seventeen; 'One must still have chaos in one to be able to give birth to a dancing star', said Zarathustra twenty-one years later (*Z*, Prologue, 5). In *Beyond Good and Evil*, internal 'war' is, together with the capacity for its direction, posited as the force which creates genius:

> The man of an era of dissolution which mixes the races together and who therefore contains within him the inheritance of a diversified descent, that is to say contrary and often not merely contrary drives and values which struggle with one another and rarely leave one another in peace – such a man ... will, on average, be a rather weak man: his fundamental desire is that the war which he *is* should come to an end ... If, however, the contrariety and war in such a nature should act as one *more* stimulus and enticement to life – and if, on the other hand, in addition to powerful and irreconcilable drives, there has also been inherited and cultivated a proper mastery and subtlety in conducting a war against oneself, that is to say self-control, self-outwitting: then there arise those marvelously incomprehensible and unfathomable men, those enigmatic men predestined for victory and the seduction of others, the fairest examples of which are Alcibiades and Caesar ... and among artists perhaps Leonardo da Vinci. (*BGE*, 200)

In 1888, the conception is asserted with absolute directness:

> One is *fruitful* only at the cost of being rich in contradictions; one remains *young* only on condition the soul does not relax, does not long for peace ... Nothing has grown more alien to us than that desideratum of former times 'peace of soul', the *Christian* desideratum; nothing arouses less envy in us than the moral cow and the fat contentment of the good conscience ... One has renounced *grand* life when one renounces war. (*T*, V. 3)

And therefore: 'Not contentment, but more power; *not* peace at all, but war' (*A*, 2).

XV

All these elements are drawn together in the theory of the superman, in whom 'passion' and 'war' are maintained and where possible enhanced but also directed, 'spiritualized', 'sublimated'. The process is designated, as we have already seen, by various different terms. The verb *sublimieren* and the noun *Sublimierung* are used, although they seem not to carry an identical meaning in every context. '*Sublimierungen*' as it is employed in the opening section of *Human, All Too Human* (quoted on p. 59) is probably to be understood in the sense in which it is employed in chemistry: the conversion of a substance from a solid state to vapour, followed by its resolidification; and as the chemical terms in this section are probably to be understood metaphorically, 'sublimations' probably means no more than 'refinements'. But the term '*sublimierte Geschlechtlichkeit*' (sublimated sexuality), used in the very next book (*AOM*, 95) in the course of an account of the transference of 'love' from personal to religious objects, seems not to be a metaphor, but to be employed in the same sense as it is in psycho-analysis. Among the other terms employed are *aufheben*, whose primary meaning is 'to lift up' but whose conceptual similarity to the Latin *sublevo* has bestowed on it a penumbra of secondary meanings which taken together corres-pond to the meanings contained in the word 'sublimate'; the nouns formed from it, *Aufhebung* and *Selbst-aufhebung*; *überwinden* (to over-come), *Überwindung* and *Selbst-überwindung*; *vergeistigen* (to spiritualize) and *Vergeistigung*; and *in Dienst nehmen* (to press into service). The content of all these terms, and not only of *aufheben* and *Aufhebung*, is clearly similar to that of 'sublimate' and 'sublimation'; and when we examine this content we see that, in general, it resembles quite closely the content of 'sublimate' and 'sublimation' as these words are used in psycho-analysis. There are also important differences, but we shall consider the equally important similarities first.

Dictionaries of psycho-analytical terms, or at any rate those I have consulted, all agree with one another in their definition of 'sublimate'. Charles Rycroft's *Critical Dictionary of Psychoanalysis* (London, 1968), for instance, gives as its basic definition the 'developmental process by which instinctual energies are discharged in non-instinctual forms of behaviour', and other dictionaries employ almost the same words, some however adding that these new forms of behaviour usually have the characteristic of being 'socially acceptable'. Now, provided one leaves the terms 'instinctual energies' and 'non-instinctual forms of behaviour' undefined, this *basic* definition agrees precisely with what Nietzsche usually means by the 'sublimation' or (*Selbst-*) *Aufhebung*, or (*Selbst-*) *Überwindung*, or *Vergeistigung* of a 'drive' or an 'affect', and by 'pressing an affect into service'. In his many accounts of the process, the 'passions' (instinctual energies) are discharged, but not *as* passions but as something else into which they have developed; and this process of development is described as their 'sublimation' or *Vergeistigung*. In scores of instances, the new form assumed by the 'passion' is accounted for by its 'social acceptability', with that expression taken in its widest sense: teasing is a 'socially acceptable' form of brute force, contest by writing tragedies was in Athens a socially acceptable form of contest by sword and spear.

Rycroft goes on to say that the 'development process' called sublimation involves three acts. The first is the 'displacement of energy from activities and objects of primary (biological) interest on to those of lesser instinctual interest'. Here Nietzsche's concept again corresponds fairly closely. The second act is the 'transformation of the quality of the emotion accompanying the activity such that it becomes "desexualized" and "deaggressified".' In this instance Nietzsche's conception corresponds, but only on a superficial level. The thought behind the aphorism 'The degree and kind of a man's sexuality reaches up into the topmost summit of his spirit' (*BGE*, 75), and the remark that it was 'precisely in the most Christian period of Europe' that 'the sexual drive sublimated itself into love (*amour-passion*)' (*BGE*, 189), and that 'making music is another way of making children' (*WP*, 800), is certainly that in these cases the 'quality' of the sexual drive is 'desexualized'; and the aggressive 'quality' in many forms of competition is certainly thought of as being very different from that in overt acts of violence: but it is precisely this change in 'quality' – if 'quality' is to be taken as synonymous with 'essence', as it surely is – which poses the difficulty for psycho-analysis which Nietzsche's theory seeks to avoid. We shall go into this again in a moment. The third act in Rycroft's definition is the 'liberation of the activity from the dictates of instinctual tension': this conception as stated is not to be found in Nietzsche, to whom 'tension' is not something one is 'liberated' from, but one of the means of liberation and, in some cases, the actual liberated state itself. But Rycroft's final observation that the concept of sublimation 'seeks to explain the evolution of the "higher functions" from the lower ones' describes what is precisely Nietzsche's objective in proposing a theory of sublimation.

There is, then, a wide area of agreement between Nietzsche's conception of sublimation and that of psycho-analysis, and anyone familiar with the latter will understand the former correctly in its general outlines. But there are also four vital differences which must also be understood if Nietzsche's conception is to be correctly understood in detail.

The first lies in the nature of the 'instinctual energies' which are 'discharged' in non-instinctual forms of behaviour: in psycho-analysis these energies are reducible to sexual libido, in Nietzsche to 'will to power'. This is stated explicitly and often, and in many differing ways: 'All "goals", "aims", "meaning" are only modes of expression and metamorphoses of the *single* will inherent in all events: the will to power. To have goals, aims, intentions, *willing* in general, is the same thing as willing to become *stronger*, willing to grow – and willing *in addition* the *means* to it' (*WP*, 675); 'All events which proceed from intention are reducible to the intention to augment power' (*WP*, 663); and in *Beyond Good and Evil* he describes his conception of 'psychology' as 'morphology and *theory of the evolution of the will to power*' (*BGE*, 23). The word 'will' in this formula, presumably taken over from Schopenhauer, was not well chosen, because it carries suggestions which are not intended. We shall see later that Nietzsche doubted the existence of distinct 'faculties' of any kind, even the 'faculty of thought', yet the word 'will' suggests very strongly the existence of a faculty of 'willing'. That this is not intended is made clear in several places, but most explicitly and in greatest detail in a long section of *Beyond Good and Evil* which, among other things, elucidates the apparent contradiction between his employment of the word 'will' and his frequent assertion that there is 'no such thing' as will. I quote it here at length because it also provides excellent evidence in support of a contention, to be put forward later, that Nietzsche's endeavour was to construct a phenomenalist philosophy:

> Willing seems to me to be above all something *complicated*, something that is a unity only as a word ... in all willing there is, first of all, a plurality of sensations, namely the sensation of the condition we *leave*, the sensation of this condition towards which we *go*, the sensation of the 'leaving' and 'going' itself, and then also an accompanying muscular sensation. ... As feelings, and indeed many varieties of feeling, can therefore be recognized as an ingredient of will, so, in the second place, can thinking: in every

act of will there is a commanding thought – and do not imagine that this thought can be separated from the 'willing', as though will would then remain over! Thirdly, will is not only a complex of feeling and thinking, but above all an *emotion*: and in fact the emotion of command. What is called 'freedom of will' is essentially the emotion of superiority over him who must obey: 'I am free, "he" must obey' – this consciousness adheres to every will, as does that tense attention, that straight look which fixes itself exclusively on *one* thing, that unconditional evaluation 'this and nothing else is necessary now', that inner certainty that one will be obeyed, and whatever else pertains to the state of him who gives commands. A man who *wills* – commands something in himself which obeys or which he believes obeys. But now observe the strangest thing of all about the will – about this so complex thing for which people have only *one* word: inasmuch as in the given circumstances we at the same time command *and* obey, and as the side which obeys know the sensations of contraint, compulsion, pressure, resistance, motion which usually begin immediately after the act of will; inasmuch as, on the other hand, we are in the habit of disregarding and deceiving ourselves over this duality by means of the synthetic concept 'I'; so a whole chain of erroneous conclusions and consequently of false evaluations of the will itself has become attached to the will as such – so that he who wills believes wholeheartedly that willing *suffices* for action. Because in the great majority of cases willing takes place only where the effect of the command, that is to say obedience, that is to say the action, was to be *expected*, the *appearance* has translated itself into the sensation, as if there were here a *necessity of effect*. Enough: he who wills believes with a tolerable degree of certainty that will and action are somehow one – he attributes the success, the carrying out of the willing, to the will itself, and thereby enjoys an increase of that sensation of power which all success brings with it. 'Freedom of will' – is the expression for that complex condition of pleasure of the person who wills, who commands and at the same time identifies himself with the executor of the command – who as such also enjoys the triumph over resistances involved but who thinks it was his will itself which overcame these resistances. He who wills adds in this way the sensations of pleasure of the successful executive agents, the serviceable 'under-wills' or under-souls – for our body is only a social structure composed of many souls – to his sensations of pleasure as commander ... In all willing it is absolutely a question of commanding and obeying, on the basis ... of a social structure composed of many 'souls'. (*BGE*, 19)

In this conception, 'will' is read back to that 'world of desires and passions' which, Nietzsche asserts, is for us irreducible 'reality' (*BGE*, 36), and its 'essence' is the sensation of commanding something within us which obeys. If, then, one recognizes a 'drive' to power, or a 'will' to power, whose essence is 'commanding and obeying', and whose conscious aspect is the 'feelings of pleasure' of the commander and obeyer, then the 'sublimation' of this drive or will does not involve any change in its essence, but only in its objectives. Thus, whatever other difficulty there may be, there is no *logical* difficulty involved in describing 'philosophy' as 'the most spiritual [*geistigste*] will to power' (*BGE*, 9) – 'spiritualization' (*Vergeistigung*) being a synonym of 'sublimation' – though to describe it as sublimated sexuality does involve the logical difficulty that the essence of the drive allegedly sublimated is nowhere in evidence.

The second difference is Nietzsche's increasing wariness of the word 'psyche'. The issue is whether the 'psyche' is a necessary postulate – necessary, that is, for designating the subject matter of 'psychology': and Nietzsche's view of it would have been that, unless one really wishes to assert the existence of 'the psyche', the word is too misleading to be useful. He was a student of Greek before he was a student of psychology, and it was probably impossible for him to separate the meaning of the word in its modern connotation from its original Greek connotation of 'soul' (quite apart from the fact that in German *Psychologie* has a native synonym in *Seelenlehre* [*Seele* — soul], and *Psycholog* [psychologist] a native synonym in *Seelenforscher*). Is 'the soul' a necessary postulate, or even a useful one? 'I am body entirely,' says Zarathustra, 'and nothing beside; and soul is only a word for something in the body' (*Z*, I. 4); this view, which Nietzsche, far from moderating, adhered to more and more literally, really makes 'psychology' a branch of physiology with no distinct and circumscribed subject matter of its own; and the necessary postulate which designates this subject matter thus becomes, not only not necessary, but definitely misleading. We therefore find, especially in the works of 1886 to 1888, that the words 'physiology' and 'physiological' are introduced where one might have expected to find 'psychology' and 'psychological', and that the object of study is increasingly, not the condition of the 'psyche', but that of the whole organism.

The third vital distinction lies in the polemical intentions served by Nietzsche's psychology. Its objective is, in the last resort, not description for its own sake (an increase in knowledge), nor of course is it advanced as the basis of psychiatric cures: it is the conceptual background to a demand for the creation of the *Übermensch*. Strictly speaking, and all the many psychological insights to be found in his writings notwithstanding, Nietzsche would not have cared a scrap whether his ideas on the sublimation of the 'passions' were correct or erroneous if they were not going to serve the only end which he ultimately cared about, namely the transcendence of modern nihilism. 'Not "humanity" but *superman* is the goal!' (*WP*, 1001) – and it is this 'goal' too which is served by his psychological/physiological investigations.

Finally, Nietzsche's psychology is radically different from Freud's in the tone of voice in which it is presented. I am not referring especially to the euphoric rhapsodizing of Zarathustra, but to the emotive and at times even moralizing formulas in which Nietzsche elects to couch what he has to say. Freud's mode of address was typically courteous and urbane, and however much his earlier readers may have been offended by his ideas, they can hardly have been offended by the way in which he expressed them or by the man himself; Nietzsche, on the other hand, *uses* politeness but is not naturally or typically polite; he is quite capable of introducing a note of contempt into what is supposed to be a statement of scientific fact. 'What determines your rank is the quantum of power that you are; the rest is cowardice' (*WP*, 858): such a sentence as this is typically effective and memorable, but also typically impolite. Ultimately, of course, this mode of address, while it has helped to make him widely read, has worked against his acceptance as a dispassionate scientific investigator.

XVI

The psychological theory, then, to recapitulate briefly, upon which the ideal of the superman is raised (but which does not constitute the whole significance of this ideal) is that the 'will to power' common to all living things is capable in man of sublimation, of turning inward and operating upon itself, so that it becomes the means by which man can transcend the rest of nature. For this to be possible two conditions must obtain: the drive in question must remain strong, if possible grow stronger, but in any case not be deliberately weakened; and the process called the 'sublimation', 'spiritualization', *'Aufhebung'* and 'pressing into service' of this drive must actually take place. Satisfaction of the former condition involves Nietzsche in all those demands that the 'passions' should be allowed their rights which have gained him the reputation of being an irrational admirer of vivid action and abundant strength of no matter what kind; satisfaction of the latter involves at least an attempt at an explanation of how the 'will to power' acquired in man the capacity to turn and operate upon itself, and this is offered in his conception of *Verinnerlichung* – becoming inward, becoming deeper, intensification.

The term first occurs in a short note published as section 376 of *The Will to Power*:

> The *Verinnerlichung* of man. *Verinnerlichung* arises when powerful drives which have been denied external discharge by the establishment of peace and society seek compensation internally, in concert with the imagination. The need for enmity, cruelty, revenge, violence turns back, 'retreats'; in desire for knowledge there is avarice and conquest; the capacity for lying and dissimulation which has retreated reappears in the artist; the drives are transformed into demons which are combated, etc.

This note cannot be dated at all precisely, but it must have preceded the second of the three long essays which comprise *On the Genealogy of Morals* (1887) entitled '"Guilt", "Bad Conscience" and the like', in which Nietzsche, among other things, ventures a 'first provisional' hypothesis on the *origin* of 'bad conscience'. Here the idea of the *Verinnerlichung* of 'powerful drives' is reduced to that of 'will to power'. The relevant passage is again rather lengthy but it offers an example of Nietzsche's expository style at its best, and shows how difficult it is to segregate one 'department' of his philosophy from another: a single passage will usually illuminate several different fields:

> I regard the bad conscience as the serious illness which man was bound to contract under the stress of the most fundamental change he had ever experienced – that change which occurred when he found himself finally enclosed within the walls of society and of peace. The situation that must have faced the sea animals when they were compelled either to become land animals or

perish was the same as faced these semi-animals which were well
adapted to the wilderness, to war, to prowling about, to
adventure – suddenly all their instincts were deprived of value
and 'suspended'. Henceforth they had to walk on their feet and
'sustain themselves', whereas previously they had been sustained by
the water: a terrible heaviness lay upon them. They felt incapable
of the simplest undertakings, in this new unfamiliar world their
former guides, the regulating and unconsciously certain drives,
deserted them – these unhappy creatures were reduced to thinking,
inferring, reckoning, co-ordinating cause and effect, to their
'consciousness', to their poorest and most fallible organ! I believe
there has never been such a feeling of misery, such leaden
discomfort, on earth – and at the same time their old instincts
had not suddenly ceased to make their demands! Only it was
hard and rarely possible to gratify them: as a rule they had to
look for new and as it were subterranean satisfactions. All instincts
which do not discharge themselves outwardly *turn inwards* – this
is that which I call the *Verinnerlichung* of man: thus it was that
man first developed what he afterwards called his 'soul'. The
entire inner world, originally as thin as if stretched between two
membranes, grew and expanded, acquired depth, breadth, height,
in the same measure as outward discharge was *hindered*. Those
fearful bulwarks with which the social organization protected
itself against the old instincts of freedom . . . brought it about that
all those instincts of wild, free, prowling man turned backwards
against man himself. Enmity, cruelty, joy in persecuting, in
attacking, in change, in destruction – all this turned against the
possessors of such instincts: *that* is the origin of the 'bad
conscience' . . . thus was inaugurated the worst and uncanniest
illness, from which man has not to the present moment recovered,
man's suffering *from man, from himself*: as the consequence of a
forcible sundering from his animal past, as it were a leap and
plunge into new circumstances and conditions of existence, a
declaration of war against the old instincts in which his strength,
joy and fearsomeness had previously reposed. Let us add at once
that, on the other hand, with the fact of an animal soul turned
against itself, taking sides against itself, something so new,
profound, unheard-of, enigmatic, contradictory *and full of future*
was introduced that the aspect of the earth was thereby essentially
altered . . . From now on man . . . awakens an interest, a tension,

a hope, almost a certainty, as if with him something were announcing, preparing itself, as if man were not a goal but only a way, an episode, a bridge, a great promise . . .

Among the presuppositions of this hypothesis on the origin of the bad conscience is, firstly, that that change was not a gradual or voluntary one and represented not an organic adaptation to novel conditions, but a break, a leap, a compulsion, a fatality against which there could be no resistance or even *ressentiment*. In the second place, however, it presupposes that the welding of a hitherto unrestrained and shapeless populace into a firm form, as it was originated by an act of violence, so it was completed by nothing but acts of violence – that the oldest 'state', consequently, appeared as a fearful tyranny, as a remorseless machine of oppression, and went on working until this raw material of people and semi-animals was at last not only kneaded and pliant, but also *formed*. I employed the word 'state': it is self-evident what is meant – some herd of blond beasts of prey, a conqueror and master race, which, organized for war and with the ability to organize, unhesitatingly lays it terrible claws upon a population perhaps tremendously superior in numbers but still formless and nomad. That is how the 'state' began on earth . . . They do not know what guilt, responsibility, respect are, these born organizers . . . It is not in *them* that the 'bad conscience' developed, that goes without saying – but it would not have developed *without them*, . . . it would be lacking if a tremendous quantity of freedom had not been expelled from the world, or at least been rendered invisible and made, as it were, *latent*, under their hammer-blows. This *instinct for freedom* forcibly made latent . . . this instinct for freedom pushed back and made to retreat, incarcerated within, and in the end discharging and venting itself only on itself: that and that alone is, in its inception, the *bad conscience*.

One should guard against thinking lightly of this phenomenon on account of its initial painfulness and ugliness. For fundamentally it is the same active force which is at work on a grander scale in those artists in violence and organizes and builds states which here, internally . . . in the 'labyrinth of the breast' . . . creates for itself a bad conscience and builds negative ideals, it is that *instinct for freedom* (in my language: will to power); with the difference that the material upon which this . . . force operates is here man himself, his entire old animal self – and *not* . . . *other* men . . .

The bad conscience is an illness, there is no doubt about that, but an illness as pregnancy is an illness . . . (*GM*, II. 16–19)

All this is still a hypothesis, and one which, as Nietzsche says, 'needs to be thought on, observed and slept on for a long time' (*GM*, II. 16). That there is no evidence for it lies in the nature of the case: the 'men' in whom the 'bad conscience' originated are held to have been no more than 'semi-animals' and the whole process to have occurred in pre-historic times; but that there is a necessity for it, or for some theory of the kind, is also true, for the phenomenon it seeks to explain does in fact exist and must therefore have originated somehow. It should be noticed that it embodies the four typical characteristics of a Nietzschean explanation described in chapter 1: it is an attempt to understand a 'metaphysical' phenomenon in naturalistic terms, it involves assertions about primitive mankind, it is not a fully worked out theory but rather the material for one, and it relies on a power relationship as the essential explicatory principle. In this instance, Nietzsche has constructed his entire hypothesis out of the 'will to power' – it is the will to power in its crudest form which creates the prehistoric 'state', and it is the will to power of those whose freedom is suddenly and radically curtailed by the creation of this 'state' whose transformations create the 'soul' and the 'bad conscience', and indeed 'man' as distinct from an animal or 'semi-animal'.

It should also be noticed that Nietzsche *approves* of 'bad conscience'. On this point one has to be simple and direct, and say that people who assert that he 'glorifies' the 'blond beast' and despises civilization have not read him, or have done so with very little application, and do not know what they are talking about. He designates 'bad conscience' as 'an illness': but those who think this must mean he condemns it do not even know that, to Nietzsche, all the best things are bad things over-come – that 'a tree, if it is to grow proudly into the sky' cannot 'do without bad weather and storms', that it was only when man suffered '*from man, from himself*' that he became '*full of future*' and altered the aspect of the earth. 'Bad conscience' made of man something other than animal, so that it was 'as if with him something [else] were announcing, preparing itself, as if man were not a goal but only a way, an episode, a bridge, a great promise.' A bridge to what, a promise of what? 'Man,' said Zarathustra, 'is a rope, fastened between animal and superman ... What is great in man is that he is a bridge and not a goal' (Z, Prologue, 4). 'Bad conscience' made it possible for man to become superman: this indicates the degree to which Nietzsche approves of it.

From primitive man in whom the 'bad conscience' originated to Goethe is a very long journey: but on even the longest journey it is the first step that counts. Of Goethe, Nietzsche says: 'he *created* himself' (T, IX, 49). In his theory of *Verinnerlichung* he attempts to account for Goethe's ability to do this: for the possibility of the *Übermensch*, who is conceptually the highest product of the will to power operating, not upon other men, but upon 'man himself'.

XVII

At the end of the last book he saw through the press, Nietzsche described himself as 'the last disciple of the philosopher Dionysus ... the teacher of the eternal recurrence' (T, X. 5). The connection between the ideas of 'Dionysus' and 'eternal recurrence' is established via the theory of will to power, of which 'eternal recurrence' is the final product. Here we shall consider the 'scientific' basis of the idea, how it affects the individual human life, and finally the grounds for associating it with the superman and the philosophy of power.

Chronologically the last topic comes first: the affective appeal of the eternal recurrence of the same events was what struck Nietzsche initially, and it was only afterwards that he sought evidence for it in science; but to discuss the affective appeal before we have become clear what the concept is supposed, concretely, to mean would be to create unnecessary difficulty.

XVIII

That all events recur an infinite number of times is held by Nietzsche to follow from the empirical fact that the universe exists and is changing. 'If the world could possibly become rigid, dry up, die, become *nothing*,' he writes in a note of 1888, 'or if it could attain a state of equilibrium, or if it could possibly have any sort of goal that involved duration, unchangeability, a once-and-for-all (in brief, and speaking metaphysically: if becoming *could* terminate in being or in nothingness), then this state must have been attained. But it has not been attained: from which it follows ... This is the only certainty we hold in our hands to serve as a corrective to a great number of universal hypotheses possible in themselves' (*WP*, 1066). This is the fundamental postulate: if any sort of end-state, whether of being or of nothingness, were possible, it would already have been reached; but, empirically, it has not been reached; therefore no such end-state is possible.

This postulate does not by itself lead to the conclusion that every event is a repetition of an identical event in the past: for that conclusion to follow, one has also to assert that the universe lacks the capacity for limitless innovation. This assertion Nietzsche makes:

> The ancient habit . . . of associating a goal with every event and a directing creating God with the world is so strong that the thinker has to make an effort not to regard the very aimlessness of the world as intentional. This is an idea – the idea that the world intentionally *avoids* a goal and even knows artifices for preventing itself from entering on a circular course – which must occur to anyone who would like to impose on the world the capacity for *eternal novelty* . . . The world . . . is supposed wilfully to *prevent* itself from returning to any of its old forms; it is supposed to possess, not only the intention of guarding against any repetition, but also the *means* for doing so.

But this way of thinking is a residue of the old belief in an infinitely creative God; the new 'scientific spirit' counters it with the 'law' that 'the world, as force, may not be thought of as unlimited, for it *cannot be so thought of* – we forbid ourselves the concept of an *infinite* force as incompatible with the concept "force"*. Therefore – the world also lacks the capacity for eternal novelty' (*WP*, 1062).

Given these two conditions – that the world is incapable either of attaining an end-state or of unending innovation – then 'eternal recurrence' must follow.

> If the world *may* be thought of as a definite quantity of force and as a definite number of centres of force – and every other idea remains indefinite and consequently *unusable* – it follows from that, that in the great dice game of existence it has to go through a calculable number of combinations. In an infinite period of time every possible combination would at some time be attained; more, it would be attained an infinite number of times. And since between every combination and its next recurrence all other combinations possible would have to transpire, and each of these

combinations conditions the entire sequence of combinations in the same series, a circle of absolutely identical series would thus be demonstrated: the world as a circle that has already repeated itself an infinite number of times and plays its game *in infinitum*. (*WP*, 1066)

This is the 'scientific' basis of the theory of the eternal recurrence of the same events. It is obviously wide open to criticism: for one thing, it is doubtful whether Nietzsche had any clear idea of what he meant by 'force' or 'centres of force'; for another, the nature of the world is something to be determined experimentally, not by an arrangement of syllogisms; and for another, the 'world', if by that is meant the totality of everything, can no more be subjected to the 'laws of logic' than eternity can be measured by a clock, and any attempt to subject it to them leads only to paradoxes and riddles. In defence of Nietzsche it must be said that the arguments I have quoted and *all* other passages which treat the recurrence as a demonstrable scientific fact are no more than notes and jottings which he deliberately left unpublished: they remained strictly speculations founded on an idea which had first occurred to him in a different context and with a different emphasis.

XIX

This idea was of the *effect on an individual* of an eternity which was the never-ending repetition of the events of his life. It is this aspect – that of the nature of the response – rather than insistence on the recurrence as a fact, which governs the first published reference to it:

What if a demon crept after you one day or night in your loneliest solitude and said to you: 'This life as you live it now and have lived it, you will have to live again and again, times without number; and there will be nothing new in it, but every pain and every joy and every thought and sigh and all the unspeakably small and great in your life must return to you, and everything in the same series and sequence ... The eternal hour-glass of existence will be turned again and again ...' Would you not throw yourself down and gnash your teeth and curse the demon who thus spoke? Or have you experienced a tremendous moment in which you would have answered him: 'You are a god and never did I hear anything more divine!' If this thought gained power over you it would, as you are now, transform and perhaps crush you; the question in all and everything: 'do you want this again and again, times without number?' would lie as the heaviest burden upon all your actions. Or how well disposed towards yourself and towards life would you have to become to have *no greater desire* than for this ultimate eternal sanction and seal?' (*GS*, 341)

What state of being would be necessary for the idea of its unending recurrence, of its eternity, to be not merely an endurable but actually the most highly desired idea? That is the question the posing of which is the *purpose* of the idea in this passage: it is only because we already know the content of future books that we know that this idea is envisaged as a true idea; in the passage itself it appears only as a suggestion, apparently offered only in order to see what kind of response will be elicited.

That the idea that all events recur is supposed to be literally true is not made clear until the end of the third part of *Zarathustra* (1884), when Zarathustra narrates a nightmare in which eternity is imagined as a road passing through a gateway:

Behold this gateway ... it has two aspects. Two paths come together here: no one has ever reached their end. This long lane behind us: it goes on for an eternity. And that long lane ahead of us – that is another eternity. They are in opposition to one another, these paths ... and it is here at this gateway that they come together. The name of the gateway is written above it: 'Moment'. But if one were to follow them further and ever further and further: do you think ... that these paths would be in eternal opposition? ... Behold this moment! ... From this gateway Moment a long, eternal lane runs *back*: an eternity lies behind us. Must not all things that *can* run have already run along this lane? Must not all things that *can* happen *have* already happened, been done, run past? And if all things have been here before: what do you think of this moment ...? Must not this gateway too have been here – before? And are not all things bound fast together in such a way that this moment draws after it all future things? *Therefore* – draws itself too? For all things that *can* run *must* also run once again forward along this long lane ... must we not all have been here before? – and must we not return and run down that other lane out before us, down that long, terrible lane – must we not return eternally? (*Z*, III. 2:2)

The 'argument' offered here in support of the idea of recurrence is that time is infinite, and this is presented as being self-evident: and this is the *only* 'argument' for the recurrence Nietzsche ever published. It would appear that when the idea came to him, as he said it did in August 1881, the infinity of time was its sole supporting notion. It will seem a very inadequate basis for so far-reaching a conclusion until we come to see why the idea itself made so powerful an appeal to him: when we have done that we shall also see that he would have embraced it even if he could have discovered no supporting arguments for it whatever.

When the recurrence is referred to again, it is stated simply as a fact. Zarathustra's emblematic animals, speaking out to him what he already knows, tell him: *'you are the teacher of the eternal recurrence'*, and go on:

> Behold, we know what you teach: that all things recur eternally and we ourselves with them, and that we have already existed an infinite number of times before and all things with us. You teach that there is a great year of becoming, a colossus of a year: this year must, like an hour-glass, turn itself over again and again, so that it may run down and run out anew: so that all these years resemble one another, in the greatest things and in the smallest, so that we ourselves resemble ourselves in each great year, in the greatest things and in the smallest. And if you should die now, O Zarathustra: behold, we know too what you would then say to yourself . . . 'Now I die and decay . . . and in an instant I shall be nothingness . . . But the complex of causes in which I am entangled will recur – it will create me again! . . . I shall return . . . *not* to a new life or a better life or a similar life: I shall return eternally to this identical and selfsame life, in the greatest things and in the smallest . . . (*Z*, III. 13:2)

The fact of eternal recurrence is announced as a species of 'glad tidings', and the remainder of the book in its original form – for it was at first intended to end with the end of the third part – is devoted to Zarathustra's solitary celebration of his new-found redemption: a celebration which concludes with a 'Song of Yes and Amen' whose lengthy refrain – 'Oh how should I not lust for eternity and for the wedding ring of rings – the Ring of Recurrence! Never yet did I find the woman by whom I wanted children, unless it be this woman, whom I love: for I love you, O Eternity! *For I love you, O Eternity!*' –

is repeated no fewer than seven times and brings the work to an exultant conclusion. But after he has recovered from this intoxication, the reader is likely to ask himself: 'What was it we were celebrating? Not, surely, the eternal recurrence of the same events!' And one could understand his incredulity, for he has probably forgotten the circumstances under which the suggestion was first put to him, and that it was put to him to test his 'state of being'. What kind of state of being would *want* 'eternity'? As the clock of the world strikes twelve and midnight arrives, Zarathustra supplies the answer in a laconic and mysterious song which chimes with the booming of the bell:

O Man! Attend!
What does deep midnight's voice contend?
'I slept my sleep,
'And now awake at dreaming's end:
'The world is deep,
'Deeper than day can comprehend.
'Deep is its woe,
'Joy – deeper than heart's agony:
'Woe says: Fade! Go!
'But all joy wants eternity,
'– wants deep, deep, deep eternity' (*Z*, III. 15:3)

Joy does not merely endure the thought of eternity, it *wants* eternity, *it does not want to end*. And what, according to a later work, is joy – or, as it is there termed, happiness? 'The feeling that power *increases* – that a resistance is overcome' (*A*, 2).

XX

At this point certain strands which seemed to lie far apart begin to be drawn together; we begin to perceive why it is that the will to power, the *Übermensch* and the eternal recurrence all make their appearance in the same book and as a consequence of the same 'breakthrough' to transcendence; and that the state of 'joy' – which 'wants itself, wants eternity, wants recurrence, wants everything eternally the same' (*Z*, IV. 19:9) – implies '*amor fati*': 'that one wants nothing to be other than it is, not in the future, not in the past, not in all eternity' (*EH*, II. 10), because this state is a product of every other state.

Did you ever say Yes to one joy? O my friends, then you said Yes to *all* woe as well. All things are chained and entwined together, all things are in love; if ever you wanted one moment twice, if you ever said: 'You please me, happiness, instant, moment!' then you wanted *everything* to return! – you wanted everything anew, everything eternal, everything chained, entwined together, everything in love, oh that is how you *loved* the world, you everlasting men, loved it eternally and for all time: and you say even to woe: 'Go, but return!' *For all joy wants – eternity!* (Z, IV. 19:10)

In the passage in which the term '*amor fati*' is first introduced (*GS*, 276), Nietzsche supplies a synonym for it by declaring that 'I want to be at all times hereafter only an affirmer [*ein Ja-sagender*]!' Being *ein Ja-sagender* is what *amor fati* means; and when he comes to designate Goethe as 'Dionysian' – that is to say, as an instance of an *Übermensch* – he endows him with it: 'A spirit thus *emancipated* stands in the midst of the universe with a joyful and trusting fatalism, in the *faith* that only what is separate and individual may be rejected, that in the totality everything is redeemed and affirmed – *he no longer denies* . . . But such a faith is the highest of all possible faiths: I have baptised it with the name Dionysus' (*T*, IX. 49).

The inadequate and unpublished 'scientific' evidence is now seen to be redundant and therefore rightly unpublished, for the 'eternal recurrence' is not really a hypothesis at all, but a statement of 'Dionysian faith', of '*amor fati*', couched in the most extreme terms: 'the highest formula of affirmation that can possibly be attained' (*EH*, section on Z, 1). Ultimately, one is not even expected to see any *literal* sense in it: ultimately it is not an assertion of fact, but an existential test of one's state of being. Can I say Yes to my life? If I cannot, why can I not? The *Übermensch* would rejoice in the idea of eternal recurrence: if I do not, why do I not?

5

Theories and Innovations: I

Logic, Theory of Knowledge, Metaphysics, Ethics, Aesthetics

I

Philosophy as traditionally taught is divided into five large compartments, each devoted to one of the five basic problems upon which men reflect. These departments are logic (reflection on the nature of reasoning), epistemology or theory of knowledge (reflection on the nature of knowledge), metaphysics (reflection on the nature of being), ethics (reflection on the nature of morality), and aesthetics (reflection on the nature of beauty). There is some artificiality in this division, and it can easily break down; but the arrangement is certainly not wholly artificial: each department does have a core of subject matter which is quite distinct. An 'encyclopaedic' philosopher will be found to contribute to each of these departments – indeed, it is in this that his 'encyclopaedicism' consists – and order can be imposed on a general survey of him by considering his views under these several heads. Nietzsche may not seem to be a suitable subject for such treatment, but in fact the unsystematic character of his philosophizing almost compels you to impose some such order upon it if you are to discuss it at all. We shall therefore consider in this chapter his theories and innovations regarded as contributions to the five traditional divisions of philosophy.

II: Logic

Nietzsche was not a logician, but he did undertake a critique of logic in the sense of raising one specific objection to the claims normally made on its behalf. This objection is worth considering in a little detail, since, whatever value it may have for the science of logic, it adds a dimension to our picture of Nietzsche himself and his attitude towards thought and truth.

Let us recall his assertion that 'nothing is "given" as real except our world of desires and passions' and that 'we can rise or sink to no other "reality" than the reality of our drives – for thinking is only the relationship of these drives to one another' (*BGE*, 36). This assessment of the relation between thought and the 'drives' is repeated elsewhere, and is in general Nietzsche's view of the matter: it is stated, for example, in a note of the winter of 1887–8 which refers to the 'misunderstanding of passion and *reason*, as if the latter were an independent entity and not rather a relationship between different passions and desires; and as if every passion did not have in it its quantum of reason' (*WP*, 387). A similar conclusion had already been drawn in *The Gay Science*, where the 'course of logical thought and inference in our present brain' is said to correspond 'to an operation and struggle of drives which are all in themselves individually very illogical and unjust' (*GS*, 111). Such a view of the nature of thought conflicts with any idea involving its objective validity: it abolishes the 'faculty' of thought altogether, and thus calls in question the objective validity of the 'science of reasoning', logic.

A long and very interesting note published as section 516 of *The Will to Power*, starting from a criticism of the Aristotelian 'law of contradiction', concludes by denying that logic has anything at all to do with truth. 'We are incapable of affirming and denying one and the same thing: this is a subjective law drawn from experience, it does not express any "necessity" *but only an incapacity*': this is the basic objection. If, as Aristotle says, the law of contradiction 'is the most certain of all principles . . . then one should consider all the more strictly what assertions it already *presupposes*'. Either 'it is supposed to assert something in regard to reality, to being, as if one already knew this from another source: namely that antithetical predicates *cannot* be ascribed to it', or 'that antithetical predicates *ought not* to be ascribed to it': in the latter case 'logic would be an imperative, *not* to knowledge of what is true, but to the positing and arrangement [*Zurechtmachung*] of a world *which we shall call true*'. The question at issue is: 'are logical axioms adequate to reality, or are they standards and means for us to *create* the real, the concept "reality"?' In order to affirm the first alternative, one would have 'to know being already, which is certainly not the case'; consequently, the law of contradiction 'contains no *criterion of truth*, but is an *imperative* in regard to that which *ought* to count as true'. Logical axioms, in fact, in so far as they are assumed to possess objective validity, repose upon a metaphysical view of the world: every law of logic and mathematics presupposes a 'self-identical A', the substratum of which is inevitably a 'thing': '*our belief in things* is the presupposition of the belief in logic'. But a 'thing' is, as Nietzsche never wearies of insisting, a construct, and if we do not grasp that fact but 'make of logic a criterion of *true being*, we are already on the road to positing as realities all those hypostases substance, predicate, object, subject, action, etc.: that is to say, to conceiving a metaphysical world'. The 'most primitive acts of thought' affirmation and denial, 'holding for true and holding for not true', are already dominated by the belief that our judgments correspond with what is true in itself; but, since thoughts are a product of sensations, this belief amounts to a belief that 'sensations teach us *truths* about things'. This belief is at least questionable; quite apart from the fact that the foundation of the law of contradiction – 'I cannot have two antithetical sensations simultaneously' – is '*quite crude and false*'. The fact of the matter is that logic, like geometry and arithmetic, 'applies only to *fictitious entities which we have created*. Logic is the attempt to comprehend the real world by means of a scheme of being we ourselves have posited: more correctly, to render it formulatable and calculable to us.'

Logic thus 'rests on presuppositions with which nothing in the actual world corresponds' (*HA*, 11); 'reality does not appear' in logic or in 'that applied logic, mathematics' at all, 'not even as a problem' (*T*, II. 3). 'Logic is fastened to the condition: assuming there are identical cases. In fact, for logical thought and inference to be possible, this condition must first be imagined as fulfilled; that is to say: the will to *logical truth* can successfully assert itself only after a fundamental *falsification* of all events has been assumed' (*WP*, 512). We have at present a 'subjective compulsion to believe in logic', but this compulsion only reveals that 'long before logic itself entered our consciousness, we did nothing but introduce its postulates into events': it is we 'who have created the "thing", subject, predicate, act, object, substance, form, after we had long been engaged on *making* identical, *making* crude and simple' (*WP*, 521). Logic is thus the 'science' of a fictitious world created by man and believed to be true. Why was it created? Because a 'logical' world, a 'calculable' world, is useful (*WP*, 507), or answers 'physiological demands' (*BGE*, 3). It may even be that the ability for '*making* identical, *making* crude and simple' was once a decisive factor in natural selection:

He who . . . did not know how to discover the 'identical' sufficiently often in regard to food or to animals hostile to him, he who was thus too slow to subsume, too cautious in subsuming, had a smaller probability of survival than he who in the case of every similarity at once conjectured identity. But it was the prevailing tendency to treat the similar at once as identical, an illogical tendency – for nothing is identical – which first created all the foundations of logic. (*GS*, 111)

The 'logical' view may even be a 'condition of human life' (*BGE*, 4). Moreover, through the fictions of logic one *dominates* reality: '*the will to make equivalent is the will to power*' (*WP*, 511).

The theory that the categories of reason are fictions, and are recognized as such, does not, however, for Nietzsche carry with it the corollary that they should be set aside (even if that were possible): for logical fictions are *necessary*. That, indeed, is why they were brought into existence; and while you may recognize that an error is an error, you ought not to condemn it simply on that account, for it may be a necessary error – necessary, that is, for the preservation and enhancement of mankind:

> The falseness of a judgment is to us not necessarily an objection to a judgment . . . The question is to what extent it is life-advancing, life-preserving, species-preserving, perhaps even species-breeding; and our fundamental tendency is to assert that the falsest judgments . . . are the most indispensable to us, that without granting as true the fictions of logic, without measuring reality against the purely invented world of the unconditional and self-identical, without a continual falsification of the world by means of numbers, mankind could not live – that to renounce false judgments would be to renounce life, would be to deny life (*BGE*, 4).

III: Theory of knowledge

> In some remote corner . . . of the universe there was once a star on which clever animals invented knowledge. It was the most arrogant and mendacious moment of 'universal history': but only a moment. Nature took but a few breaths and the star grew cold; and the clever animals had to die. – Someone might invent such a fable as this and yet still not have illustrated well enough how pitiful, how shadowy and fleeting,

how aimless and capricious the human intellect appears within
nature. There were eternities in which it did not exist; when it
has gone again nothing will have happened. For there exists
for that intellect no mission extending beyond the life of man . . .

Here, at the beginning of an unfinished and unpublished essay of
1873, 'On Truth and Falsehood in an Extra-Moral Sense', is the essence
of what was also Nietzsche's final attitude towards the nature of human
knowledge: it is before all else an *instrument*, designed in accordance
with, and limited to the satisfaction of human needs. In the sense in
which philosophers are accustomed to use the word, therefore, there
is *no* 'knowledge'.

The consequences of this fact permeate the published works, especially the later ones; the grounds by which it is established are confined
largely to the posthumously-published notebooks, and *The Will to
Power* contains very many epistemological speculations which have no
parallel in the published books. In so far as failure to publish a line of
speculation indicates in general that Nietzsche was not yet satisfied
with it, we must say that he never arrived at a formal 'theory of
knowledge'; but his thinking on this subject is unmistakable, and can
be detected at every stage of his development; so that, in this case, it
seems that the unpublished notes served to clarify to his own mind
and bring clearly into the open that which was presupposed in much
of what he had already published. If we too avail ourselves of this
explicit clarification we can present Nietzsche's 'theory of knowledge'
briefly and in an orderly fashion.

The world is in a constant state of change: in philosophical jargon,
it is 'becoming' and not 'being'. But a 'becoming' world cannot be
'known'. This is the conceptual basis of Nietzsche's denial of the possibility of knowledge: we can 'know' only the simulacra of being which
we ourselves have constructed.

Continual transitions forbid us to speak of an 'individual' etc.;
the 'number' of beings is itself in flux. We would know nothing
of time or of motion if we did not, in a crude fashion, believe
we observed 'that which is at rest' beside 'that which is in
motion'. The same applies to cause and effect, and without the
erroneous conception of 'empty space' we would never have
arrived at the conception of space. The law of identity has as its
background the 'appearance' that there are identical things.
A world in a state of becoming could not in a strict sense be

'comprehended' or 'known'; only in so far as the 'comprehending'
and 'knowing' intellect discovers a crude ready-made world
put together out of nothing but appearances, but appearances
which, to the extent that they are of the kind that have
preserved life, have become firm – only to this extent is there
anything like 'knowledge': i.e. a measuring of earlier and later
errors by one another (*WP*, 520)

Thinking itself is possible only on the basis of an 'assumption of
beings . . . logic deals only with formulas for that which remains the
same': but this assumption 'belongs to our perspectives'. Because 'the
world in a state of becoming' is 'unformulatable', and 'knowledge and
becoming exclude one another', 'knowledge' must be something other
than knowledge: 'there must first be a will to make knowable, a kind
of becoming must itself create the *illusion of beings*' (*WP*, 517).
  Knowledge is 'not "to know" but to schematize – to impose upon
chaos as much regularity and form as suffices for our practical requirements'; in the evolution of reason what was decisive was 'the requirement, not to "know", but to subsume, to schematize, for the purpose
of intelligibility and calculation'; the evolution of reason is 'adaptation
[*Zurechtmachung*], invention, in order to produce similarity, identity –
the same process every sense impression goes through' (*WP*, 515).
Knowledge, again, is 'a *determining, designating, making-conscious of
conditions (not a fathoming* of entities, things, "things in themselves")'
(*WP*, 555); and this is true of all knowledge, deductive as well as
empirical: 'An illusion that something is *known* when we possess a
mathematical formula for an event: it has only been *designated, described*;
nothing more!' (*WP*, 628). In brief: 'The whole apparatus of knowledge is an apparatus for abstraction and simplification – directed, not
at knowledge, but at obtaining possession of things: "end" and "means"
are as remote from its essence as are "concepts". With "end" and
"means" one obtains possession of the process (– one *invents* a process
which is graspable), with "concepts", however, of the "things" which
constitute the process' (*WP*, 503).
  This conception of the nature of knowledge is repeated and re-
formulated scores of times, and we need not labour it further. Out of
it emerge all his other suggestions as to why the 'knowledge' we have
is of the kind it is and not of some other kind – suggestions which
would be redundant if our 'knowledge' of reality and the nature of
reality coincided. Since 'there are no facts', all knowledge of facts is

interpretation, 'introduction of meaning – *not* "explanation"' (*WP*, 604): and the attempt to discover what we know thus resolves itself into an attempt to discover why we interpret as we do.

One line of investigation begins from the necessity we are under to think in words, and the illusion this gives us that a word is an explanation: 'man has for long ages believed in the concepts and names of things as in *aeternae veritates* . . . he really thought that in language he possessed knowledge of the world. The sculptor of language was not so modest as to believe that he was only giving things designations, he conceived rather that with words he was expressing supreme knowledge of things' (*HA*, 11). Words are also the chief agents in our construction of 'facts', that is to say the imposition of 'being' on the flux of 'becoming': through words and the concepts formed from them we are 'continually tempted to think of things as being simpler than they are, as separated from one another, as indivisible, each existing in and for itself' (*WS*, 11). And the structure into which all our words are fitted, that is to say grammar, fixes in advance according to what scheme our thinking as a whole will be directed – which explains the 'singular family resemblance between all Indian, Greek and German philosophizing . . . Where, thanks to a common . . . grammar . . . there exists a language affinity it is quite impossible to avoid everything being prepared in advance for a similar evolution and succession of philosophical systems: just as the road seems to be barred to certain other possibilities of world interpretation' (*BGE*, 20).

The basis of *our* grammar, Nietzsche insists, is the subject-predicate relationship. The consequence of introducing this relationship into all our thinking is that we impose the idea of subject and object, deed and doer, on to the world itself: 'In every judgment there lies the entire, full, profound belief in subject and predicate or in cause and effect (namely, as the assertion that every effect is an activity and that every activity presupposes an agent)' (*WP*, 550). The cause of the relationship itself is our belief in the existence of the ego, of an 'I' which we are, and which is the primal 'subject' and causal agent: '"Subject", "object", "predicate" – these distinctions are *created* and are now imposed as a schematism upon all apparent facts. The fundamental false observation is that I believe it is *I* who do something, suffer something, "have" something, who "have" a quality' (*WP*, 549). But the ego is, as here indicated, an error; it is indeed the simplest and most primitive 'assumption of being': but, through becoming the basis of language construction, it leads ineluctably to the most comprehensive of all such assumptions: 'I fear we are not getting rid of God because we still believe in grammar', the reason being that language 'sees everywhere deed and doer . . . believes in the "ego", in the ego as being, in the ego as substance, and . . . *projects* its belief in the ego-substance on to all things – only thus does it *create* the concept "thing" . . . Being is everywhere thought in, *foisted on*, as cause; it is only from the conception "ego" that there follows, derivatively, the concept "being"' (*T*, III. 5). 'Things' are projections of the ego as causal agent, and God is only the biggest 'thing'.

When he seeks to penetrate further and discover why this initial assumption of an ego is made, Nietzsche discovers it in physiology, in the life-forms of the races of man: 'the spell of definite grammatical functions is in the last resort the spell of *physiological* value judgments and racial conditions' (*BGE*, 20). The kind of knowledge we possess is determined by what we are physically, and 'it is improbable that our "knowledge" should extend further than what exactly suffices for the preservation of life' (*WP*, 494). We 'know' precisely what we need to 'know' for our survival: 'we have . . . no organ whatever for *knowledge*, for "truth": we "know" . . . precisely as much as may be *useful* in the interest of the human herd, the species.' Naturally, we do not necessarily 'know' correctly even that which is really 'useful' to us: 'what is here called "utility" is . . . perhaps precisely that fatal piece of stupidity through which we shall one day perish' (*GS*, 354).

With which observation we are back with the thought that the 'clever animal' which invented knowledge 'had to die', and that when the human intellect has gone again 'nothing will have happened'.

IV: Metaphysics

Nietzsche wanted to be a phenomenalist, and you fail to appreciate a whole dimension of his greatness unless you see that his philosophy is at heart a phenomenalism. But his antecedents again and again undermined his capacity to fulfil this desire, and he remained until the end and against his will a writer of metaphysics. Or perhaps it was his artistic nature, which wanted to produce powerful effects, which continually pushed him back into metaphysics. An account of Nietzsche as a phenomenalist – or, better, an edition which excised everything that was not strict phenomenalism – would contain the hard core of his philosophy, including his ethical philosophy, which is an attempt at a phenomenalism of morals, but almost all the 'poetry', almost everything pertaining to him as 'the lyrist of cognition', would be gone, and with it a great part of his 'influence'.

Philosophy is not exactly a majority interest, and there is no reason it should be; but even the minority who do read the subject are for the most part attracted to it by the same force which attracts them to *art*: philosophy which possesses no affective content is really philosophy for professionals, for men and women who specialize in it as a livelihood or are committed amateurs, and there is no more reason it should have any popular following than that the study of the properties of elastic gases and fluids ('pneumatics') should have such a following.

Recall how Nietzsche, according to his own account, was attracted to philosophy: he bought *The World as Will and Idea* and allowed the 'energetic and gloomy genius' of Schopenhauer to 'operate upon me . . . Here I saw a mirror in which I beheld the world, life and my own nature in a terrifying grandeur . . . here I saw sickness and health, exile and refuge, Hell and Heaven' (*Retrospect of my Two Years at Leipzig*). If this has in it the ring of truth, as it surely does have, is that not because it is, in all essentials, an account of how most of us were first attracted to philosophy? But if the name of, say, Beethoven, were substituted for that of Schopenhauer, would it not still ring true? It is an affective response to a work of art which is being described – the work of art in this instance being a metaphysical philosophy. This seems to me no accident: I would even go so far as to say that it is metaphysics which has hitherto recruited philosophers, and has made of philosophy a subject of 'general interest' which has been studied by non-professionals in the same way as music is studied by people who have no intention of becoming professional musicians.

Now, it was part of Nietzsche's complex attitude towards art to suggest that artists are falsifiers, in the sense that art is a means of disguising the real nature of existence; and in so far as metaphysics is art it is open to the same objection: that is why Nietzsche wanted to get past metaphysics. But, at the same time, metaphysics supplied him with an outlet for the side of his nature which could be satisfied only with artistic expression: and so, until the end of his active life, and perhaps sometimes without being fully aware of it, he continued to express ideas which have to be called metaphysical.

I will give two examples of Nietzsche writing metaphysics after 1876, when he had in intention turned away from it. The first is the passage written in 1885 and printed by the editors of *The Will to Power* as the last section of the book (1067): a rhapsody on universal 'will to power':

> And do you know what 'the world' is to me? Shall I show it to you in my mirror? This world: a monster of energy, without beginning, without end; an immovable, brazen enormity of energy, which does not grow bigger or smaller, which does not expend itself but only transforms itself; as a whole of unalterable size, a household without expenses or losses, but likewise without increase or income; enclosed by 'nothingness' as by a boundary; not something flowing away or squandering itself, not something endlessly extended, but as a definite quantity of energy set in a definite space, and not a space that might be 'empty' here or there, but rather as energy throughout, as a play of energies and waves of energy at the same time one and many, increasing here and at the same time decreasing there; a sea of energies flowing and rushing together, eternally moving, eternally flooding back, with tremendous years of recurrence, with an ebb and a flood of its forms; out of the simplest form striving towards the most complex, out of the stillest, most rigid, coldest form towards the hottest, most turbulent, most self-contradictory, and then out of this abundance returning home to the simple, out of the play of contradiction back to the joy of unison, still affirming itself in this uniformity of its courses and its years, blessing itself as that which must return eternally, as a becoming that knows no repletion, no satiety, no weariness – : this my *Dionysian* world of the eternally self-creative, the eternally self-destructive, this mystery-world of the twofold delight, this my 'beyond good and evil', without aim, unless the joy of the circle is itself an aim; without will, unless a ring feels goodwill towards itself – do you want a *name* for this world? A *solution* for all your riddles? A *light* for you too, you best concealed, strongest, least dismayed, most midnight men? – *This world is the will to power – and nothing beside!*
> And you yourself are also this will to power – and nothing beside!

This is only an unpublished note; yet it was not something hastily thrown off and forgotten, for it replaces an earlier, erased excursus on the same theme. What does it mean? What, even if we ignore and discount the 'poetic' form of delivery as a piece of self-indulgence, does it mean to say that the 'world' is 'will to power'? *Whose* power?

Power over *what*? Or, if these questions are misdirected, what is 'power' intended to mean? Energy, in the sense in which we speak of 'electrical power'? If so, what does 'will' mean? Not, certainly, a 'drive' or a 'complex of drives and emotions', since the detection of these phenomena would indicate that the 'world' is an organism, which is patently not what is meant by a 'sea of energies flowing and rushing together'. Or, if these questions too are misguided, what is there in this passage which could be verified or disproved? Is it not the kind of utterance which is neither true nor false, but rather a release of an internal tension, like 'Yippee!'? Finally, if the phrase 'the world' in this passage were, wherever it occurs, replaced by 'the last movement of the *Hammerklavier* sonata', or by 'the process of combustion', or by any phrase designating something characterized by the appearance of energetic action, would the sense of the passage as a piece of description suffer in any way? In other words, is it not a description of *the appearance of energetic action* itself, and of no other specific thing? In short, the passage seems to possess no specific meaning of the kind obviously intended. What it *sounds* like is a description of Schopenhauer's undifferentiated 'will' as the ground of being with mental images evoked by the word 'power' added to it: in other words, an extension, impermissible to Nietzsche, of the will to power beyond the realm of phenomena into the word-intoxicated realm of metaphysics.

The second example is his persistent worrying of the ancient problem of appearance and reality. For the sake of his theory of knowledge and critique of logic, he needs the postulate that 'being is an empty fiction' (*T*, III. 2), and he rightly sees as a corollary to this that 'the "apparent" world is the only real one' (*ibid.*); what he does not see, apparently, is that the distinction between 'being' and 'becoming', and between 'appearance' and 'reality', is altogether irrelevant to the phenomenalism to which he had, in intention, committed himself when he repudiated metaphysics. Moreover, for all his continuing concern with this metaphysical problem, he never seriously considers whether the solution to it he discovered at the age of twenty was in any way inadequate: so far as I can see, he never subjected it to the slightest critical inspection. The solution in question comes from F. A. Lange's *History of Materialism*, which Nietzsche first read in 1866 and subsequently recommended as a work offering great enlightenment. Lange argues that all knowledge is knowledge of the phenomenal (apparent) world – the fact of our knowing a thing being the proof that that thing is a phenomenon – and that consequently all the ideas we have, including the ideas of a dichotomy between an apparent and a real world and the content of that real world, can only be phenomena. Nietzsche accepted this argument and repeated it, in differing formulations, again and again throughout the remainder of his life: 'The "real world", however it has been conceived of hitherto – it has always been the apparent world *once more*' (*WP*, 566), he wrote in a note of the winter of 1887–8, and this formulation may stand as a paradigm of all the others. Now this 'proof' is no more than the assertion that we cannot *imagine* a 'real' world that does not turn out to be the world we know once more: it does not touch upon the question whether a 'real' world might not be a necessary postulate even if we cannot imagine what it might be like. Fundamentally, Nietzsche realizes this, but he has no interest in emphasizing it because all his interest is directed towards asserting the limitation of our knowledge to knowledge of phenomena and then to decrying as instances of 'world-denial' and 'decadence' all attempts to establish the existence of anything beyond or behind phenomena: 'To talk about "another" world than this is quite pointless, provided that an instinct for slandering, disparaging and accusing life is not strong within us: in the latter case we *revenge* ourselves on life by means of the phantasmagoria of "another", a "better" life . . . To divide the world into a "real" and an "apparent" world . . . is only a suggestion of *décadence* – a symptom of *declining* life' (*T*, III. 6). This is all very well as far as it goes, but it does not go nearly far enough. To reduce the problem of appearance and reality to a psychological (or physiological) problem is to do no more than trifle with it: the question whether, aside from the *motive* one may have for believing in the existence of a 'real' world, reason does or does not *compel* us to posit some such thing, is not even touched upon: and the reason Nietzsche halts at this problem with a solution he discovered ready-made when he was hardly out of his teens is, I think, that he had ceased to be interested in metaphysics and could not be bothered to give much serious thought to what had come to seem to him irrelevant issues. What Lange's argument really establishes (if you go along with it) is a basis for an exclusive occupation with phenomenalism – not because everything is proved to be phenomenon, but because within this discipline the dichotomy of 'appearance' and 'reality' no longer plays any role. If Nietzsche grasped this, determined to devote himself to phenomenalism, but was against his will diverted from this path back on to that of metaphysics, the unsatisfactory character of his speculations about reality and appearance would be explained.

There is a parallel between Nietzsche's development in this regard and the historical scheme of Comte. According to Comte, mankind began by explaining phenomena theologically (in terms of the operations of gods and spirits), moved on to metaphysical explanations (in terms of impersonal essences and faculties), and finally arrived at phenomenalism (explanation as the description of the relations between phenomena). This course, whether or not it represents a valid account of human intellectual evolution, certainly describes Nietzsche's: one might call him a 'classic case' of the progression from theology to metaphysics to phenomenalism. It is because this is so – because this progression is so marked that even his backslidings into metaphysics cannot obscure it – that a determination to see him as a front-line Protestant theologian, or as the 'last metaphysician of the West' who demonstrated the impossibility of metaphysics, while it may bring out and highlight some very interesting aspects of him, is a falsification of him as a whole.

V: Ethics

Consideration of Nietzsche's ethics offers at once a first-rate instance of his phenomenalism. He sought to discover what 'morality' was, and he did so, not by trying to define its 'essence', but by observing 'moral phenomena' and comparing them.

He wrote endlessly on this topic and to such effect that many think of him as primarily a moral philosopher – though sometimes this amounts to thinking of him as the philosopher who wanted to invert our moral judgments. This, as I have already insisted, is false as stated, and even when corrected to 'make us revise our idea of the nature of good and evil' still a misleading simplification. Nietzsche's objective, as a moral philosopher, was to subject the phenomenon morality to objective scrutiny. If we are to examine how he goes about it, we have to be selective: to no department of his work does the caution that an introduction to him is a map of a city and not a visit to it apply with greater force.

To begin, then, at the beginning: the first introduction Christian children have usually had to the concepts 'good and evil' – as opposed to 'being good' and 'being naughty' in the nursery sense – has been in the shape of the tree of the knowledge of good and evil, whose fruit, when eaten by Eve and Adam, makes them godlike (Genesis 3). What do they make of this story, and of the equivocal character 'the Lord

God' who plays a prominent role in it? Certainly they feel sorry for Adam and Eve, whom they no doubt think of as children (for they are treated like children), and probably they are disturbed by the arbitrary tyranny of the Lord God; but the sexual interpretation of the story (which is in any case consistent with only part of it) of course passes them by; it is only from other sources that they learn that the forbidden tree was an apple tree, and they cannot understand the role played by the serpent (a child does not have to be especially bright to see that, if the Lord God made everything, as it has just been emphatically insisted he did, he must have made the serpent. Therefore . . .). They must, however, necessarily have learned one new thing from it: that there is something in the world called 'good and evil', and that Adam and Eve now know what it is. 'Good' and 'evil': not 'being good' and 'being naughty', for Adam and Eve were being good in the Garden of Eden until they ate the fruit of the tree, and by eating the fruit they were being naughty – yet it was not until after they had eaten it that they had 'knowledge of good and evil'. Good and evil are something outside of and distinct from them, and are not synonymous with good and naughty acts: they are something waiting to be discovered, a possible object of knowledge.

Now the way in which I have imagined a child reasoning is the way in which almost all moral philosophers have reasoned hitherto: they have believed that there is good and evil *in the world*, that the world possesses moral significance, that there exists a 'moral world-order'. How to define a 'good act' has exercised the intelligence of many of them: one has said that a good act is an act the cause of (intention behind) which is good, another has said that it is an act the consequence of which is good, a third has said that it is an act performed in obedience to the dictates of duty, a fourth has said something else again: but all have assumed that 'good' itself *exists*, as a fact, and that one can recognize whether an intention is good or the consequence of an act is good as one can recognize whether a wall is white.

Is there a flaw in this reasoning common to children and moral philosophers and the author of Genesis? There is at any rate a difficulty which might suggest where a flaw might lie. After they have consumed the forbidden fruit, we are told, Adam and Eve know good and evil: but we are not told in what that knowledge consists. We are told that it makes them 'godlike' and embarrassed at being undressed: but *what* it is we are not told. The secret is never divulged: Socrates, 'the wisest of men', admits that he is not in on it. He says he can recognize what he thinks are good and wicked acts; he knows, or thinks he knows, what being good and being naughty are, which is what any child knows; but he does not know what 'good' is. He tries to define it, and fails. Well over two thousand years later a modern Socrates rebukes a young man who says 'I know the difference between right and wrong' with 'You don't say so! What! no capacity for business, no knowledge of law, no sympathy for art, no pretension to philosophy; only a simple knowledge of the secret that has puzzled all the philosophers, baffled all the lawyers, muddled all the men of business, and ruined most of the artists: the secret of right and wrong. Why, man, you're a genius, a master of masters, a god! At twenty-four, too!' (*Major Barbara*).

This, indeed, is the great difficulty about it, and the child who reads the story of the Fall and believes it has acquired a new piece of information from it has subsequently to learn that it has done nothing of the sort: that its 'knowledge of good and evil' is precisely what it was before, namely a knowledge of 'good and wicked' *acts*. 'Good' and 'wicked' are still descriptions of acts, not of entities: that is the truth of the matter; and once it is grasped, 'morality' ceases to be something given and becomes a problem.

I call this act 'good' and that 'wicked': what, if I am not in possession of the 'knowledge of good and evil', do I mean? He calls this act I have called good wicked: how can that be? Is it a difference of opinion, or of taste? Why am I getting so hot under the collar about it: why do I set so high a value on my moral opinions or tastes that I cannot tolerate any others? Why are the words 'immoral', 'wicked', 'evil' so heavily charged? 'We must destroy evil', says the moralist, and although his sentiments do not accord with those of Jesus ('Resist not evil') they usually elicit an affirmative response – unless, that is, the moralist happens to be, for instance, a disciple of the Prophet, and by evil means *you*.

All this suggests that morality, knowledge of good and evil, is not a simple matter at all, and certainly not the simple question of possessing a 'moral sense': and Nietzsche's investigation commences from this fact. 'When I visited men,' says Zarathustra, 'I found them sitting upon an old self-conceit. Each one thought he had long since known what was good and evil for man. All talk of virtue seemed to them an ancient wearied affair; and he who wished to sleep well spoke of "good" and "evil" before retiring. I disturbed this somnolence when I taught that *nobody yet knows* what is good and evil' (Z, III. 12: 2).

He began, I think, with the observation that the moral judgments of Christendom were different from those of classical antiquity; and not merely different but in many instances antithetical. This fact alone sufficed, when he came to reflect on its implications, to prove that the 'moral sense', if it existed, was not unchanging; and that if the world possessed 'ethical significance' that significance was not obvious, since whole civilizations could fail to see it. If the morality of Christendom was morality as such, Graeco-Roman morality was immoral: but to use 'moral' and 'immoral' in this way implies the possession of a criterion of 'the moral' independent of and preceding all moral phenomena (such as 'Christian morality' and 'Graeco-Roman morality'), and he decided he did not possess such a criterion. He generalized: there is no morality, there are different moralities.

This conclusion denies the existence of any essential good, and asserts that morals are phenomena, to be studied like any other phenomena, that is by comparing one phenomenon with another. (He was later to assert that 'there are no moral phenomena at all, but only a moral interpretation of phenomena' (*BGE*, 108): but 'moral interpretation' is also a phenomenon, so this assertion in no way affects the issue.) A description and typology of morals is the task he sets himself; and it is, he says, a quite different task from that undertaken by previous philosophers:

> Moral sensibility is as subtle, late, manifold and refined in
> Europe today as the 'science of morals' pertaining to it is still
> young, inept, clumsy and coarse-fingered . . . One should, in all
> strictness, admit *what* will be needed here for a long time to
> come . . . assembly of materials, conceptual comprehension and
> arrangement of a vast domain of delicate value-feelings and
> value-distinctions which live, grow, beget and perish – and
> perhaps attempts to display the more frequent and recurring
> forms of these living crystallizations – as preparation of a *typology*
> of morals . . . one has not been so modest hitherto. Philosophers
> one and all . . . have demanded something much higher, more
> pretentious, more solemn of themselves . . . they wanted to
> furnish the *rational ground* of morality . . . How far from their
> clumsy pride was that apparently insignificant task left in dust
> and mildew, the task of description . . . the real problems of
> morality . . . come into view only if we compare *many*
> moralities. (*BGE*, 186)

The need for a description of morality derives from the fact that, although there are different moralities, they must all have something in common by which they can be recognized as moralities: Christian morals and Graeco-Roman morals must have some common characteristic which makes them both morals and not, for instance, aesthetic tastes. This characteristic, Nietzsche says, is obedience to a command. 'Every morality is, as opposed to *laisser aller*, a piece of tyranny against "nature", likewise against "reason" . . . The essential and invaluable element in every morality is that it is a protracted constraint . . . a protracted *obedience* in *one* direction . . . "Thou shalt obey someone and for a long time: *otherwise* thou shalt perish . . ." – this seems to me to be nature's imperative' (*BGE*, 188). And again: 'To be moral, virtuous, ethical, means to obey a long-established law or tradition. Whether one obeys gladly or reluctantly is immaterial: it is enough that one obeys' (*HA*, 96). The nature of the command – what it is a command to do – is secondary: the primary and defining fact is the fact of obedience to it. And, Nietzsche goes on: 'He is called "good" who acts according to custom as if by nature . . . easily and gladly' (*ibid.*). Later he rephrases 'as if by nature . . . easily and gladly' more specifically as 'unconsciously' and, taking the law of Manu, the foundation of Hindu morality, as an example, tries to account for the origin of a 'moral law'. Such a law-book as that of Manu, he says:

> Originates as does every good law-book: it summarizes the experience, policy and experimental morality of long centuries . . . A law-book never tells of the utility of a law, of the reason for it . . . for in that way it would lose the imperative tone, the 'thou shalt', the precondition of being obeyed . . . At a certain point in the evolution of a people its most enlightened . . . class declares the experience in accordance with which the people is to live – that is, *can* live – to be fixed and settled. Their objective is to bring home the richest and completest harvest from the ages of experimentation and *bad* experience. What, consequently, is to be prevented above all is the continuance of experimenting.

The rationale of the procedures devised for this 'lies in the intention of making the way of life recognized as correct . . . unconscious: so that a complete automatism of instinct is achieved – the precondition for any kind of . . . perfection in the art of living' (*A*, 57). Automatism of instinct in the obedience of these commands is 'conscience'; and our conscience always tells us what is right because 'right' is by definition the content of our conscience. It is, of course, in childhood that we usually receive all the basic 'moral commands', which are presented to us, as 'every good law-book' is presented, 'without any given reason' (*WS*, 52).

Much of this is epitomized in a few sentences by Zarathustra:

> Zarathustra has seen many lands and many peoples: thus he
> has discovered the good and evil of many peoples. Zarathustra
> has found no greater power on earth than good and evil. No
> people could live without evaluating; but if it wishes to
> maintain itself it must not evaluate as its neighbour evaluates.
> Much that seemed good to one people seemed shame and disgrace
> to another . . . I found much that was called evil in one place
> was in another decked with purple honours . . . A table of values
> hangs over every people. Behold, it is the table of its overcomings;
> behold, it is the voice of its will to power. What it accounts
> hard it calls praiseworthy; what it accounts indispensable and
> hard it calls good; and that which relieves the greatest need, the
> rare, the hardest of all – it glorifies as holy. Whatever causes it
> to rule and conquer and glitter, to the dread and envy of its
> neighbour, that it accounts the sublimest, the paramount, the
> evaluation and the meaning of all things . . . if you only knew a
> people's need and land and sky and neighbour, you could surely
> divine the laws of its overcomings, and why it is upon this
> ladder that it mounts towards its hope (*Z*, I. 15)

A people gives itself commands so that it may *prevail*: 'morality' is a codification of the conditions under which it can continue to exist and the means by which it can enhance its power; and the reason there have been different 'moralities' is that these conditions and means have differed.

Now, still comparing moral phenomena, Nietzsche himself undertakes the typology of morality he has demanded: he says there are two types of morality, and I quote at length from the passage in which he says what they are:

> There is *master morality* and *slave morality* – I add at once that in
> all higher and mixed cultures attempts at mediation between the
> two are apparent and more frequently confusion and mutual

misunderstanding between them, indeed sometimes their harsh juxtaposition – even within the same man, within *one* soul. The moral value-distinctions have arisen either among a ruling order . . . or among the ruled, the slaves and dependants of every degree. In the former case, when it is the rulers who determine the concept 'good', it is the exalted, proud states of soul which are considered distinguishing and determine the order of rank . . . in this first type of morality the antithesis 'good' and 'bad' means the same thing as 'noble' and 'despicable' – the antithesis 'good' and '*evil*' originates elsewhere . . . It is immediately obvious that designations of moral value were everywhere first applied to *human beings*, and only later and derivatively to *actions*: . . . the noble type of man feels *himself* to be the determiner of values, he does not need to be approved of, he judges 'what harms me is harmful in itself', . . . he *creates values* . . . In the foreground stands the feeling of plentitude, of power which seeks to overflow, the happiness of high tension, the consciousness of a wealth which would like to give away and bestow – the noble human being too aids the unfortunate, but not, or almost not, from pity, but more from an urge begotten by superfluity of power. The noble human being honours in himself the man of power, also the man who has power over himself, who understands how to speak and how to keep silent, who enjoys practising severity and harshness upon himself and feels reverence for all that is severe and harsh . . . belief in oneself, pride in oneself, a fundamental hostility and irony for 'selflessness', belong just as definitely to noble morality as does a mild contempt for and caution against sympathy and the 'warm heart' . . . It is otherwise with the second type of morality, *slave morality*. Suppose the abused, oppressed, suffering, unfree, those uncertain of themselves and weary should moralize: what would their moral evaluations have in common? Probably a pessimistic mistrust of the entire situation of man will find expression . . . The slave is suspicious of the virtues of the powerful: he is . . . *keenly* mistrustful of everything 'good' that is honoured among them – he would like to convince himself that happiness itself is not genuine among them. On the other hand, those qualities which serve to make easier the existence of the suffering will be brought into prominence and flooded with light: it is here that pity, the kind and helping hand, the

warm heart, patience, industriousness, humility, friendliness
come into honour – for here these are the most useful qualities
and virtually the only means of enduring the burden of existence.
Slave morality is essentially a morality of utility. Here is the
source of the famous antithesis 'good' and '*evil*' – power and
danger were felt to exist in evil, a certain dreadfulness, subtlety
and strength which could not admit of contempt. Thus, according
to slave morality, the 'evil' inspire fear; according to master
morality it is precisely the 'good' who inspire fear and want to
inspire it, while the 'bad' man is judged contemptible. The
antithesis reaches its height when, consistently with slave morality,
a breath of disdain finally also comes to be attached to the 'good'
of this morality . . . because within the slaves' way of thinking
the good man has in any event to be a *harmless* man . . . (*BGE*, 260)

Notice, first of all, that Nietzsche is not saying that every morality
must be a 'master' or a 'slave' morality, nor that every man is either a
master or a slave: on the contrary, he stresses as soon as he has introduced these terms that 'all higher and mixed cultures' are a compound
of the two. 'Master' and 'slave' moralities are *types*, that is classes of
'moral commands', and not descriptions of moral codes at present
existing. When he wants to find an example of a morality a description
of which would coincide with its description as a type he has to retreat,
as usual in other contexts, into prehistory. The example he chooses is
again Hindu morality. The 'Aryan' conquerors of what then became
India are pictured as being faced with the need to survive among and
rule over a population very much more numerous: to this end four
'races' are bred – the priestly, the warrior, the trading and farming,
and the menial race (Sudras) – and the morality inculcated into each of
these 'castes' is not only suitable to the function each has to perform
but is also directed towards keeping down and weakening the native
population, which is excluded from the caste system and branded with
the name 'Chandala' – untouchable. 'Perhaps there is nothing which
outrages our feelings more than *these* protective measures of Indian
morality', Nietzsche goes on.

The third edict, for example . . . that 'concerning unclean
vegetables', ordains that the only nourishment permitted the
Chandala shall be garlic and onions, in view of the fact that
holy scripture forbids one to give them corn or seed-bearing
fruits or *water* or fire. The same edict lays it down that the water

they need must not be taken from rivers or springs or pools, but only from the entrances to swamps and holes made by the feet of animals. They are likewise forbidden to wash their clothes or to *wash themselves*, since the water allowed them as an act of charity must be used only for quenching the thirst. Finally, the Sudra women are forbidden to assist the Chandala women in childbirth, and the latter are likewise forbidden to *assist one another* . . . Manu himself says: 'The Chandala are the fruit of adultery, incest and crime . . . They shall have for clothing only rags from corpses, for utensils broken pots, for ornaments old iron, for worship only evil spirits; they shall wander from place to place without rest. They are forbidden to write from left to right and to use the right hand for writing: the employment of the right hand and of the left-to-right motion is reserved for the *virtuous*, for people of *race*'. These regulations are instructive enough: in them we find for once *Aryan* humanity, quite pure, quite primordial – we learn that the concept 'pure blood' is the opposite of a harmless concept. It becomes clear, on the other hand, in *which* people the hatred, the Chandala hatred for this 'humanity' has been immortalized, where it has become religion, where it has become *genius* . . . Christianity . . . represents the *reaction* against that morality of breeding, of race, of privilege – it is the *anti-Aryan* religion *par excellence*: Christianity . . . the victory of Chandala values, the evangel preached to the poor and lowly, the collective rebellion of everything downtrodden, wretched, ill-constituted, underprivileged against the 'race' – undying Chandala revenge as the *religion of love* . . . (*T*, VI. 3–4)

In Indian morality certain actions are 'good' which to our way of thinking are repellent, and we find it difficult to understand how the stigmatization of a host of people as 'untouchable' could be a question of conscience: yet that is what it was. Moral commands exist and have existed which are not only different from those we usually hear but so very different that we find it hard to recognize them as moral commands, and talk about 'superstition' and the like: but the command not to kill a cow is no more superstition than the command to have only one wife at a time is superstition – both have a remote origin in the conditions under which a nation could best survive, prosper and prevail.

This remains the case whether one is considering a 'master' or a 'slave' morality; their origin is to be found in the same need to survive and grow more powerful; and it might therefore seem that there is no essential difference between them, only a difference of means. But this, it will be noted, Nietzsche denies: he says there *is* an essential difference, and it can be summarized in the distinction 'good and bad' and 'good and evil', the former being the moral antithesis of *Herrenmoral*, the latter of *Sklavenmoral*. The two types of morality stand towards one another in the relation of *primary* and *reactive*: master morality originates in naïve and direct 'will to power', slave morality in a reaction to master morality. The point is brought out explicitly in the *Genealogy of Morals*:

> The slave-revolt in morals begins when *ressentiment* . . . becomes creative and gives birth to values . . . While every noble morality develops from a triumphant affirmation of itself, slave morality from the outset says No to what is 'outside', what is 'different', what is 'not itself': and *this* No is its creative act . . . its action is . . . reaction. . . . The man of *ressentiment* . . . has conceived 'the evil enemy', 'the *Evil One*', and this indeed is his basic idea, from which he then evolves, as a corresponding and opposing figure, a 'good one' – himself! This is . . . quite the contrary of what the noble man does, who conceives the basic idea 'good' spontaneously . . . out of himself, and only then creates for himself the concept 'bad'. This 'bad' of noble origin and that 'evil' out of the cauldron of unsatisfied hatred . . . how different these words 'bad' and 'evil' are, although they are both apparently the opposite of the same concept 'good'. But it is *not* the same concept 'good': one should ask rather precisely *who* is 'evil' in the sense of the morality of *ressentiment*. The answer, in all strictness, is: *precisely* the 'good man' of the other morality, precisely the noble, powerful man, the ruler. (*GM*, I. 10–11).

The reference to 'good' in this passage is slightly misleading, inasmuch as it is the *effect* of the 'good man' of master morality which the other finds 'evil', rather than that which really constitutes 'the good' for him. Recall the definition of 'good' given in *The Anti-Christ*: 'All that heightens the feeling of power, the will to power, power itself in man' (*A*, 2). Now, this is intended as an *objective* definition: that which people call 'good' is in fact that which heightens the feeling of power: that is Nietzsche's proposition, and it applies equally to both types of morality. Where they differ is in the nature of *that which* heightens the feeling of power: and it is from that point of view that 'slave morality' can be recognized as originating in a feeling of powerlessness, as a reaction to which feeling its criteria of 'good' are first established.

There are two further points which it will be interesting to discuss briefly.

Nietzsche had a theory that the words for 'good' coined in the various languages had all originally meant 'noble', 'aristocratic' in the social sense, and that the words for 'bad' had originally meant 'plebeian', 'low' in the social sense. The 'most convincing example of the latter' which he can find is the German *schlecht* (bad), which is etymologically identical with *schlicht* (plain, simple) (*GM*, I. 4): it is certainly a striking example, almost as striking as our own villein/villain. On the other side, he suggests that *gut* (good) may derive from Goth, the conquering and therefore noble race (*GM*, I. 5), though here he is on shakier ground. He also derives the Latin *bonus* (good) from 'warrior' and *malus* (bad) from 'dark-haired', meaning the pre-Aryan occupants of Italy. But the origin of the theory fairly clearly lies in Greece, and specifically in the preoccupation of Theognis with the distinction between the 'good' nobility and the 'bad' common people. Nietzsche's first publication was an article on Theognis, and he refers to him in *GM*, II. 5 in the midst of his discussion of the etymology of 'good' and 'bad'. Theognis represents in an exaggerated form the assumption of a Greek aristocrat that the typical character traits of the aristocracy are good (truthfulness, for instance) and those of the common people bad (lying, for instance); and Nietzsche manages in this connection to trace back *esthlos* (good) to 'noble' and thence to 'truthful'.

He has been represented as seconding the opinion of Thrasymachus (in *The Republic*) that 'justice is nothing else than the interest of the stronger', and applying it to 'good' in general. We have seen already that this is not his idea of what 'justice' is, and it is not his idea of 'good' either. Consider the matter in this way: a definition of 'good' might be arrived at by answering the question 'when people say a thing is good what does "good" mean?' The answer to this question, even the correct answer, would perhaps not be a sufficient and compelling definition, but any definition which was obviously and flagrantly not the correct answer would certainly be suspect. Now, how does Thrasymachus's definition, as supposedly adapted by Nietzsche, stand up? 'When people say a thing is good, "good" means the interest of the stronger': is that not obviously the *wrong* answer? Is it not obviously wrong even if the original 'justice' is substituted for 'good' – for how can 'the weaker' possibly agree that justice *as such* consists in the ignoring or frustration of their interest? Now try Nietzsche's definition: 'When people say a thing is good, "good" means that which heightens the feeling of power.' Leaving aside whether it is or is not the right answer, it is not obviously wrong, and is not merely a repetition of Thrasymachus's answer. In short, it is not the case that Nietzsche maintains that 'good' is the interest of the stronger.

VI: Aesthetics

Even Carlyle, who could take far more 'German ponderousness' than most of us, was irritated into a protest at the seemingly endless theorizing and argufying about the nature of 'the beautiful' and 'the sublime', the distinction between 'nature' and 'art', the dichotomy of 'classic' and 'romantic', and all the rest of it, which he found in the writings and correspondence of Goethe and Schiller. Even he reached a point where he had had enough: we are likely to reach it much sooner. In no department of life does the theoretical dissection of experience so soon become tedious as it does in the aesthetic department, and the reason is our very great partiality for making aesthetic judgments. If you reflect on a normal day in your life, you will find that the occasions for making other kinds of judgment – moral judgments, for instance – are exceedingly few, but that you are making aesthetic judgments almost all the time. It seems, indeed, that, while the capacity for moral judgment has to be acquired, aesthetic judgment is almost 'second nature', and is for that reason very little amenable to modification through argument: if you 'do not like' something, it will be hard to *argue* you into liking it. Now this kind of response to existence – the 'aesthetic' response – which seems to be so much a part of us that it is hard to imagine what a human being who lacked 'aesthetic judgment' would be like, or how he would look upon the world and his own experience, is in art as it were fenced off and isolated: whatever other objectives, conscious or otherwise, a work of art may be intended to serve, it must serve an aesthetic end – it must be intended to elicit an aesthetic response, that is to say, the kind of response for which we have in general so great a partiality. How irritating, therefore, it is when that which is specifically designed as a tonic for, or even an orgy of, our aesthetic feelings is subjected to an analysis to which aesthetic feeling cannot respond; and how much more irritating when that aesthetic feeling itself is removed from the realm of enjoyment into the non-aesthetic and sometimes positively anaesthetic 'science of aesthetics'.

Strictly speaking, the essential purpose of this 'science' is to discover why beauty is beautiful; but on a second level it accepts 'the beautiful' and the other aesthetic categories as given, and asks why they exist and whether they exist objectively in the world or are a subjective human response to or interpretation of that which is in itself aesthetically neutral; and on a third level it inquires into the nature and purpose of the human creation of beauty, that is to say the nature and purpose of art. Because of the very large part played in our lives by our aesthetic responses and judgments, no philosophy with encyclopaedic ambitions can possibly afford to overlook them; and if the philosopher is also an artist, as Nietzsche was, his interest in them may be very lively. Nietzsche in fact wrote about aesthetics at all periods of his life and at (for him) great length. I shall here concentrate on his three main interests and present what appear to be his basic conclusions with respect to them: first, his attempt to solve the problem of why beauty is beautiful and ugliness is ugly; then, his answer to the question what art is and what purpose it is intended to serve; finally, his investigations into the nature of tragedy.

Nietzsche had no doubt that beauty is in the eye of the beholder, but for all that it is not a matter of arbitrary taste: 'Nothing is beautiful, only man,' he writes: 'on this piece of naïvety rests all aesthetics, it is the *first* truth of aesthetics. Let us immediately add its second: nothing is ugly but *degenerate* man – the domain of aesthetic judgment is therewith defined' (*T*, IX. 20). Our feeling for the beautiful cannot be divorced from 'man's pleasure in man': in the beautiful 'man sets himself up as the standard of perfection', and does so in obedience to his '*deepest* instinct, that of self-preservation and self-aggrandizement', of which this aesthetic taste is a 'sublimated' expression (*T*, IX. 19). 'Man believes that the world itself is filled with beauty – he *forgets* that it is he who has created it. He alone has bestowed beauty on the world . . . Man really mirrors himself in things, that which gives him back his own reflection he considers beautiful: the judgment "beautiful" is his *conceit of his species*' (*ibid.*). The ugly, on the other hand,

is understood as a sign and symptom of degeneration: that which recalls degeneration, however remotely, produces in us the judgment 'ugly'. Every token of exhaustion, of heaviness, of age, of weariness, every kind of unfreedom, whether convulsive or paralytic, above all the smell, colour and shape of dissolution, of decomposition, though it be attenuated to the point of being no more than a symbol – all this calls forth the same reaction, the value judgment 'ugly'. (*T*, IX. 20)

'Beauty' is thus subjective, inasmuch as it exists only in the mind of man; but this subjectivity does not imply a limitless arbitrariness in what is found beautiful: men find the same things beautiful, not because 'beauty' is there to be seen, but because they are all men.

This simple solution to the problem of why beauty is beautiful is rendered even simpler by the expulsion of any kind of special or metaphysical 'sense' of beauty. In a passage in *The Gay Science*, Nietzsche asserts: 'My objections to Wagner's music are physiological objections: why conceal them under aesthetic formulas? My "fact" is that I no longer breathe easily as soon as this music begins to affect me' (*GS*, 368). When he reprinted the passage in his polemical compendium *Nietzsche contra Wagner* he reinforced the point by inserting between the two sentences quoted above: 'For aesthetics is nothing but applied physiology' (*NCW*, II). Whether this is an entirely satisfactory statement is disputable: but it is entirely consistent with the anti-metaphysical, phenomenalist tenor of his philosophy. A 'sense of beauty', even if it is a product of evolution, is too much like a 'moral sense', or even a 'will' or 'soul', to pass through Nietzsche's phenomenalist sieve. That he can no longer breathe easily is the 'fact' he records; he maintains that 'ugliness' is always associated with the experience of physiological unpleasantness on the part of the beholder of it, and that 'the effect of the ugly can be measured with a dynamometer' (*T*, IX. 20).

What all this means essentially in terms of 'aesthetics' is that Nietzsche denied Kant's dictum that 'that is beautiful which gives pleasure without interest' – a dictum he quotes in the *Genealogy of Morals* (III. 6) in order to refute it. Kant, he says, like all philosophers, considered the question of the beautiful entirely from the point of view of the spectator of it, and never from that of its creator. (He means, in this place, the artist; but since in Nietzsche's view all beauty is created by man, there is no such thing as a pure 'spectator'.) This point of view, however, is not propitious for an understanding of the nature of beauty, and is especially inadequate in Kant's own case since, Nietzsche maintains, Kant was in any event altogether unresponsive to beauty and had no experience of it even as a 'spectator': Kant, and aestheticians in general, have simply been naïve and inexperienced when they have found the essence of the aesthetic condition to lie in its disinterestedness: 'When our aestheticians never weary of maintaining, in favour of Kant, that under the spell of beauty one can view *even* undraped female statues "without interest", we may laugh a little at their expense' (*ibid.*). Against Kant he quotes Stendhal's definition of the beautiful as '*une promesse de bonheur*', which he interprets as an antithetical definition to the Kantian, inasmuch as the 'interest of the spectator' is very definitely involved.

Asking 'who is right, Kant or Stendhal?' he looks for an answer in the case of Schopenhauer, who, he says, 'interpreted the expression "without interest" in the most personal fashion as a result of an experience which must have been one of the most regularly recurring.' Schopenhauer says of aesthetic contemplation 'that it operates precisely against *sexual* "interest" . . . he never wearied of glorifying *this* liberation from the "will" as the great merit and utility of the aesthetic condition'. But this interpretation is false even from the point of view of the Kantian definition which Schopenhauer believed he was being faithful to, for, like Stendhal, 'he too was pleased by the beautiful as a consequence of "interest", even as a consequence of the strongest, most personal interest: that of the tortured man who is freed from his torture' (*ibid.*). And the supposed fact upon which it is founded is probably not a fact either, for it overlooks the possibility 'that that peculiar sweetness and plenitude which is characteristic of the aesthetic condition might have its origin in precisely the ingredient "sensuality" . . . so that, with the advent of the aesthetic condition, sensuality would have been, not abolished, as Schopenhauer believed, but only trans-figured and no longer enter consciousness as sexual excitation' (*GM*, III. 8).

Nietzsche then promises to return to this point 'another time . . . in connection with even more delicate problems of the – hitherto so untouched, so unrevealed – *physiology of aesthetics*': he never did so formally, but his writings of the following year (1888) are none the less full of what could well be called a 'physiology of aesthetics'. We have already quoted a few of his suggestions from *Twilight of the Idols*, and in this same volume he returns to Schopenhauer and his theory that beauty is 'redemption from the "will"' in general and especially from the 'focus of the will', sexuality, and comments that nature contradicts Schopenhauer. '*To what end* is there beauty at all in the sounds, colours, odours, rhythmic movements of nature? what *makes* beauty *appear?*' Fortunately, he adds, a philosopher also contradicts him: 'No less an authority than . . . Plato . . . maintains a different thesis: that all beauty incites to procreation – that precisely this is the *proprium* of its effect, from the most sensual regions up into the most spiritual' (*T*, IX. 22).

In short, the aesthetic condition is associated with 'interest' in the closest way; the interest is biological:

> That which we instinctively find *repulsive*, aesthetically, is proved by mankind's longest experience to be harmful, dangerous, worthy of being suspected: the suddenly vocal aesthetic instinct (e.g. in disgust) contains a *judgment*. To this extent the beautiful stands within the general category of the biological values of what is useful, beneficial, life-enhancing . . . It is senseless to want to posit something as beautiful or ugly apart from this. *The* beautiful exists as little as *the* good, *the* true. In each particular case it is a question of the *conditions for the preservation* of a certain kind of man . . . (*WP*, 804)

If we turn from the aesthetic condition as such to the production and appreciation of works of art, we find Nietzsche adopting the same attitude: art, too, serves the purpose of supporting and maintaining life. And as we were able to simplify his interpretation of the aesthetic condition by contrasting it with Kant's definition, so we can simplify his interpretation of art by contrasting it with Keats's 'beauty is truth, truth beauty': for to Nietzsche this is precisely the opposite of the truth.

In *The Birth of Tragedy* he describes 'the highest and truly serious task of art' as 'to deliver the eye from gazing into the terrors of night and to rescue the subject from the spasms of the activities of the will through the healing balm of illusion' (*B T*, 19). The language is still Schopenhaueran, but the sense of what is meant derives, not from Schopenhauer, but from Nietzsche's own reflections on the nature and purpose of art – reflections whose conclusions remained unchanged for the rest of his life. Truth, as we have noted often enough before, is not beautiful but ugly, dreadful, hard to endure: art is a mask set over the face of truth. 'The Greek knew and felt the terrors and horrors of existence: in order to be able to live at all he had to set before it the glittering dream-image of the Olympians' (*B T*, 3): this is one formulation, and it is succeeded by scores more, all asserting essentially the same thing, namely that art is an illusion the objective of which is to falsify and obscure an unendurable reality and thus make it endurable and life possible:

> Art is mightier than knowledge, for art desires life, and knowledge attains as its final goal only – annihilation. ('On the Pathos of Truth', 1872)

> If we had not approved of the arts and invented this kind of cult of the untrue, the insight into universal untruth and mendaciousness which has now been granted us by science – the insight into the delusion and error which is a condition of knowing and sentient existence – could in no way have been endured. *Honesty* would have led to disgust and suicide. But now our honesty is confronted by an opposing power which helps us to avoid such consequences: art, as the *good* will to illusion . . . As an aesthetic phenomenon existence is still *endurable* to us and, through art, eye and hand and above all a good conscience are given us so that we may be *able* to make of ourselves such a phenomenon (*GS*, 107)

> Art and nothing but art! It is the great possibilizer of life, the great seductress to life, the great stimulant of life . . . art is *worth more* than truth. (*WP*, 853, I and IV – an unused draft for a preface for a new edition of *The Birth of Tragedy*)

> In a philosopher it is baseness to say 'the good and beautiful are one'; if he should even go on to add 'the true also' he ought to be thrashed. Truth is ugly. We possess *art* so that we *shall not perish of truth* (*WP*, 822)

At first Nietzsche interpreted this insight into the character of art as it were the wrong way round: in *The Birth of Tragedy* he declared that 'only as an *aesthetic phenomenon* is existence and the world *eternally justified*' (*B T*, 5; cf. 24). This dictum, however, depends, as the context in which it appears makes clear, on the existence also of that which produces the universal art-work, and necessitates some conjecture as to why it (or He) produces it; and this leads either to a Schopenhaueran conception of the 'will' as the productive force (as in *The Birth of Tragedy*), or to a fantastical and, in Nietzsche's case at any rate, never wholly serious picture of a 'suffering god' who fashions the world as a kind of cure for his sickness. The latter conception is an extrapolation of the familiar idea that artistic creation is a consequence of some shortcoming or sense of insufficiency in the artist – a conception to which Nietzsche gives voice in such aphorisms as: 'A Homer would never have created an Achilles, a Goethe would never have created a Faust, if Homer had been an Achilles and Goethe had been a Faust' (*GM*, III. 4), and 'It is the exceptional states which condition the artist: those which are profoundly related to and involved with morbid phenomena: so that it does not seem possible to be an artist and not be sick' (*WP*, 811); and whatever may be said in its favour, it is no more likely or seriously convincing an explanation of the origin of the world than is the notion that we are all figments of a divine dream, for both ideas are to the last degree anthropomorphic. Nietzsche, however, was never seriously involved with this dubious notion, because he came quite quickly to the view that 'existence and the world' is not in itself an 'aesthetic phenomenon' at all, but that it is man who interprets it 'aesthetically' (just as he interprets it 'morally'; just as all knowledge is interpretation): so that the correct formula, if one needed a formula, would be 'aesthetic interpretation of phenomena is an attempt at the eternal justification of existence and the world'.

It is in the light of this redefinition of the relation between the aesthetic condition and that with which it is associated that we can, I believe, come to a true understanding of Nietzsche's much misunderstood contention that – to put it at its simplest – all art is praise. And that will in turn lead us to an understanding of what is on the whole the most interesting aspect of his examination of the nature of art: his conception of tragedy.

We must begin by making a temporary distinction between Nietzsche's desire to affirm and his thesis that art is affirmation, and we must make it firmly because some of the questionable measures to which the former seduces him can obscure the essential soundness of the latter.

Nietzsche desires to affirm life, and he expresses this desire in such passages as those beginning 'I want to learn more and more to see what is necessary in things as the beautiful in them' (quoted on p. 68), 'Did you ever say Yes to one joy?' (quoted on p. 125), 'A spirit thus *emancipated*' (quoted on p. 126), and 'My formula for greatness in a human being is *amor fati*' (quoted on p. 32). Now I have suggested that the pathos of such passages as these is the *religious* pathos, which has survived the destruction of the religion to which it was originally attached. When, in his influential essay on 'Rilke and Nietzsche' in

The Disinherited Mind, Erich Heller says that 'Neither Rilke nor Nietzsche praises the praiseworthy. They praise', he is surely right, but I suggest he is not attributing to them any very novel, not to speak of unique, tendency. The Christian praises God, but not because God is praiseworthy: he praises Him. The Jew praises Jehovah, but not because things have gone well: he praises Him. 'Allah is good, Allah is merciful' is in Islam said in response, not to good fortune, but to bad: it is an affirmation of the goodness of life, all appearance notwithstanding. These attitudes are typical of the religious response to existence as it has evolved in the West under the influence of Semitic monotheism: and at the end of his active life Nietzsche was still as much affected by it as he had been at the beginning – only then, of course, it had to find a new and inevitably more devious mode of expression.

It was these two needs – the need to affirm ('praise') existence and the need for a new way of doing so – which at last produced the unique manifesto *Ecce Homo*, which is a sustained attempt to view his own life under the aspect of *amor fati* and thus to affirm it in every part. The content of this book is determined by one fact and two hypotheses: the fact is that Nietzsche's life was uncommonly full of illness, pain, loneliness and disappointment; the hypotheses are that 'one must need strength, otherwise one will never have it' (*T*, IX. 38) and that 'what does not kill me makes me stronger' (*T*, I. 8). With the aid of these hypotheses Nietzsche plays a dialectical game with the sufferings and mistakes of his life.

He says that on 'this perfect day' – his forty-fourth birthday – on which he has begun to write his autobiography, 'I looked behind me, I looked before me, I never saw so many and such good things at once', and asks '*how should I not be grateful to my whole life?*' His gratitude is expressed by showing how what has been bad in his life has really been good:

> The perfect cheerfulness and brightness, even exuberance of spirit reflected in the said work [*Daybreak*] is in my case compatible not only with the profoundest physiological weakness, but even with an extremity of pain. In the midst of the torments which attended an uninterrupted three-day headache accompanied by the laborious vomiting of phlegm – I possessed a dialectical clarity *par excellence* and thought my way very cold-bloodedly through things for which when I am in better health I am not enough of a climber, not refined, not *cold* enough. (I. 1)

For one who is typically healthy . . . being ill can even be a
stimulant to life, to more life. Thus, indeed, does that long period
of illness seem to me *now*: I discovered life as it were afresh . . .
I constructed my philosophy out of my will to health, to *life* . . .
it was in the years of my lowest vitality that I *ceased* to be
pessimist . . . (I. 2)

During my time at Basel my whole spiritual diet . . .was a
perfectly senseless misuse of exceptional powers . . . It was only
sickness which brought me to reason. (II. 2)

I have never felt so happy with myself as in the sickest and
most painful periods of my life. (III, section on *HA*, 4)

And there are very many more of such explanations of 'how one
becomes what one is'. As a human response to suffering – and especially
in its total freedom from *ressentiment* and self-pity – it is wholly admir-
able, indeed exemplary: but the dialectic involved in it is none the less
open to the objection that the terms 'health' and 'sickness' have, as they
are employed here, undergone a silent redefinition which greatly
enfeebles their meaning. 'Sickness', of whatever kind, must at the very
least be that which undermines and harms 'health', which makes
'unhealthy': if it does not do that it is not sickness. There are degrees
of sickness, of course (or, as it is more commonly phrased, degrees of
health): but if the words are used correctly, it makes no sense to say
of a person that he is at the same time sick and healthy – a healthy
invalid is a *contradictio in adjecto*. But this is how Nietzsche describes
himself throughout *Ecce Homo*: which is to say that 'health' and 'sickness' do not in this book mean what they usually mean. 'Health'
appears to signify, not the absence of sickness, but the capacity to
resist and exploit sickness: but in that case his 'health', i.e. *this capacity*,
is never undermined, so that he is never really 'sick', and the sicknesses
which he describes are not really sicknesses. But the reality is that
Nietzsche really was sick, desperately and painfully sick; his existence
was punctuated by periods of total incapacitation; and, far from
accepting this state of things with cowlike equanimity, he was often
infuriated by the thought that he was passing through the prime of life
in an invalid and half-dead condition. When he was writing *Ecce Homo*,
his illness, far from having been overcome, was in its terminal stage,
and two months after the book was finished reached its predestined
end: thereafter Nietzsche wrote no more about his 'essential healthiness'

or about anything else, having become incapable of any intellectual activity whatever. It is in the light of these facts that one has to view the juggling with the concepts 'health' and 'sickness' in *Ecce Homo* and the dialectical scheme of which they are components.

It may seem that this scheme is not very different from the dialectical conception of the 'artist' as one whose activities are a compensation for some deficiency, but the likeness is slightly misleading. When Nietzsche writes that a Homer would not have created an Achilles if Homer had been an Achilles, he is not implying any sickness in the artist but, precisely, a lack, a deficiency: Homer falls short of being an Achilles; if he *had* been an Achilles he would have felt no need to invent him. When he writes that it seems not to be possible to be an artist and not to be sick, on the other hand, he lays himself open to the objection raised above: he must be redefining 'sick' in a way which makes 'sickness' something not really harmful – and in any event not a three-day headache or some other recognizable malaise. Perhaps what he means is expressed more clearly when he says, at the end of *The Birth of Tragedy*: 'how much must a people [the Greeks] have suffered to be able to become so beautiful!' or in *Ecce Homo*: 'I know of no more heart-rending reading than Shakespeare: what must a man have suffered to feel such a need to be a buffoon!' (*EH*, II. 4) – for here, of course, he is not speaking of 'sickness' at all. Moreover – and this consideration will make a convenient bridge from 'life-affirmation' to 'art as affirmation' – he was never able to make up his mind whether 'great art' really was, or could be, a product of a deficiency.

'The aesthetic conditions,' he says in a note of 1888, are 'twofold. The full and bestowing, in antithesis to the seeking, desiring' (*WP*, 843). This seems to him to be a 'fundamental distinction'; and in a note of 1885–6 he says that, in regard to all aesthetic values, he avails himself of this distinction: 'I ask in each individual case: "Has hunger or superfluity become creative here"' (*WP*, 846). This note was employed as part of section 370 of *The Gay Science* (Book Five, 1887), where its implications are spelt out in more detail:

> Every art, every philosophy may be viewed as an aid and remedy [*Heil- und Hilfsmittel*] in the service of growing and striving life: they always presuppose suffering and sufferers. But there are two kinds of sufferer: firstly he who suffers from *superabundance of life*, who desires a Dionysian art and likewise a tragic view of and insight into life – and then he who suffers from *poverty of life*,

who seeks in art and knowledge either rest, peace, a smooth sea,
delivery from himself, or intoxication, paraxism, stupefaction,
madness. The twofold requirement of the *latter* corresponds to all
romanticism in art and knowledge. (cf. *NCW*, V)

The 'antithesis' here is between 'Dionysian tragedy' and 'romanticism', and Nietzsche never wearied of explaining that the error he
committed in youth when he admired Wagner and, in *The Birth of
Tragedy*, designated Wagnerian music-drama as a rebirth of tragedy,
was to mistake the romantic for the Dionysian. The romantic artist 'is
an artist whom great dissatisfaction with himself makes creative' (*WP*,
844), and in his case one may well speak of art's being a product of
'sickness'; but this idea makes far less sense in the case of the 'Dionysian'
artist who 'suffers', certainly, but from a 'superabundance of life'.

We shall return to 'Dionysian tragedy' in a moment: what should
be clear now is that all artists, the romantic and the Dionysian, the
sick and those who suffer from abundance, employ their art as a means
of affirming life – some kind of life. Rilke is nowhere closer to Nietzsche
than when he declares this fact in the well-known poem beginning
'O sage, Dichter, was du tust? – Ich rühme' (O tell, Poet, what it is
you do? – I praise): for he is here repeating in other words what
Nietzsche says again and again in such formulations as: 'Artists continually *glorify* – they do nothing else: they glorify all those conditions
and things which have the reputation of making men feel good or
great or intoxicated or merry or happy or wise' (*GS*, 85), and 'There
is no such thing as pessimistic art . . . Art affirms. Job affirms. – But
Zola? But the Goncourts? – The things they exhibit are ugly: but *that*
they exhibit them comes from *pleasure in this ugliness* . . . There is no
help for it! You deceive yourselves if you say otherwise. – How
liberating is Dostoyevsky!' (*WP*, 821).

The ground upon which Nietzsche establishes his certainty of this –
for it *is* something of which he appears to be quite certain – is an
examination, not of individual artists or works of art, nor of his own
response to them, but of the nature of 'the aesthetic interpretation of
phenomena' as such, which rules out as impossible a work of art that
is not an affirmation of existence. Art is the enjoyment of the aesthetic
condition; the aesthetic condition is a means of interpreting phenomena
in such a way as to make them endurable and in a sense self-justified:
art is therefore necessarily a celebration of the 'rightness of things', an
affirmation, 'praise'. I think that everyone's experience bears out this

thesis: in art, that is to say by aesthetic interpretation, anything can be 'made enjoyable' and thus justified: and that is the inescapable purpose of art, and even – or rather, especially – of that form of art which is the aesthetic interpretation of the worst things, within which the spectacle of death, catastrophe and unmerited and useless suffering becomes a source of the highest gratification and satisfaction and which knows how to employ even the blackest pessimism as a 'stimulant to life': the art of tragedy.

A faithful exposition of Nietzsche's idea of tragedy can be lengthy and abstruse, or it can be short and simple. My taste is for the short and simple. Nietzsche inherited two conceptions of tragic drama: Schopenhauer's and Aristotle's. Schopenhauer's idea is that in tragedy 'the misery of existence is brought before us, and the final outcome is . . . the vanity of human striving . . . the sensation of the will's turning away from life is aroused in us' (*Parerga and Paralipomena*, II. 227); Schopenhauer values tragedy as a demonstration of the badness of existence and a stimulant to resignation. Aristotle's idea is that tragedy is the arousal and catharsis of emotion, and especially the emotions of pity and fear: he values tragedy as a sort of purgation. Nietzsche rejected both conceptions as inconsistent with what he believed to be the origin and the customary effect of tragedy, and with the general character of art as life-affirmative.

His theory that Greek tragedy, and thus all tragedy, originated in the rites of Dionysus was first published in *The Birth of Tragedy*, and gave currency to the aesthetic concepts 'Apollonian' and 'Dionysian'. Apollo is the god of individuation, dream and illusion, Dionysus the god of intoxication and the forces of nature; Apollo creates form, Dionysus is that out of which form is created. The 'Apollonian Greek', the creator of aesthetic forms which still stand as the paradigm of 'beauty', is to be understood as the self-conquest of the 'Dionysian Greek', whose characteristic mode of expression is the ritual orgy. To illuminate this contrast Nietzsche compares Homer, 'the type of the Apollonian naïve artist', with Archilochus, who 'appals us by his mocking cry of hatred, by the drunken outbursts of his desires' (*B T*, 5). The former represents 'a perfect victory of Apollonian illusion' (*B T*, 3); the latter, 'the first Greek lyrist' and therefore also a musician, 'has become wholly one with the primal unity, its pain and contradiction' and produced 'a copy of this primal unity as music', which 'under the Apollonian dream inspiration' assumes a second form as 'a symbolic dream image' (*B T*, 5). This image is the lyricist's 'I', the centre and subject of lyric as opposed to epic poetry. Tragedy is then conceived of as having originated in a manner analogous to the origination of the lyric: the chorus, 'the symbol of the whole Dionysiacly excited throng' whose intoxication unites it with the forces of nature, 'discharges itself again and again in an Apollonian world of images'; and thus the chorus is 'the womb of the entire so-called dialogue, i.e. the entire world of the stage, of the actual drama' (*BT*, 8). The 'I' is in this case the god Dionysus: 'It is an unimpeachable tradition that Greek tragedy in its oldest form depicted only the sufferings of Dionysus', but, Nietzsche claims, 'Dionysus never ceased to be the tragic hero . . . all the famous figures of the Greek stage . . . are only masks of that original hero Dionysus' (*BT*, 10). Thus tragic drama is 'the Apollonian materialization of Dionysian insights and effects' (*BT*, 8).

The most immediate consequence of the Dionysian tragedy is that 'the gulfs between man and man fade before an overwhelming feeling of unity which leads back to the heart of nature'; and the 'metaphysical comfort' with which 'every true tragedy leaves us' is 'that life is at the bottom of things, despite all the changes of its appearances, indestructibly powerful and joyful' (*BT*, 7). The aesthetic pleasure we derive from tragedy – that is to say, from the spectacle of ugly and painful things – is to be explained by analogy with musical dissonance: 'the joy which is produced by the tragic myth originates in the same way as the joyful sensation of dissonance in music. The Dionysian, with its primordial joy even in pain, is the common womb of music and of the tragic myth' (*BT*, 24). In brief: in *The Birth of Tragedy*, 'the *tragic-Dionysian* condition' is conceived of as 'a supreme condition of affirmation of existence . . . from which even the greatest pain cannot be subtracted' (*WP*, 853).

It is from this point of view that Nietzsche consistently criticizes Schopenhauer's and Aristotle's ideas of tragedy:

> I have on repeated occasions laid my finger on the great
> misunderstanding of Aristotle in believing he recognized as the
> tragic affects two *depressive* affects, terror and pity. If he were
> right, tragedy would be an art dangerous to life . . . Art,
> elsewhere the great stimulant of life, an intoxication with life, a
> will to life, would here, in the service of a movement of decline,
> as it were the handmaid of pessimism, become *harmful to health*
> (– for that one 'purges' oneself of these affects through their
> arousal, as Aristotle seems to believe, is simply not true) . . . and if

Schopenhauer were right that tragedy is a lesson in resignation . . .
this would be the conception of an art in which art denies itself.
Tragedy would then signify a process of disintegration . . .
Tragedy would be a symptom of decline. This theory can be
refuted in the most cold-blooded way: namely, by measuring
the effect of a tragic emotion with a dynamometer and
discovering what in the last resort only the absolute
mendaciousness of a systematizer can misunderstand: – that
tragedy is a *tonic*. (*WP*, 851)

The evolution of 'Dionysus' from the god of intoxication and
abandonment to an ideogram for the affirmation of life even in its
most painful manifestations takes place even with *The Birth of Tragedy*
itself; and subsequently the name is used exclusively with this connotation. The point is important for a full understanding of Nietzsche's
conception of tragedy and of how large it loomed in his conception of
himself. *Ecce Homo* ends with the sentence: 'Have I been understood? –
Dionysus against the Crucified . . .' and a note published as section 1052
of *The Will to Power* and entitled '*The two types: Dionysus and the
Crucified*' clarifies what this antithesis means:

To determine: whether the typical *religious* man is a form of
décadence . . . but are we not here omitting one type of religious
man, the *pagan*? Is the pagan cult not a form of thanksgiving
or an affirmation of life? Must its highest representative not be
an apologia for and deification of life? . . . It is here I place the
Dionysus of the Greeks: religious affirmation of life, the whole
of life . . . Dionysus against the 'Crucified': there you have the
antithesis . . . the problem is that of the meaning of suffering:
whether a Christian or a tragic meaning. In the former case it is
supposed to be the way to a holy form of being; in the latter,
being is counted as holy enough to justify even a monstrous degree
of suffering . . . The god on the cross is a curse on life, a signpost
to redemption from it; – Dionysus cut to pieces is a *promise* of
life: it will be eternally reborn and come back from destruction.

Tragedy, 'Dionysus' and eternal recurrence thus became associated
and at last fused in his mind as powerful symbols or 'ciphers' of life-
affirmation; and this whole concatenation is summed up, together with
a repudiation of the two principal conceptions of tragedy he had
inherited, with incomparable style and conciseness in the closing
paragraphs of *Twilight of the Idols*:

It is only in the Dionysian mysteries, in the psychology of the Dionysian condition, that the *fundamental fact* of the Hellenic instinct expresses itself – its 'will to life'. *What* did the Hellene guarantee to himself with these mysteries? *Eternal* life, the eternal recurrence of life; the future promised and consecrated in the past; the triumphant Yes to life beyond death and change; *true* life as collective continuation of life through procreation, through the mysteries of sexuality. It was for this reason that the *sexual* symbol was to the Greeks the symbol venerable as such, the intrinsic profound meaning of all antique piety. . . . In the teachings of the mysteries, *pain* is sanctified: the 'pains of childbirth' sanctify pain in general . . . For the eternal joy in creating to exist . . . the 'torments of childbirth' *must* also exist eternally. . . . All this is contained in the word Dionysus . . . The profoundest instinct of life, the instinct for the future of life, for the eternity of life, is in this word experienced religiously . . . It was only Christianity, with *ressentiment against* life in its foundations, which made of sexuality something impure . . . The psychology of the orgy as an overflowing feeling of life and energy within which even pain acts as a stimulous provided me with the key to the concept of the *tragic* feeling . . . Tragedy is so far from providing evidence for pessimism among the Hellenes in Schopenhauer's sense that it has to be considered the decisive repudiation of that idea and the *counter-verdict* to it. Affirmation of life even in its strangest and sternest problems, the will to life rejoicing in its own inexhaustibility through the *sacrifice* of its highest types – that is what I called Dionysian, *that* is what I recognized as the bridge to the psychology of the *tragic* poet. *Not* so as to get rid of pity and terror, not so as to purify oneself of a dangerous emotion through its vehement discharge . . . but, beyond pity and terror, *to realize in oneself* the eternal joy of becoming – that joy which also encompasses *joy in destruction* . . . And with that I again return to the place from which I set out – the *Birth of Tragedy* was my first revaluation of all values: with that I again plant myself in the soil out of which I draw all that I will and *can* – I, the last disciple of the philosopher Dionysus – I, the teacher of the eternal recurrence . . . (*T*, X. 4–5)

Nietzsche described himself as 'the first tragic philosopher' (*EH*,

III, section on *B T*, 3), and it is as a tragic philosopher that he has often been described by others: but only in the light of his specific interpretation of the nature of tragedy can we see what that expression really means, and how his desire to affirm life and his thesis that art is affirmation do, in this interpretation, come together in one tremendous concept.

6

Theories and Innovations: 2

The Philosophical Task, Psychology, Critique of Christianity

I: The Philosophical Task

What we have examined up to now may be called the details of Nietzsche's philosophy: what we now have to examine is his conception of philosophy *as such*, and of himself as a 'philosopher'. He had very firm and explicit ideas about the nature of the activity called philosophizing and about what kind of man ought to be called a philosopher and what kind ought not to be: these ideas conflict with many commonly held views, and he has often as a consequence been denied the name of philosopher, so it is with this that it is probably best to begin.

Consider first the idea of philosophy which finds expression in the phrase 'to do philosophy'; in Gilbert Ryle's claim that the diagnosis of 'systematically misleading expressions' is 'what philosophical analysis is' and that 'this is the sole and whole function of philosophy'; and in Anthony Flew's statement, in his *Introduction to Western Philosophy* (London, 1971), that 'philosophy, as the word is understood here, is concerned first, last and all the time with argument' – and contrast it with that expressed in Nietzsche's assertion that 'it is only great pain, that slow protracted pain which takes its time and in which we are as it were burned with green wood, that compels us philosophers to descend into our ultimate depths and to put from us all . . . that wherein perhaps our humanity previously reposed' (*GS*, Preface, 3); that 'philosophy, as I have hitherto understood and lived it, is a voluntary living in ice and high mountains – a seeking after everything strange and questionable in existence, all that has hitherto been excommunicated by morality' (*EH*, Foreword, 3); and that 'philosophy reduced to "theory of knowledge" . . . is philosophy at its last gasp, an end, an agony, something that arouses pity' (*BGE*, 204). The difference could, indeed, hardly be greater: all that these two attitudes appear to possess in common is the word philosophy.

Now it is not possible, without redefining this word, to deny the name philosopher to Professors Ryle and Flew; and I think it was Wittgenstein who first habitually employed the locution 'to do philosophy': so perhaps it is Nietzsche who is misusing the word and misapplying it to himself. This is, indeed, a conclusion which many people have drawn: Nietzsche, it has often been said, was not a philosopher.

Whether we think he was or not is a consideration of some importance, both for our attitude towards him and our attitude towards philosophy. If we think he was something other than a philosopher we shall read him with less care and accord him less respect than we otherwise would, for 'philosopher' is not only an appellation but also a description containing a value judgment – the judgment being that the man you apply the word to is sane and seriously intentioned. 'Philosopher' cannot in the ordinary way be used as a term of derogation – you cannot sensibly use the phrase 'a mere philosopher', for instance, and 'a mad philosopher' is a joke expression meaning 'not a philosopher but mad'. To say of Nietzsche that he 'was no philosopher' is more than a negative description, it is intended to lower him in our estimation (especially when it is followed by 'he was a mere aphorist' or 'merely a lay preacher'). On the other hand, if you become convinced that what Nietzsche 'does' also has a right to be called philosophy, and that his conception of what a philosopher is or should be is also legitimate, then your own conception of philosophy and philosophers is bound to be modified in some way: probably you will have to look for an idea of philosophy which would accommodate both Nietzsche and the diagnosis of systematically misleading expressions.

The main reasons Nietzsche has seemed to many not to be a philosopher are worth looking at because, in arguing against and, I believe, refuting them, we can bring out a number of aspects of his life and work which might otherwise be overlooked and show that his apparent extreme individuality disguises many points of similarity with other philosophers. There are, in my judgment, five such main reasons.

The first is the way in which he wrote. His books are typically (though not invariably) a kind of conversation or, when not conversation, monologue: he talks to you or to himself, but in any event the tone is that of speech, and the sentences are usually of the kind it is possible to speak and not of the kind that can only be written down. His ideas are presented in such a way as to make it seem that they have just occurred to him. There is a lot of intellectual jokery. Presentation, as would be the case in real conversation, is unsystematic, though the degree of disorderliness can be exaggerated: there is often more order than appears to a hurried reader. Sometimes the connection between ideas amounts, as again in real conversation, to no more than association of ideas: there are gaps in a line of reasoning, stages missed out, and certain conclusions drawn can be seen to follow from their premises only when you have filled in the gaps (this is often a product of impatience, but sometimes a device to make the reader do a bit of thinking for himself). Even *The Birth of Tragedy* struck its first readers as remarkably unacademic in appearance for a 'work of scholarship', and the general view was no doubt that expressed by the Bonn professor who told his students: 'anyone who has written anything like that is dead as a scholar [*wissenschaftlich tot*].' But *The Birth of Tragedy* is the most conventional of all Nietzsche's books, and the question 'how can anyone who writes like this be a philosopher?' has very often been the reaction to most of them.

The argument against this objection is that Nietzsche's style and ideas suit one another. When you know him well you come to see that the manner of presentation, the preservation of the immediacy with which problems become present in the mind, is correct given the nature of the problems. Orderliness and systematism would be unreal, as a systematic and orderly earthquake would be unreal. Moreover, it is surely right to say that we have unlearned, or are unlearning, that false seriousness which confuses profundity and seriousness with an outward display of them. Sterne defined 'gravity' as 'a mysterious carriage of the body to conceal the defects of the mind'; Goethe called Sterne 'the freest spirit of his century', and Nietzsche trumped that assertion with 'the freest writer of all time' (*AOM*, 113) and, in *Zarathustra*, introduced 'the Spirit of Gravity' quasi-embodied, and with a pun on gravity, as the archenemy of mankind. Nietzsche combated false seriousness, and in his works exemplified his freedom from it.

The second reason is that he invented no philosophical system. This used to be the strongest objection and is now antiquated, but we have no guarantee it will not some day arise from the dead again. Hegel, the arch-systematizer of all time, produced so powerful a prejudice in favour of systems that any system-philosopher necessarily counted as more truly a philosopher than any unsystematic problem-philosopher. The reaction against Hegel became a reaction against the system-philosopher. Nietzsche attacked system-philosophy, but as he had no system of his own this attack was regarded as sour grapes.

The third is that his writings contain inconsistencies and contradictions, which the writings of a real philosopher are supposed never to do. The reply to this is that most real philosophers do contradict themselves, and that Nietzsche does so to no greater or less degree than the rest. The reason many people with an interest in philosophy do not know this is that they read books about philosophers instead of reading the philosopher's own books; that books about philosophers tend to remove, reduce and ignore inconsistencies in the interest of summary; and that system-philosophers are more amenable to summary than a problem-philosopher such as Nietzsche. Summarizing is, of course, what books about philosophers are for: a book about a philosopher which told you all a philosopher said would duplicate the work of the philosopher and would thus be redundant: but their omissions can produce a somewhat simplistic idea of how a 'real' philosopher thinks. If you ask anyone to name a real philosopher, the chances are he will answer 'Kant'. Professor Norman Kemp Smith says, in his *Commentary to Kant's 'Critique of Pure Reason'*, that 'Kant flatly contradicts himself in almost every chapter' of that book: 'there is hardly a technical term which is not employed by him in a variety of different and conflicting senses'. He suggests that the 'chief reason for the contradictory character' of the contents of Kant's chief work is 'inseparably bound up with what may perhaps be regarded as Kant's supreme merit as a philosophical thinker . . . his open-minded recognition of the complexity of his problems, and of the many difficulties which lie in the way of any solution which he is himself able to propound'. Self-contradiction 'inseparably bound up with' a philosopher's 'supreme merit' is self-contradiction viewed in rather a different light from that in which it is viewed when it is proposed as an objection to a philosopher's being called a philosopher at all.

The fourth reason is that Nietzsche was a solitary, worked alone, and did not teach philosophy. This has been supposed to make him a suspect kind of philosopher, an inferior or 'amateur' kind, a *philosophe*, a 'lay preacher', an 'aphorist', even a prophet of some sort, but in any event not a real philosopher. The counter is that, although the idea of

169

philosophy and the idea of the academic life are certainly closely associated, many real philosophers have not been academics. Spinoza ground lenses, Hume did secretarial work, Locke worked at the Board of Trade (for a time), Schopenhauer was a capitalist parasite and did no work. The word 'amateur', when applied to a philosopher, is no more derogatory as such than it is when applied to a poet or a composer: original philosophizing is more like an art than a craft, and it is only with respect to a craft that 'amateur' and 'professional' are evaluative descriptions implying a difference in quality.

The final reason is more contentious and needs to be discussed at slightly greater length. British and American philosophy at the present time, however its practitioners define it, is invariably some sort of occupation; and that means that a philosopher is a man who undertakes that occupation, just as a 'bus driver' is a man who undertakes the occupation of driving a bus. Philosophy is a job: and just as you cannot correctly or justly call yourself a bus driver unless your job is bus driving, so you cannot call yourself a philosopher unless your job is philosophy. Moreover, philosophy is the sort of job from which it is possible to be exceedingly detached – to judge at least from the statements of some British philosophers. A degree of non-involvement does, indeed, follow from the conception of philosophy as an occupation which one becomes a philosopher by undertaking: if diagnosing systematically misleading expressions *is* philosophy, then you are 'doing' philosophy only when you are doing that – and for what proportion of his life is anyone doing that? Now this seems to me a conception of philosophy not only inadequate in itself but one which upsets what Nietzsche would call the 'order of rank' among philosophers and philosophical problems in a disastrous way (disastrous for philosophy, that is).

Perhaps the dispute might be said to hinge on whether the statement 'Plato is a greater philosopher than John Stuart Mill, and would still be so even if all Plato's conclusions could be proved false and all Mill's proved true' is considered true or false. In my opinion it is true, because a 'great philosopher' is not a man who does something superlatively well but a man who *is* something to a superlative degree. Musical composition provides an analogy. To learn the technique of composition does not make you a composer: composition is the invention of new music and a composer is a man with the capacity to do this. He is thus, not a man who does something, but a man who *is* something, and a 'great composer' is a man who is this something to a superlative degree. 'A philosopher', according to this conception, is not a man who undertakes a certain kind of occupation, but a certain kind of man. What kind of man is he was revealed by Socrates when he said 'The unexamined life is not worth living'. This assertion has been repeated numberless times as if it were self-evidently and objectively true – although, if you are so constituted as to be happy living an unreflective, instinct-directed life, it is patently untrue for you. Socrates' assertion holds good only for the type of man he was: it is the same kind of assertion as 'Life is nothing without music'; and those who have adopted it as their motto and slogan have revealed by doing so that they too are of that type. The man of whom Socrates is the exemplar – the type for whom the unexamined life is not worth living – is the philosophical type; being that type of man, he may find himself attracted to a certain type of occupation, but that occupation does not define him: on the contrary, it is he who defines the occupation – one should not say that Plato is a philosopher because he undertakes a certain kind of occupation, one should say that a certain kind of occupation is philosophy because Plato undertakes it. It is only thus, it seems to me, that we can avoid a continual redefinition of what constitutes 'philosophy' and a 'philosophical problem': we have to be content to define a philosophical problem no less widely than as the content of our experience realized on the level of clear consciousness and become the object of rational thought, and a philosopher as a man in whom experience is habitually and as it were by 'second nature' the object of conscious reflection.

If we turn from the question of whether Nietzsche was a philosopher to Nietzsche's conception of what a philosopher is, we shall find that his initial idea corresponds closely to our own idea that a philosopher is a certain kind of man rather than a man who follows a certain kind of occupation. In his early writings he tends to admire those philosophers whose circumstances placed them in isolation, and this tendency receives full expression in *Schopenhauer as Educator*, in which the details of Schopenhauer's philosophy are all but ignored, while all the emphasis is placed on his independence: 'I profit from a philosopher only in so far as he can be an example to me . . . But this example must be supplied by his outward life and not merely in his books' (*UIII, 3*) – as it was, Nietzsche contends, in Schopenhauer's outward life. The example Schopenhauer supplied seems to have consisted in living in solitude and opposing the current ideas of his time; the former takes on for the early Nietzsche what is virtually a moral quality: 'Where there have been powerful societies, governments, religions, public opinions – in short, wherever there has been tyranny – there the solitary philosopher has been hated; for philosophy offers an asylum to man into which no tyranny can force its way' (*ibid.*); the latter is conceived of as at once an heroic and a painful way of life: 'he will destroy his earthly happiness through his courage; he will have to be an enemy to those he loves and to the institutions which have produced him; he may not spare men or things, even though he suffers when they suffer; he will be misunderstood and for a long time thought an ally of powers he abhors' (*UIII*, 4). This is presented as a picture of the kind of man exemplified by Schopenhauer, but, as he himself remarks in *Ecce Homo* (III, section on *U*, 3), it is really a likeness of Nietzsche; and the same is true of the picture of his other favourite philosopher, Heraclitus, the 'proud and lonely truth-finder' (*The Pre-Platonic Philosophers*, 10) whose solitary figure is to be glimpsed behind that of the 'Wanderer' (*HA*, 638; *WS*, Prologue and Epilogue; *GS*, 380) and who is the ultimate model for Zarathustra. In these versions of himself, Nietzsche depicts the philosophical nature as being essentially at odds with and isolated from its own time, and conceives that 'to live like a philosopher' one has 'to live a solitary life in hostile isolation from the multitude' (*On the Future of our Educational Institutions*, 1): and the final and most comprehensive summation of all that is implied in this attitude is *Thus Spoke Zarathustra*.

Such an isolated and remote figure is clearly not going to consider it his purpose in life to hold down a chair of philosophy or, indeed, a job of any kind: his function is to be 'the man of the most comprehensive responsibility who has the conscience for the collective evolution of mankind' (*BGE*, 61), and as such he is not to be confused with 'the philosophical labourers and scholars in general' (*ibid.*, 211). This distinction appears to have been forced on Nietzsche by his conception of the world as having been deprived of values and become as it were masterless through the death of God. In one of the earliest sections of *Human, All Too Human* he had written that 'since the belief that a God directs the fate of the world has disappeared . . . mankind itself must set up oecumenical goals embracing the entire earth'; and for such 'universal rule' not to be self-destructive, mankind 'must first of all attain to an unprecedented *knowledge of the preconditions of culture*'. It is in this that there lies 'the tremendous task facing the great spirits of the coming century' (*HA*, 25). A few years later the solitary philosopher is seen as the voice and conscience of mankind in this matter, and he is consequently not to be confounded with anything less: 'It may be required for the education of a philosopher that he himself has also once stood on all those steps on which his servants, the scientific labourers of philosophy, remain standing . . . all these are only preconditions of his task: this task itself demands something different – it demands that he *create values . . . Actual philosophers . . . are commanders and lawgivers . . .* it is they who determine the Wherefore and Whither of mankind' (*BGE*, 211). In case it should be thought that he is here describing himself, he adds the three questions: 'Are there such philosophers today? Have there been such philosophers? *Must* there not be such philosophers? . . .' (*ibid.*) Such philosophers are philosophers of the future, just as *Beyond Good and Evil* itself is, as its subtitle says, a 'prelude to a philosophy of the future'. 'All the sciences,' Nietzsche says else-where, 'have from now on to prepare the way for the future task of the philosopher: this task understood in the sense that the philosopher has to solve the *problem of values*, that he has to determine the *order of rank of values*' (*GM*, I, note).

Now, the reader may recall at this point my earlier suggestion that if he read Nietzsche as if he were writing about physiology, medicine and the natural sciences he would never really misunderstand him; and he may wonder how this can possibly be reconciled with the conception of the philosopher just outlined. Bearing in mind that this conception is of a future ideal rather than a present reality, we may be able to reconcile them by drawing a distinction between the philo-sopher's subjective estimate of himself and of his significance and the task which he actually performs. Nietzsche often speaks of this task as being modest compared with the pretention to wholesale 'wisdom' of the priest and 'sage'; but that does not exclude the possibility that it may be the philosopher's pride to have seen through such pretentions. 'It was *modesty*,' he writes, 'which in Greece invented the word "philo-sopher" and left the splendid arrogance of calling oneself wise to the actors of the spirit – the modesty of such monsters of pride and self-glorification as Pythagoras, as Plato' (*GS*, 351). One might also note the 'modesty' involved in his exhortation to 'philosophers and friends of knowledge' not to take themselves too much in earnest. 'After all, you know well enough that it cannot matter in the least whether precisely *you* are in the right, just as no philosopher hitherto has been in the right, and that a more praiseworthy veracity may lie in every little question-mark placed after your favourite words and favourite theories (and occasionally after yourselves) than in all your solemn gesticulations and smart answers before courts and accusers!' (*BGE*, 25).

At the present stage of things the philosopher's task – which is to 'attain to an unprecedented knowledge of the preconditions of culture' – involves above all the establishment of 'little unpretentious truths' (*HA*, 3); the 'collection of material' as preparation for a 'typology of morality', a task for which philosophers have hitherto not been sufficiently 'modest' (*BGE*, 186); discussion of the influence of such 'little things' as 'nourishment, place of residence, climate, entertainment, the whole casuistry of selfishness', which are in fact 'beyond all comparison more important than anything which has been considered important hitherto' (*EH*, II. 10): in short, 'physiology, medicine and natural science'. The philosopher of the present day should be an experimenter and not a dogmatist: 'Objection, evasion, happy mistrust, delight in mockery are signs of health: everything unconditional belongs in pathology' (*BGE*, 154). It is not too much to say, indeed, that the idea of the philosopher of the present day as a sort of collector of small facts which are in reality more important than the big facts and grand conceptions previously the subject of philosophical interest, is responsible for the 'aphoristic' form of many of Nietzsche's books and for his whole tendency to reduce discourse to aphoristic brevity.

II: Psychology

Even where Nietzsche has no great standing as a philosopher it is usually allowed that he was a notable and interesting psychologist, the word understood in the wide sense of student of human behaviour and 'human nature'. With this view anyone who reads him will agree: but the term 'psychologist' understood in the sense just given needs to be defined more narrowly if we are to see in exactly what way he can be said to have contributed to the science – or putative science – of psychology.

Examination of the large body of work in which he appears as psychologist reveals that he 'practised psychology' in seven different ways: I mean there are seven fairly distinct activities he undertakes which can be termed psychological investigation. We shall look briefly at each of them.

Critic of philosophical psychology Philosophy has been and is involved with psychology in two ways. One is through the department of philosophy called speculative or rational psychology: the endeavour to develop a science of the self on *a priori* principles without recourse to empirical observation or experiment. This sounds like, and perhaps ought to be, something belonging to the past: the philosophical psychology of Heidegger, however, is of this kind, and it thus remains a contemporary phenomenon wherever Heidegger's influence extends. (Heidegger insists he is *not* writing psychology, and in view of what the word currently implies he is no doubt justified in saying so: but the language of *Sein und Zeit* makes it quite clear that, when he discusses 'man', he *is* writing psychology, only it is 'rational psychology'.) The other way is through the psychological assumptions which almost every philosopher has made and has necessarily had to make before he could begin to philosophize at all. With many philosophers, the first thing that leaps to the eye is the degree to which their speculations rely on psychological 'truths' which they have accepted almost without question, and often without realizing how much they have taken for granted. To the seventeenth and eighteenth centuries in general, 'man' seems to have presented no great problem, and in the case of a philosopher whose real interests were science, or epistemology, or ethics, or politics, the psychology of the human being, upon which his speculations really rested, was limited to simplistic statements of the 'All men desire . . .' variety, or the dividing of the mind into the 'part which perceives' and the 'part which thinks'. (British philosophers are very instructive in this regard: while, with their essays concerning human understanding and treatises of human nature, they were apparently grappling with the fundamental problems of psychology, in actuality they were content with the most superficial answers. Hobbes and Bentham – to take two great minds unalike in almost every other respect – both drew the most far-reaching conclusions from strikingly inadequate psychological premises.) The former type of philosophical psychology – speculative or rational psychology – is never mentioned by Nietzsche, so far as I know: it was in any case antiquated by the time he began to write, and the idea of constructing anything using only *a priori* principles would, of course, have seemed to him a misguided one. But the superficiality evidenced by previous philosophers in psychological matters constantly exercises his attention: and when he asks 'What philosopher at all before me has been a *psychologist?*' and replies 'There was no psychology whatever before me' (*EH*, IV. 6) we must see how much truth there is in this apparently wild assertion. 'Psychology' here means what it later came to mean in general: the investigation of the problems presented by human behaviour and of the nature of human beings; as such it is a *philosophical* undertaking, and in so far as it has become a science, it is a science which owes its form or forms to its philosophical origin. While, therefore, we cannot possibly agree that before Nietzsche there was no such thing as psychological acumen – he himself is concerned to indicate it where he notices it in men of the past – it is reasonable to say that he was at any rate one of the first to pursue psychology in the modern sense, and to place upon it the sort of emphasis which is now common. On the question whether any previous *philosopher* was a psychologist, it seems to me that Nietzsche is justified in his self-estimate: comparatively speaking none was. His criticism of his predecessors is quite often misguided and lacking in proper understanding, but when he seizes on their psychological inadequacies it is usually sound and valuable.

Writer of 'maxims' The original edition of *Human, All Too Human* is dedicated on the title page 'to the memory of Voltaire' on the hundredth anniversary of his death (30 May 1778), and in a note on the reverse of the title-page Nietzsche says that the book would not have been published at that time if the proximity of 30 May 1878 had not aroused the desire to do homage to 'one of the greatest liberators of the spirit'. A long quotation from Descartes stands 'in place of a preface', and the second supplement contains an aphorism in which it is maintained that the books of Montaigne, La Rochefoucauld, La Bruyère, Vauvenargues, Chamfort and Fontenelle 'contain more *actual ideas* than all the books of German philosophers together' (*WS*, 214). To put the matter into a simplifying formula, one can say that in *The Birth of Tragedy* and the *Untimely Meditations* Nietzsche was fundamentally concerned with German affairs, in *Human, All Too Human* he deserted to the French, 'the nation which has up till now given modern mankind its best books and its best men' (*WS*, 216). Previously the poles between which his writings had moved had been Greece and Germany, now he discovered that 'the nature of the Frenchman is much more closely related to the Greek than is the nature of the German' (*HA*, 221). The form of the new book, though not unprecedented in German, is far more typical of the French *moralistes* whom Nietzsche singles out for praise; and its subject matter – 'reflection on the human, all too human – or, as the learned expression has it, psychological observation' (*HA*, 35) – is said in the preface of 1886 to be something practised in France but 'certainly not in Germany'. In *Human, All Too Human*, in fact,

Nietzsche first assumed for the purpose of psychologizing the mask of the French writers of 'moral maxims' of whom, in the English-speaking world at least, La Rochefoucauld is the most famous instance.

This order of psychological observation makes its point and effect by the deliberate employment of the two characteristics exemplified very well in La Rochefoucauld's famous maxim, '*Dans l'adversité de nos meilleurs amis nous trouvans quelque chose, qui ne nous deplaist pas*': namely, brevity and 'cynicism'. The two things of course go naturally together: the statement is supposed to strike suddenly and stingingly, like an arrow; and Nietzsche never henceforth wholly neglected the advantages of this form of communication. Brevity also makes for memorability and thus for durability, and this too persuaded him to adopt and develop the form: 'To create things upon which time tries its teeth in vain; in form and in *substance* to strive after a little immortality – I have never been modest enough to demand less of myself. The aphorism, the apophthegm, in which I am the first master among Germans, are the forms of "eternity"; my ambition is to say in ten sentences what everyone else says in a book – what everyone else *does not* say in a book . . .' (*T*, IX. 51). The 'cynical' aspect of such aphorisms deserves a little reflection. It marks them as belonging to a primitive stage of psychology: to that stage at which not only the reader but the aphorist too has grown up with an ideal picture of mankind in his heart and mind upon which every piece of realism appears as a blot. La Rochefoucauld too finds it 'shocking' that we should find something not displeasing in the adversities of our best friends: he too finds it 'immoral': and his 'cynicism' consists in stating it simply as a fact, without any explicit or implied rebuke. There are, it is true, very many people to whom any such remark would still appear cynical: to whom the word 'cynical' is almost synonymous with 'frank', 'outspoken' – indeed, almost synonymous with 'true': but psychology has learned to accept such facts simply as facts – it has no desire to shock because it is not itself shocked. Now Nietzsche, when he imitates La Rochefoucauld and produces brief and 'cynical' *exposés* of 'human nature', reveals in doing so that, his relatively late date notwithstanding, he still belongs to an early era of psychological investigation: that his psychological insights have to penetrate an idealized image of man. It should be remarked that this style of psychologizing belongs chiefly to the period of *Human, All Too Human* to *The Gay Science*, and that even in the last-named book the tone of voice has already grown a good deal less urbane; and one might note the remark, in *Beyond Good and Evil*, that 'cynicism is the only form in which common souls come close to honesty' (*BGE*, 26) – a remark which may itself seem very 'cynical'. Psychologizing in the form of 'moral maxims' was something he never entirely abandoned, but it seems to have been of most importance to him during the period in which the polite cynicism of La Rochefoucauld appeared as a means of liberation from everything heavily Germanic.

Here are a few examples of what we have been discussing, all taken from *Human, All Too Human*:

Sleep of virtue   When virtue has slept it will arise more vigorous. (*HA*, 83)

The index of the scales   We praise or blame according to whether the one or the other offers a greater opportunity for our power of judgment to shine out. (*HA*, 86)

Preference for specific virtues   We do not place especial value on the possession of a virtue until we notice its total absence in our opponent. (*HA*, 302)

Arrogance of the meritorious   Arrogance on the part of the meritorious is even more offensive to us than the arrogance of those without merit: for merit itself is offensive. (*HA*, 332)

The danger in our own voice   Sometimes in the course of conversation the sound of our own voice disconcerts us and misleads us into making assertions which in no way correspond to our opinions. (*HA*, 333)

Test of a good marriage   A marriage proves itself a good marriage by being able to endure an occasional 'exception'. (*HA*, 402)

Psychologist of culture   What I mean by this phrase is an investigator of the psychological conditions underlying the phenomena of religion, art, philosophy and the other 'higher' activities of man. A splendid short example of Nietzsche as a psychologist of culture is provided by the brief essay on sublimated cruelty partly quoted on p. 103. To seek the psychological origin of a 'cultural fact' was almost an instinct with him, and it produced some of his finest and most characteristic writing. His first grand success in this field was to overturn the 'sweetness and light' school of thought about the ancient Greeks by substituting for it the psychological theory that Greek culture was a product of sublimated barbarity; he went on to apply the principle thus formulated – i.e. that 'higher activities' are sublimated 'lower' ones' – to virtually the whole of human culture. We have dealt with this at length in chapter 4: but to show how far he was prepared to go in his search for a psychological explanation of a cultural fact I will also quote from his attempt to establish the 'psychological type' of Jesus contained in *The Anti-Christ*:

> The attempts I know of to extract even the *history* of a 'soul' from the Gospels seem to me proofs of an execrable psychological frivolity. Monsieur Renan, that buffoon *in psychologicis*, has appropriated for his explication of the type Jesus the two *most inapplicable* concepts possible in this case: the concept of the *genius* and the concept of the *hero*. But if anything is unevangelic it is the concept hero. Precisely the opposite of all contending, of all feeling oneself in struggle has here become instinct: the incapacity for resistance here becomes morality ('resist not evil': the profoundest saying of the Gospel, its key in a certain sense), blessedness in peace, in gentleness, in the *inability* for enmity . . . To make a *hero* of Jesus! – And what a worse misunderstanding is the word 'genius'! . . . To speak with the precision of the physiologist a quite different word would rather be in place here: the word idiot. We recognize a condition of morbid susceptibility of the *sense of touch* which makes it shrink back in horror from every contact, every grasping of a firm object. Translate such a physiological *habitus* into its ultimate logic – as instinctive hatred of *every* reality, as flight into the 'ungraspable', into the 'inconceivable', as antipathy towards every form, every spacial and temporal concept, towards everything firm, all that is custom, institution, Church, as being at home in a world undisturbed by reality of any kind, a merely 'inner' world, a 'real' world, an 'eternal' world . . . 'The kingdom of God *is within you*' . . . *Instinctive hatred of reality*: consequence of an extreme capacity for suffering and irritation which no longer wants to be 'touched' at all because it feels every contact too deeply. *Instinctive exclusion of all aversion, all enmity, all feeling for limitation and distancing*: consequence of an extreme capacity for suffering and irritation which already feels all resisting, all need for resistance, as an unbearable *displeasure* . . . and knows blessedness (pleasure) only in no longer resisting

anyone or anything, neither the evil nor the evil-doer – love as the sole, as the *last* possibility of life . . . These are the two *physiological realities* upon which, out of which the doctrine of redemption has grown. I call it a sublime further evolution of hedonism on a thoroughly morbid basis . . . The fear of pain, even of the infinitely small in pain – *cannot* end otherwise than in a *religion of love* . . . (*A*, 29–30)

'*Psychiatrist*' I put the word in quotation marks because, of course, it is not quite the right word, but I cannot think of a better one. Nietzsche now and then offers 'advice' of the kind which might be called psychiatric – advice on how to live better or more happily. It does not bulk especially large in his work but it is none the less quite distinct from the sort of psychological investigation we have considered up to now. Zarathustra's 'discourses' are frequently advice of this description, though it usually needs unriddling; and the famous admonition that 'the secret of realizing the greatest fruitfulness and the greatest enjoyment of existence is: to *live dangerously*' (*GS*, 283) seems to me to be entitled to be called 'psychiatric advice', even though it is not the sort of soothing syrup and anaesthetic many psychiatrists are paid to dispense. As an example of a more conventional piece of psychiatry I quote from the section of *Daybreak* called 'Self-mastery and moderation and their ultimate motive':

I find no more than six essentially different methods of combating the vehemence of a drive. Firstly, one can avoid opportunities for gratification of the drive, and through long and ever longer periods of non-gratification weaken it and make it wither away. Then, one can impose upon oneself a strict regularity in its gratification . . . one has then gained intervals during which one is no longer troubled by it – and from there one can perhaps go over to the first method. Thirdly, one can deliberately give oneself over to the wild and unrestrained gratification of a drive, in order to generate disgust with it, and with disgust to acquire a power over the drive . . . Fourthly, there is the intellectual artifice of associating its gratification in general so firmly with some very painful thought that, after a little practice, the thought of its gratification is itself at once felt as very painful . . . Fifthly, one brings about a dislocation of one's quanta of strength by imposing on oneself a particularly difficult and strenuous labour, or by deliberately subjecting oneself to a new stimulus

and pleasure and thus directing one's thought and plays of
physical forces into other channels . . . Finally, sixth: he who can
endure it and finds it reasonable to weaken and depress his *entire*
bodily and psychical organization will naturally thereby also
attain the goal of weakening an individual violent drive . . . (*D*, 109)

Precursor of other psychologists A necessarily posthumous effect of
Nietzsche's psychologizing, but one which for the contemporary
reader none the less stands out as distinct from the rest, is that of his
anticipation of subsequent psychologists and movements in psychology.
Freud remarked in his *Selbstdarstellung* on the agreement between
Nietzsche's 'premonitions and insights' and the results of psycho-
analysis. The agreements and disagreements have already been
discussed (see pp. 110–15); here it might be noted that Freud was
referring not only to the estimate of sexuality but also to the insight
expressed, for example, in the aphorism: '"I have done that", says
my memory. "I cannot have done that" – says my pride, and remains
adamant. At last – memory yields' (*BGE*, 68) – which is a description
of 'repression'.

In general, Nietzsche's views on sex are remarkable, however, less
for their anticipation of Freud's than for what one can only call their
casual enlightenment: they were certainly more striking to his contemporaries than they are to us – we, indeed, are more likely to overlook them than be struck by them. Only in the last half-year of his
active life does he give vent to such strident proclamations as 'The
preaching of chastity is a public incitement to unnaturalness. Every
expression of contempt for the sexual life, every befouling of it through
the concept "impure", is *the* crime against life – is the intrinsic sin
against the holy spirit of life' (*EH*, III. 5): before this time his attitude
is far more that expressed in the aphorism on the usefulness of adultery
(quoted on p. 178), or in the remark that, in sexual intercourse, 'one
person, by doing what pleases him, gives pleasure to another person –
such benevolent arrangements are not to be found so very often in
nature!' (*D*, 76). The core of the chapter 'Of Chastity' in *Zarathustra*
(*Z*, I. 13) is 'Those to whom chastity is difficult should be advised
against it'. Contrary to what one might perhaps have expected, there
is in general an absence of tension and emphasis in Nietzsche's published remarks on sex, so that often you will not notice, unless you
make a point of doing so, that his views on this or that subject assume
that sexual conduct is an entirely personal, extra-moral matter, and

N

that he has simply taken this for granted. In this field, and perhaps in this alone, his attitude seems to have been 'Do what you like'. Unquestionably he did not accord sexuality the same importance as Freud did.

Similarities between the psychology of Adler and Nietzsche's psychology of will to power have often been noted and anyone at all versed in Adlerian psychology will readily recognize 'inferiority complex' and 'compensation' in very many of Nietzsche's psychological explanations of human conduct. But the degree of similarity can be exaggerated. Adler's conscious attempt to lower the temperature of psychological theory and discussion, to take the melodrama out of it, stands in direct contrast to Nietzsche's histrionic and dramatizing manner; and the social aspect of Adlerian psychology – the desire for 'social success' and the frustration of this desire as a cause of neurosis – while not wholly absent from Nietzsche is certainly not what is meant by 'will to power'.

Other psychological theories are also anticipated in Nietzsche's writings, though it would probably be wrong to think that he exercised any direct influence on their inventors, who are unlikely to have read him. I offer here two examples.

He frequently insists on the superficiality of *consciousness*: 'everything that becomes conscious is a terminal phenomenon, a conclusion – and causes nothing' (*WP*, 478); 'It is to be shown to how great a degree everything conscious remains *on the surface*' (*WP*, 676); 'In the total process of adaptation and systematization, consciousness plays no role' (*WP*, 226); 'That which we call our "consciousness" is innocent of any part in the essential processes of our preservation and growth' (*WP*, 646); and so forth. This insistence, taken together with his 'physiologism' (see below), appears as a conceptual anticipation of the foundations of Behaviourism.

A feature of *Daybreak* is an investigation of the psychology of fear, and among the suggestions offered is one that, in order to understand another person, 'that is to say *to reproduce his feelings in ourselves*', it is a very common practice 'to generate this feeling in ourselves according to the *effects* it exhibits in the other person by imitating with our person the expression of his eyes, his voice, his walk, his bearing (or even merely their reflection in words, paintings and music) . . . A similar feeling will then arise in us as a consequence of an ancient association between movement and sensation . . . We have acquired great skill in this art of understanding the feelings of others, and in the presence of another person we are always and almost involuntarily practising it'; the reason for our great skill is the length of time we have been engaged on perfecting it: for many millennia man saw 'a danger in everything strange and alive: at the sight of it he at once imitated the expression of the features and bearing and drew his conclusions as to the kind of evil intention behind this expression and this bearing' (D, 142). This theory of the emotions is not so much an anticipation as a complete statement of the well-known theory subsequently propounded by William James and Carl Lange: the theory that our emotions are our awareness of our physical reactions to events – that we feel afraid, for instance, because we are trembling, and not the other way round.

Psychologist of will to power This has been discussed in an earlier chapter and need not be repeated. 'Will to power' as the basic psychological drive in man, of which all other human activities are sublimations, is Nietzsche's specific psychological 'theory', developed in the series from *Human, All Too Human* to *The Gay Science*, stated in *Zarathustra*, and explained and developed in the series from *Beyond Good and Evil* to *Ecce Homo*. The view of Nietzsche which asserts that he was constantly changing his mind, or that his 'philosophy' is a programme of continual self-reversal and oscillation between opposites, is really refuted by the evolution of this theory, whose content it is obliged to ignore.

What is desired, according to this theory, is the feeling of increased power. The negative aspect, that is to say the feeling of impotence, of being subject to the power of another, produces as its characteristic effect the phenomenon of *ressentiment* – and this is the chief corollary of the theory of will to power. Nietzsche developed the psychology of resentment almost as luxuriently as he did that of power: the essence of it is that the powerless man feels resentment against those whose power he feels and against this state of powerlessness itself and out of this feeling of resentment *takes revenge* – on other people or on life itself. The objective of the revenge is to get rid of the feeling of powerlessness: the forms it takes include all moralities in which punishment is a prominent feature; all doctrines of future damnation (of the powerful) and salvation (of the powerless); the socialist millennium, with the class at present oppressed on top and the present ruling class exterminated or in labour camps; anarchism, which Nietzsche saw as a peculiarly direct and uncomplicated expression of the resentment of impotence; in short, every kind of open or disguised revenge. At its simplest and most personal, resentment is the opposite of magnanimity. The magnanimous man is essentially the man whose feelings and actions are prompted by an inner power: he is a happy man – his magnanimity is a consequence of his happiness. The resentful man is the reverse of this: his feelings and actions are prompted by an inner impotence, and his resentment and the effects it produces are a consequence of his unhappiness. Here again you will find that Nietzsche is consistent: *ressentiment*, as he terms it, and the products of *ressentiment*, are always bad, and he would like to see the world rid of them.

Physiologist　From *Zarathustra* onwards Nietzsche shows an increasing tendency to try to reduce psychology to physiology. The idea that there is really no such thing as a 'psychic phenomenon' is one which was bound to occur to the psychologist who wanted to abolish 'will', 'soul', 'ego', and indeed all 'spiritual causes', and thought itself as a distinct faculty. Zarathustra declares that 'since I have known the body better . . . the spirit has been only figuratively spirit to me' (*Z*, II. 17); what he means is indicated in the chapter called 'Of the Despisers of the Body': '"I am body and soul" – so speaks the child . . . But the awakened, the enlightened man says: I am body entirely, and nothing beside; and soul is only a word for something in the body. The body is a great intelligence, a multiplicity with one sense . . . Your little intelligence . . . which you call "mind" is also an instrument of your body, a little instrument and toy of your great intelligence . . . There is more reason in your body than in your best wisdom . . . The creative body created mind for itself, as a hand of its will' (*Z*, I. 4). All the 'physiology' which follows in succeeding works is really no more than a development of the implications of these statements. I have already quoted (p. 179) from the analysis of Jesus in which the attempt to establish a 'psychological type' becomes, almost unawares, a discussion of its *physiology*; that this must happen in the case of the later Nietzsche follows from his denial of 'spiritual causes', for if there are no spiritual causes, all causes must be physical. 'We have always believed we knew what a cause is', he writes in *Twilight of the Idols* (VI. 3):

> but whence did we derive our knowledge, more precisely our belief we possessed this knowledge? From the realm of the celebrated 'inner facts', none of which has up till now been

shown to be factual. We believed ourselves to be causal agents in the act of willing . . . It was likewise never doubted that all the *antecedentia* of an action, its causes, were to be sought in the consciousness and could be discovered there if one sought them – as 'motives': for otherwise one would not have been *free* to perform it, *responsible* for it. Finally, who would have disputed that a thought is caused? that the ego causes the thought? . . . of these three 'inner facts' through which causality seemed to be guaranteed the first and most convincing was that of *will as cause*; the conception of a consciousness ('mind') as cause and later still that of the ego (the 'subject') as cause are merely after-products after causality had, on the basis of will, been firmly established as a given fact, as *empiricism* . . . Meanwhile we have thought better. Today we do not believe a word of it. The 'inner world' is full of phantoms and false lights: the will is one of them. The will no longer moves anything, consequently no longer explains anything – it merely accompanies events, it can also be absent. The so-called 'motive': another error. Merely a surface phenomenon of consciousness, an accompaniment to an act . . . And as for the ego! It has become a fable, a fiction, a play on words: it has totally ceased to think, feel and will! . . . What follows from this? There are no spiritual causes at all!

This conclusion, and all that follows from it, is already implicit in Zarathustra's admonition to the despisers of the body, and leads to – or better, would surely have led to if Nietzsche had continued to speculate – the repudiation of 'psychology' as a distinct science of the 'psyche' – simply because the psyche had already gone the way of the soul – and its replacement by physiology.

In the *Genealogy of Morals* (I, note), Nietzsche says that 'every table of values, every "thou shalt" known to history or ethnology, requires first of all a *physiological* illumination and interpretation – in any event, it requires this before it requires a psychological one; and they all await a critique on the part of medical science.' At the end of any inquiry into Nietzsche as a psychologist one arrives back at his assertion that he has really been trying to write nothing but physiology, medicine and natural science; that the drive to see things in this light has been active in this domain too.

III: Christianity

At the end of his active life, Nietzsche chose to define his position and himself in relation to Christianity: he described himself as the Anti-Christ and used as the title of his autobiography a phrase identified with Jesus and ended it with a formula calculated to set his own and the Christian world-outlook in diametrical opposition: 'Have I been understood? – *Dionysus against the Crucified* . . .' (*EH*, IV. 9).

In so far as his philosophy is, as a whole and in all its parts, incompatible with Christianity, this assertion of the fact now needs no further elucidation. But as Nietzsche's specific attack gained so great a degree of notoriety, and as he himself insisted so strongly on his anti-Christianity, we ought to consider his relation to the religion in which he was raised separately and as a distinct issue.

Nietzsche employs the word 'Christianity' almost indifferently to denote three distinct things: the mode of being manifested in the practice of Christ, the religion named after him, and the scheme of beliefs appropriated by this religion. We shall make an exposition of his ideas easier for ourselves if we reserve the word 'Christianity' for the second of these phenomena, and call the first 'Christianness' and the last 'Christian belief': we can then summarize Nietzsche's position by saying, firstly, that he stood in radical opposition to all three, but that the nature of this opposition was different in each case.

Christian belief he considered 'mere lies and deception' (*WP*, 159). The Christian's world of ideas, he said, 'contains nothing which so much as touches upon actuality' (*A*, 39); belief in God, soul, sin, redemption, grace, punishment, spirits, the kingdom of God, the Last Judgment, eternal life – to cite part of the list offered in *The Anti-Christ* (15) – is dismissed as palpably false and impossible. But this system of beliefs was, he implies, not at first sincerely held: it was the means by which Christianity (in the sense in which we are using the word) triumphed over the other cults of the ancient world:

> Christianity [here meaning 'Christian belief'] as the formula for outbidding all the subterranean cults, those of Osiris, of the Great Mother, of Mithras for example – *and* for summing them up: it is in this insight that the genius of Paul consists. His instinct in this matter was so sure that, doing ruthless violence to the truth, he took the ideas by which those Chandala religions

exercised their fascination and placed them in the mouth of the 'Saviour' he had invented . . . so as to *make* of him something even a priest of Mithras could understand . . . he grasped that to disvalue 'the world' he *needed* the belief in immortality, that the concept 'Hell' will master even Rome (*A*, 58)

Later, 'when it went in search of power among barbarian peoples', Christianity 'had need of *barbarous* concepts and values' (*A*, 22): again the implication is that Christian belief was originally a means employed by Christianity for acquiring power. The details of this belief, and its absurdities, are not of very great moment to Nietzsche, because they could have been different from what they were without affecting the nature of Christianity or of Christianness: and it is with these that he is chiefly concerned.

Christianity is a *ressentiment* religion of Jewish origin, 'the revaluation of all Aryan values, the victory of Chandala values, the evangel preached to the poor and lowly, the collective rebellion of everything downtrodden, wretched, ill-constituted, under-privileged against the "race"' (*T*, VIII. 4). In Christianity 'the instincts of the subjugated and oppressed come into the foreground: it is the lowest classes which seek their salvation in it' (*A*, 21). The needs which brought Christianity into existence were those felt by the Jews as an oppressed people; the feelings of *ressentiment* against the power under which they suffered, and the 'slave morality' produced by the pressure of that suffering itself – the view of life which evolves out of a life of suffering – gave this religion its characteristics. Subsequently it became 'a collective movement of outcast and refuse elements of every kind', who with its aid hoped to 'come to power'; it 'turned to the disinherited of life of every kind' (*A*, 51). The great formula which defines Christianity is that of Paul: 'God hath chosen the *weak* things of the world, the *foolish* things of the world, *base* things of the world and things which are *despised*' (*ibid.*): and Christian values are an expression of the *rancune* of the weak, foolish, base and despised.

Among the characteristics which Nietzsche postulates as having derived from the '*ressentiment* against life' which lies at the bottom of Christianity none seems to him more revelatory than the Christian attitude towards sex: 'It was only Christianity, with *ressentiment against* life in its foundations, which made of sexuality something impure' (*T*, X. 4), is the motif upon which he plays a hundred variations. Christianity was also responsible for the invention of 'sin': 'only

Christianity brought sin into the world. Belief in the remedies against sin which it offered has now been gradually shaken down to its deepest roots: but *belief in the illness* which it taught and disseminated still remains' (*WS*, 78). If one subtracted every other objection to Christianity raised by Nietzsche, one could probably reconstruct his polemic against it entirely out of his objections to the concept of sin, 'that form *par excellence* of the self-violation of man' (*A*, 44), and its presuppositions and consequences.

Christian morality is a 'slave morality' of a pure type. It is a further development of the 'slave revolt in morality' inaugurated by the Jews (*BGE*, 195; *GM*, I. 7). The slave revolt in morality 'begins when *ressentiment* itself becomes creative and gives birth to values: the *ressentiment* of creatures to whom the real reaction, that of the deed, is denied' (*GM*, I. 10). The Jews 'brought about that miracle of reversal of values' which consists essentially in fusing together the concepts 'rich, godless, evil, violent, sensual' into a single concept and for the first time coining 'the word "world" as a term of reproach' (*BGE*, 195). Judaeo-Christian morality is thus in part a slave morality in which the characteristics typical of this species of morality – the emphasis on pity, for example, or on the relief of suffering – are to be found in exemplary purity; but it is also an aggressive creation of *ressentiment* and impotence, and as such has fashioned for itself a purely imaginary state of affairs in which the powerful have been overcome and the powerless have come to dominate. Whether these imaginings take the unpleasant form of Tertullian's gloating over the spectacle of the 'heathen' roasting in hellfire, or the touching form of the *Magnificat* – 'He hath put down the mighty from their seats, and exalted them of low degree' – their origin in an imaginary revenge is the same, and the world they envisage equally unreal. And it is because he views the French Revolution, democracy, socialism and anarchism exclusively as 'slave revolts' that Nietzsche speaks of them as the direct outcome of Christianity.

Christian belief and Christianity are antithetical to Christianness. '"Christianity" has become something fundamentally different from that which its founder did and desired' (*WP*, 195); 'The entire Christian doctrine of that which *ought* to be believed . . . is mere lies and deception: and precisely the opposite of that which gave the Christian movement its beginning' (*WP*, 159); 'Paul re-erected in the grand manner precisely that which Christ had annulled through his life' *WP*, (167); 'what did Christ *deny*? – Everything today called Christian'

(*WP*, 158). Christianness is the practice exemplified in the life of Jesus and 'even today *such* a life is possible, for certain men even necessary: genuine . . . Christianity will be possible at all times' (*A*, 39). Christianness is the 'incapacity for resistance' become morality – '"resist not evil!": the profoundest saying of the Gospel' – the consciousness of 'blessedness in peace, in gentleness, in the *inability* for enmity' (*A*, 29); the 'glad tidings' are 'that there are no more opposites' (*A*, 32), in the Gospel 'the concept guilt and punishment is lacking; likewise the concept reward. "Sin", every kind of distancing relationship between God and man, is abolished – *precisely this is the "glad tidings"*' (*A*, 33). The life of Jesus was the *practice* of Christianness, and so was his death: 'He does not resist, he does not defend his rights, he takes no steps to avert the worst that can happen to him – more, *he provokes it* . . . And he . . . suffers, he loves *with* those, *in* those who are doing evil to him . . . *Not* to defend oneself, *not* to grow angry, *not* to make responsible . . . But not to resist even the evil man – to *love* him' (*A*, 37). An absolute disinclination for enmity and contention, not merely externally but within oneself; refusal to resist, even within one's heart; freedom from every feeling of *ressentiment*; the ability to love without discrimination: this *constitutes* the 'kingdom of God' which is 'within you'. Christian belief is irrelevant to, and Christianity the opposite of the practice resulting from such a state of being: which is what is implied in Nietzsche's most famous dictum concerning Jesus: 'there has been only one Christian, and he died on the Cross' (*A*, 34).

It will be clear that Nietzsche had a good deal more respect for Christianness than he had for Christianity or Christian belief; but it should also be clear why for that very reason he felt the need to state that towards the practice of Christ too he stood in rooted opposition. 'Dionysus against *the Crucified*' says plainly enough that what is being set in opposition to the Dionysian world-outlook is not Christian belief or Christianity – whose falsity and reprehensibility he had already demonstrated time and again – but precisely the God on the Cross, the embodiment of Christianness. His conception of the psychological (or physiological) origin of the practice of Jesus has already been outlined (see p. 179), but Nietzsche's opposition to him does not depend upon whether this conception is correct or not: it depends only on the contention that Christianness and the Dionysian outlook represent antithetical responses to the fact of suffering. 'The tragic man affirms even the harshest life: he is sufficiently strong, full, and capable of deification to do so; the Christian denies even the happiest lot on earth:

he is sufficiently weak, poor, disinherited to suffer from life whatever form it assumes' (*WP*, 1052); and therefore, all personal respect for Jesus notwithstanding, 'the god on the cross is a curse on life' because Christianness is a flight from the suffering necessarily entailed by life (*ibid.*). The opposition is still between the sublimation of passion and its extirpation; between acceptance of the preconditions of existence and refusal to accept them; between affirmation and denial of life.

7
Interpretations and Influence

Nietzsche's famous 'influence' and the equally famous disagreement over his 'meaning' are obviously allied phenomena, and both testify to the variety of response his works can elicit. In both cases, too, one can speak of legitimate or illegitimate influences or interpretation: of supposed influence which can be seen as such only by a demonstrable misreading of him, and of interpretation which is demonstrably untrue to the texts upon which it is supposedly based. Here I propose to suggest, firstly, some of the reasons for disagreement over what Nietzsche means and for what I consider misreadings; and then indicate the principal directions in which he has exercised influence.

II

Perhaps the most common reason for differing and incompatible notions of what Nietzsche means is *knowing about but not knowing him*. Because his name is so familiar there are many people who would be ashamed to admit they have no idea what his books contain even though they have never read them and could not name them. They do not know his works, but they know about them: what they know about them is inevitably confused and half or more than half wrong. Nietzsche is, of course, not alone in suffering from this sort of misrepresentation, but he is rather more open to it than most philosophers, partly because of his greater notoriety (an effect of his literary quality and contemporary relevance), partly because of the aforementioned fact that he is widely regarded as not being a 'real' philosopher. If you have never read a single line of, say, Leibniz, you will probably feel you are something less than a Leibniz expert: in the case of Nietzsche, however, you can 'gather' what he was on about without reading him because it is only 'real' philosophers like Leibniz who require close attention if they are to be understood.

The notion that Nietzsche was not a real philosopher is a cause of disagreement about him in another sense also, for it imposes the necessity of deciding what, in that event, he really was. The most common conclusion is that he was really a writer of unconscious confessions. (According to Nietzsche all philosophers are writers of unconscious confessions, but that is not what is meant by those who think Nietzsche was not a philosopher.) What he wrote has to be unriddled into what he 'really' wrote, and that leads on to psychoanalysis and the reduction of his works to biographical data. In the process his philosophy vanishes. A further undesirable outcome is that his terminology is misunderstood because it is not read as the terminology of a philosopher.

A third reason is 'encyclopaedicism'. Nietzsche has suffered at the hands of the scholarly philosopher whose speciality is the history of philosophy. A summary of Nietzsche in three paragraphs must result in caricature. Often the encyclopaedic view sees him in quite the wrong surroundings and context: as 'coming after' Schopenhauer, for instance. The encyclopaedic view in general blunts and smudges what is individual in a philosopher for the benefit of what he has in common with the other members of the 'line' of which he is in some respects part.

A fourth reason is the combative urge. Some of the disagreement about Nietzsche can be explained by the violence which has attended it. Many good men who devote their lives to the things of the spirit have a quantity of natural spleen and aggressiveness which they can get rid of only on the battlefields of the intellect: for seventy years Nietzsche has constituted one such battlefield. The acerbity and splenetic indignation attending many disputes over him would be incomprehensible if one did not realize that their motive has been first and foremost the discharge of spleen and acid; and even when this quality of malevolence has been absent, there has still been a suspiciously high quantity of contradiction and schoolmasterly correction of others, as though the main objective was the assertion and demonstration of a fancied superiority over one's colleagues and rivals.

Fifth: extreme selectivity. You already know all about Nietzsche and you select from his works half a dozen passages which confirm your view of him: these, you say, represent his true position. You do not have to be a fool to do this: you can be Georg Lukács and do it. The catch is that someone else has selected half a dozen different passages and advanced the same claim in respect of *them*.

Sixth: taking the part for the whole – a form of selectivity but produced by mistaken emphasis rather than unrepresentative selection. You halt at a particular point of view and fail to see where that point of view is called in question; or you are so taken with the discovery of 'contradictions' that you overlook the continuing attempt to get past them; or you keep your eyes on the 'will to power' and fail to see the nihilism which made that theory necessary. The first mistake leads to the attribution to Nietzsche of views he did not hold or held only provisionally and 'experimentally'; the second deprives his philosophy of positive content; the third deprives it of its inexhaustibility, and makes it hard to understand how he could have exerted so varied an influence on contemporary philosophy and literature.

A seventh reason for disagreement is a failure to grasp the degree to which the Nazi interpretation of Nietzsche was fraudulent. I have already indicated how he came to publish formulations and incitements which can reasonably, if with some freedom of expression, be called 'fascist'; and the extent to which Hitler was 'influenced' by him will be dealt with in a moment; but the 'Nazification' of Nietzsche is a consideration different from either of these. Eichmann surprised his judges by repeating Kant's definition of the 'categorical imperative' in Kant's own words: but in Germany everyone above a certain minimum of intelligence knows a bit of philosophy and has a little respect for it. National Socialism had to pose as a 'philosophy of life' (*Weltanschauung*), and its leaders thought it expedient to provide it with some sort of philosophical backing and justification: indeed, to put it in that way is to put it too coldly – they themselves felt the need for a 'philosophy'. One result was a 'reinterpretation' of as many German artists and thinkers of the past as could possibly be pressed into service, and Nietzsche was of course among them. The 'fascist' and anti-democratic expressions were there to hand, and references to 'will' and 'war' were also useful: yet it might none the less be thought peculiarly difficult to make Nietzsche of all people into a 'national socialist' – and so it was. His books were, as wholes, quite useless for the purpose; even his 'aphorisms' were useless as wholes: what was required was the lifting of individual sentences and parts of sentences – not out of a mistaken 'interpretation' but from the desire to falsify. It was not ignorance or error which was at work here: Bäumler (*Nietzsche der Philosoph und Politiker*, 1931) and Richard Oehler (*Friedrich Nietzsche und die Deutsche Zukunft*, 1935) knew very well – none better – that Nietzsche was not a nationalist or an anti-Semite; did not consider the French depraved or the Slavs subhuman; called himself a 'good European' as a polemical antithesis to 'good German'; advocated racial mixture; and would have seen in Hitler's politics the *rancune* of the disinherited and dis-possessed and in the triumph of his philosophy a confirmation that the age of nihilism had arrived. They knew, none better, that he criticized the whole conception of 'politics', the 'political party', the 'modern state' even to the point – or rather far past the point – at which his criticism becomes unreasonable and one needs to put in a word in their favour. Bäumler contributed a postscript to each volume of Kröner's pocket edition of Nietzsche's works, Oehler compiled the indices of both the major collected editions, the second of them (that of the *Musarion* edition) comprising two and a half volumes. Neither needed to pose as a 'Nietzsche expert' but really was one; and herein lay the fatality for Nietzsche's reputation – for if the compiler of a two and a half volume index to Nietzsche's writings does not know what they contain, who does? It was because the leading Nietzsche scholars inside Germany said that Nietzsche was four-fifths a Nazi that the Nazis themselves believed it.

In the last analysis these are all relatively trivial grounds for disagree-ment: there remain those large-scale studies in which a serious, informed and entirely honest attempt is made to encompass the whole of Nietz-sche but which still embody differences of view which seem irreconcil-able. You sometimes find it difficult to believe the same man is under discussion: the fascist beast attacked in one book is surely not the child of the Enlightenment defended in another? When you see this an uncanny suspicion begins to agitate your mind: you begin to suspect that Nietzsche cannot be encapsulated at all, even within the biggest capsule; that he forever eludes final definition. And that leads you to an even uncannier suspicion: that the sort of reception they have received may be due to something fundamental to the works them-selves; that this irreconcilability between different interpretations is actually appropriate in the case of a philosopher so widely regarded as self-contradictory. You begin to believe that, by some unconscious grasp and trick of genius, Nietzsche has managed, not only to assert the paradoxical nature of rationality, but actually to bring it about that the way in which this assertion was received should demonstrate its

truth. This belief would itself amount to no more than another interpretation, but that would, of course, not constitute an objection to it.

Finally: from the passage of time. In Nietzsche's own day his writings
were ignored – not because his contemporaries were so much denser
than we are, but because events had not yet demonstrated their relevance. The world as seen by Nietzsche is in many respects the world
as it is now, and almost everything written about him before the
Second World War is consequently out of date. He has always been
ahead of his commentators: and, almost certainly, he still is.

III

Turn to 'influence' and you find an even greater plentitude and variety.
On the broadest scale, Nietzsche influenced the entire 'cultural climate'
of this century: certain ideas are present in a large number of heads
which probably would not have been present, and certain things are
taken for granted which would probably not have been taken for
granted, if he had never existed and published books. On the narrowest
scale, he gave fresh currency to a few old words and fresh impetus and
relevance to a few ancient ideas. Some of his 'influence' is definable
only vaguely: his name has become associated with certain feelings, so
that the utterance of the name tends to bring these feelings to life; and
a good part of it comes from his personality, or from an idea of his
personality, and not from his writings at all.

Gisela Deesz wrote a whole book on *The Development of the Image
of Nietzsche in Germany* – it covers only that one country, and it was
published in 1933, since when in that one country alone 'Nietzsche's
image' has undergone considerable further development. Here we are
clearly going to be limited to the merest sketch of 'Nietzsche's influence'; and we are going to have to divide it up, somewhat arbitrarily,
into different 'types' of influence, because only if we do that shall we
be able to see our way clear at all.

First, then, Nietzsche exercised influence as *an exemplary personality*.
The 'front generation' – the German version of the 'lost generation' –
very justly repudiated and turned away in disgust from the style of
life of which the war and the defeat had been the outcome. They did
so for differing, sometimes even antithetical reasons. Some had had
enough of Imperial Germany, of the mystique of the *Reich* and its
destiny, of discipline, virtue and war; they wanted to be Westernized
or Easternized (Sovietized), they wanted to be anything but German:

and it was these who created the typical characteristics of the Weimar Republic, with its experimentalism in the arts, its desperate modernity, its reliance on foreign models (English parliaments, Russian conspiratorial 'communism', French cabarets, American night clubs), its neurotic vitality, and its decadence. Some, on the other hand, had not had nearly enough of war; they had acquired a taste for *Kameradschaft* and submersion in a mass, for marching and shooting and being told what to do: to them the end of hostilities meant the opening up of a life quite devoid of meaning, and it was from them that the *Freikorps, Wehrverbände,* and other para-military organizations of the Right acquired their membership. But there were others too who took neither course, who wanted neither the old nor the foreign, but something essentially new: and to many of these the figure of Nietzsche made an appeal. It was not his writings which were decisive but the personality and way of life which shone through them. To many members of the front generation Nietzsche seemed to have been an incarnate rejection of bourgeois life, and an incarnate experiment in living in the kind of world they believed they were now living in and in making the most of it. This effect corresponded closely enough to the reality of Nietzsche's existence to constitute a legitimate influence; but it was always in danger of passing over into reverence for a myth. The Nietzsche admired by Stefan George was already a figure of mythology: a construct whose essential purpose was to serve as a predecessor of George himself. The study of Nietzsche by George's follower Ernst Bertram carries the frank subtitle 'Attempt at a Mythology', and in this Nietzsche ceases to be a real human being and becomes the sacrificial god which in his days of madness he imagined himself to be. The unrealism of this attitude itself had its followers in such people as Werner Sombart (1863–1941), who wrote that Nietzsche was 'merely the last singer and seer who, descending from heaven, announced to us the tidings that from us would be born the Son of God whom he called superman' (quoted in Hans Kohn, *The Mind of Germany*, London, 1960). It is not, I think, a matter of 'interpretation' to regard utterances of this description as being altogether subjective and having a minimum of relevance to the works of the real Nietzsche.

It was not, however, only as a myth that Nietzsche exercised influence on Stefan George: in common with very many other Germans, including a necessarily incalculable number who were not writers, he was influenced by Nietzsche's cosmopolitanism. The student of German literature must again and again be brought up against the provincialism and narrow parochialism of even the best German writers in the age following the death of Goethe: imitation of foreign models and parish-pump obsessions have, indeed, always been the twin poles of German literature (as they have been of German life), and this has never been more the case than during the mid-nineteenth century. This parochialism was one of the things Nietzsche was reacting against when he 'deserted' Wagner and subsequently declared, in *The Wagner Case*, that Wagner, far from being typically German, was really an epigone of the French Romantics of the 1840s. His own works represent an 'un-German' indifference to national interests and an impartial concern with the life and literature of all European nations. It is true to say that no prominent German writer, with the possible exception of Heine, had introduced his readers so forcibly to the idea of a pan-European culture as Nietzsche did, and this had the effect of to some extent liberating German literature from its former self-absorption.

Nietzsche's cosmopolitanism also had its effect on Rilke, but in his case a more profound influence is perceptible and has long been recognized. Rilke's early and unsuccessful writings are full of an undigested and superficial Nietzscheanism; later he came to see that what really attracted him to Nietzsche was the latter's 'Dionysian' acceptance of life in all its manifestations, and this then became the underlying theme of all his work. That Rilke's Orpheus approximates very closely to Nietzsche's Dionysus is now a commonplace of Rilkean commentary.

An idea of the comprehensiveness of Nietzsche's 'influence' might be conveyed by mentioning here the extent to which H. L. Mencken borrowed from him. Mencken made no secret of his indebtedness, but even drew attention to it by the frequency with which he referred to Nietzsche and by accusing others who might not wish the fact to be too widely known of also being indebted to him. (He claimed, for instance, to have discovered 'numerous and inescapable' borrowings in Theodore Roosevelt's *The Strenuous Life*.) Except for their both being writers of genius it is hard to imagine two men more different from one another than Rilke and Mencken: yet both were to a great extent educated by Nietzsche, though by different aspects of him. And in case it should be thought that Mencken's idea of him was a parody or vulgarization I quote here a few lines from the *Treatise on Right and Wrong*: Nietzsche's 'furious attack upon the Christian ideal of humility and abnegation', says Mencken, 'has caused Christian critics to denounce him as an advocate of the most brutal egoism, but in point of fact he proposed only the introduction of a new and more heroic form of renunciation, based upon abounding strength rather than upon hopeless weakness; and in his maxim "Be hard!" there was just as much sacrifice of immediate gratification to ultimate good as you will find in any of the *principia* of Jesus.'

Historically, the earliest sort of 'influence' Nietzsche exercised was as a prophet of brutal aggressiveness, with 'power' understood in a political sense. It was the propagation of this idea of him which, whatever its individual collaborators may have thought, constitutes the chief effect of the 'Nietzsche Archive' and its work. Elizabeth Nietzsche (Förster-Nietzsche after her marriage to Bernhardt Förster) was an anti-Semitic nationalist of the kind described in chapter 2 and exemplified very well by her husband. During the First World War she organized, through the Archive, a mass edition of *Zarathustra* and had it distributed in the front line: what the troops made of it I do not know, but what they were *supposed* to make of it is clear – it was supposed to inspire them to ruthlessness. After Hitler came to power Elizabeth quite naturally placed the Archive at the disposal of the Third Reich: Hitler visited it on the occasion of Nietzsche's ninetieth birthday (15 October 1934), and was photographed beside a bust of Nietzsche; he also attended a memorial ceremony for Elizabeth on 11 November 1935, three days after her death. In 1937 a typically Nazi building was erected at Weimar to house the Archive and as a centre for 'instruction in the spirit of Zarathustra'. In all of this one can see a drive to recognition, to social acceptability and 'success', and this drive comes entirely into the open in such endeavours as the successful attempt at formal reconciliation with Bayreuth. What Nietzsche had written about Wagner's 'decadence' and the 'anti-Semitic abortions' at Bayreuth he had still written and his words were still in print: Elizabeth, however, thought it very important that the 'Archive' should be on a friendly footing with the Wagner Festival and arranged a meeting at which she recited Nietzsche's aphorism '*Sternenfreundschaft*', the sense of which is that friends may go their separate ways without thereby becoming enemies; whereupon, it appears, everyone agreed to let bygones be bygones. In principle, of course, one does not object to this burying of the hatchet, particularly as 'Bayreuth' and the 'Archive' were in fact at one on all important issues and had no real ground for continuing to quarrel: one's objections arise over the concrete fact that, whereas 'Bayreuth' still represented in its essentials the spirit of Wagner himself, the 'Archive' had for years been the subject of the justified accusation of never having embodied the spirit of Nietzsche at all – so that in this case 'reconciliation' meant a sort of public surrender on the part of the 'Nietzscheans' and a further befogging of Nietzsche's considered and consistent criticism of the nature of the *Reich*. The motive for it is, however, clear: Elizabeth's desire for solid success. I do not imagine that Wagner's heirs gave a damn *what* Nietzsche thought about Bayreuth: Wagner had in any case written him off as insane at the time of *Human, All Too Human*, and in the world of 'German culture' Bayreuth counted for enormously more than the Nietzsche Archive. This last consideration was, of course, the spur to Elizabeth's ambition for a 'reconciliation' – and the Wagnerians let her have her way because to them the issue was of no consequence whatever.

The issue which Elizabeth's success in the Third Reich does raise, however, is whether Nietzsche actually exercised any 'influence' over Hitler, and if so in what it consisted. This is to many people a vital consideration, for if it could be shown that Hitler's opinions, and hence his actions, originated in a reading of Nietzsche this would constitute a very grave objection to Nietzsche – the gravest, indeed, that could very well be imagined. During the years of his power, the general consensus of opinion outside Germany was roughly that Wagner, Nietzsche and Hitler stood in much the same relationship to one another as Marx, Engels and Lenin: this misapprehension was made possible by general ignorance, not only of what Nietzsche wrote, but also of what Hitler's opinions really were – for *Mein Kampf*, although as explicit as one could desire, is almost unreadable and the very opposite of a 'popular exposition' of its author's ideas. All this notwithstanding, it ought to have been known, for instance, that Nietzsche was not an anti-Semite and that his name does not occur in *Mein Kampf* – although the activities of the Archive and of such experts as Bäumler and Richard Oehler admittedly made a stronger impression than such negative evidence could have. Since the end of the war Hitler's intellectual background has come in for a great deal of scrutiny, and has been seen to consist very largely of subterranean and near-subterranean anti-Semitic and 'folkish' literature for which the term illiterate rubbish would be a compliment: Hitler in fact fed his mind, not on Wagner and Nietzsche, but on precisely the kind of trash one would expect from a perusal of *Mein Kampf*, which is for the most part the same kind of trash drawn out longer. People who have not read *Mein Kampf* – most people, that is – have no conception how bad

a book it is, how ill-written, how *low*: the chapters on party organization and propaganda methods are, given their objective (political
power) and presupposition (nothing is true, everything is permitted),
excellent; and the statement of the author's future foreign policy is an
admirably direct and unhypocritical expression of the general ambitions
of German nationalism; but these elements count for nearly nothing
in the overall impression made by the book, which is one of a fixed,
almost maniacal obsession with the danger to the purity of the German
race represented by the Jew. Hitler, who thought he could tell any lie,
is here incapable of lying: here he writes with a 'burning sincerity'
that he was never able to conceal for any motive whatever. Anti-
Semitism was clearly a substitute for what in a normally constituted
man are erotic fantasies and sexual dreams and ambitions: and the
author of *Mein Kampf* is so possessed by it, and derives such enjoyment
from giving it rein, that he becomes utterly careless of the impression
he is making on the reader. When you consider that the book was
supposed to be a combined autobiography, political testament and
instruction manual, and that its objective was to help leader and party
to power in a nation in which they as yet counted for very little (the
party was banned and Hitler in prison at the time it was written), the
amount of straight pornography which was allowed to remain on its
pages is astonishing: 'racial purity', for instance, is not thought of in
any esoteric or historical sense, or as something comparable to general
hygiene: it is something German girls lose when they are raped by
Jews, as they are in the pages of *Mein Kampf*. Indeed, the book contains
so much that a man with political ambitions might be expected to do
everything he could to conceal rather than everything he could to
advertise, that one is driven to suspect that in the depths of his soul
Hitler wanted to destroy his own career at its outset. (This is not a
wild surmise: his life is punctuated by hazardous actions interpretable
as attempts at suicide.) What saved him was not that millions of
Germans shared his fantasies, but that only those already victims of
the same obsession were drawn very far into his book: what Hitler
was really like, and what his 'opinions' really were, remained comparatively unknown.

To feel fairly convinced, then, that Nietzsche played no very great
part in Hitler's intellectual education it is sufficient to have read *Mein
Kampf*. Whether he played any part at all must remain a matter for
conjecture. Werner Maser says in his analysis of *Mein Kampf*: 'Nietzsche
. . . is frequently included in Hitler's pre-1925 reading [i.e. before he

wrote *Mein Kampf*]. There is nothing in *Mein Kampf*, however, to indicate the extent to which Hitler really knew Nietzsche's writings. Percy Schramm's remark that Hitler had perhaps been impressed by Nietzsche's titles *The Will to Power* and *Beyond Good and Evil* is possibly not far from the truth. There is no proof one way or the other' (*Hitler's Mein Kampf: An Analysis*, trans. R. J. Barry, London, 1970; Schramm is quoted in *Hitler's Tischgespräche im Führerhauptquartier 1941–1942*, 2nd edn, Stuttgart, 1965). According to Maser, therefore – and my own reading confirms this – the only reasonable probability is that Hitler acquired from Nietzsche a few words to which he had given new currency – such words as *Macht* and *Wille* – and the pathos of his exhortation to go beyond contemporary morality and 'become hard'. I cannot find evidence of any 'influence' that goes beyond this.

We have already discussed the extent to which Nietzsche was a precursor of modern psychology: he anticipated developments, but whether he actually influenced them is doubtful. Direct influence, sometimes to the point of imitation, is clear in very many imaginative writers, of whom Thomas Mann and Shaw are only the greatest. (For a detailed account of Mann's relationship with Nietzsche perhaps I may be permitted to advertise my own *Thomas Mann*, London, 1971.) Where his influence has been most comprehensive, however, is, as might be expected, in the field of philosophy.

Jaspers defined existentialism as 'a philosophy which does not cognize objects' but 'elucidates and makes actual the being of the thinker' (*Die Geistige Situation der Zeit*). Sartre defined this philosophical movement as the consequences of believing that 'existence precedes essence' (*Existentialism is a Humanism*). In both these senses, existentialism is anticipated in Nietzsche: when he writes that 'it makes all the difference in the world whether a thinker stands in personal relation to his problems . . . or can only feel and grasp them impersonally, with the tentacles of cold, prying thought', and when he writes that 'man is the animal *whose nature has not been fixed*'. Jaspers's formula is, indeed, no more than an unnecessarily oblique and 'difficult' way of saying that 'every great philosophy' has been 'a confession on the part of its author and a kind of involuntary and unconscious memoir' (*BGE*, 6). To Heidegger, Nietzsche was the metaphysician who demonstrated the impossibility of metaphysics. If by the 'contemporary philosophical situation' one means the situation on the Continent, and in other parts of the world where Continental, as distinct from British and American philosophy has been influential, Jaspers's view that this situation 'is determined by the fact that two philosophers, Kirkegaard and Nietzsche, who did not count in their times . . . have continually grown in significance' (*Reason and Existenz*, New York, 1955) is clearly justified. Here Nietzsche's 'philosophy of power' hardly counts at all: what has been influential is his breaking down of the categories of reason, his denial of systematism, and his insistence on the need for a new beginning.

8

Poetry, Philologica, Compositions, Letters

I: Poetry

Nietzsche's importance for the present day resides wholly in his philosophical thinking and in the attitude he represents – or even embodies – towards the concept 'a philosopher'. His productions and activities other than philosophical are of secondary interest, although some knowledge of them is of course necessary for a picture of the complete man.

Just as Wagner's earliest reputation was that of the opera composer who wrote his own libretti, so Nietzsche's was that of the philosopher who wrote poetry: in both cases it was the combination in one man of capacities not usually found together which occasioned wonderment, and in both cases also the wonderment subsequently decreased when it became clear that one of these capacities was a good deal inferior to the other.

Nietzsche's quality as a poet is, in my judgment, to be correctly assessed by reversing the cliché that poetry is language 'heightened' and made more intense: in his case, poetry is a relaxation from the intensity of his normal prose medium, and whenever he breaks into verse the temperature at once goes down. 'Verse', indeed, rather than poetry, is what he had a talent for: and not merely verse, but *light verse*. He never attempted, and clearly never felt any desire to attempt the larger forms; and although he experimented with eccentric metres and, from the time of *Zarathustra* onwards, with a kind of *vers libre*, his usual conception of 'a poem' was of something embodying strong regular rhythm and clear powerful rhyme – and of something, moreover, which says what it has to say without gravity, lightly, quickly:

Heraklitismus
Alles Glück auf Erden,

Freunde, gibt der Kampf!
Ja, um Freund zu werden,
Braucht es Pulverdampf!
Eins in Drein sind Freunde:
Brüder vor der Not,
Gleiche vor dem Feinde,
Freie – vor dem Tod!

(All happiness on earth, friends, comes from struggle! Indeed, you cannot even be a friend without powder-smoke! Friends are at one in three things: brothers in the face of danger, equals in the face of the enemy, undismayed – in the face of death!) Nietzschean light verse at its best: no surplussage; imitative four-square rhythm which fits the lines to any number of popular four-square tunes ('Onward, Christian Soldiers', for instance); comical allusion to philosophy (Heraclitus) and religion ('Eins in Drein' – one in three); nothing difficult or 'modern'; a serious poem at bottom, but not an earnest one.

Ecce Homo
Ja! Ich weiss, woher ich stamme!
Ungesättigt gleich der Flamme
Glühe und verzehr ich mich.
Licht wird alles, was ich fasse,
Kohle alles, was ich lasse:
Flamme bin ich sicherlich.

(Yes, I know whence I have sprung! Insatiable as a flame I burn and consume myself. Whatever I seize hold on becomes light, whatever I leave, ashes: certainly I am a flame.) Imitative rhythm which flickers along unstoppably (except for the pause at 'mich' there is nothing to make the tongue stumble no matter how fast you recite the poem); comic allusion to philosophy (Heraclitus again) and religion (Behold the man!); again something serious said lightly.

Both poems, and the others like them, are evidently modelled on the comic side of Heine, and are not inferior to it:

Doktrin
Schlage die Trommel und fürchte dich nicht,
Und küsse die Marketenderin,
Das ist die ganze Wissenschaft,
Das ist der Bücher tiefster Sinn. . . .
Das ist die Hegelsche Philosophie,

Das ist der Bücher tiefster Sinn.
Ich hab sie begriffen, weil ich gescheit,
Und weil ich ein guter Tambour bin.

(Beat the drum and don't be afraid, and kiss the woman who follows
the camp: that is the whole of science, that is the deepest meaning of
books.... That is the Hegelian philosophy, that is the deepest meaning
of books. I have grasped it because I am clever and because I am a
good drummer.) Heine's all-pervading sexiness is missing from Nietzsche, but the technique of 'Doktrin' is the same as that of 'Heraklitismus'
and 'Ecce Homo': imitative rhythm (in this instance imitative of a drum-
beat), humorous philosophical allusion (much less apposite in Heine),
lightness of touch masking seriousness.

The similarity of Nietzsche's most characteristic verse to Heine's
extends further than similarity of technique. Consider this famous
poem: its subject is the same as that of Goethe's 'Nur wer die Sehnsucht
kennt', namely a hopeless longing for one far away:

Ein Fichtenbaum steht einsam
Im Norden auf kahler Höh'.
Ihn schläfert; mit weisser Decke
Umhüllen ihn Eis und Schnee.
Er träumt von einer Palme,
Die fern im Morgenland
Einsam und schweigend trauert
Auf brennender Felsenwand.

(A fir-tree stands alone on a bare height in the north. It sleeps; ice and
snow cover it with a white blanket. It dreams of a palm-tree which,
far away in the orient, sorrows alone and in silence on a burning cliff-
face.) Direct statement of the feeling to be conveyed is suppressed and
concealed under allusiveness; seriousness of intention is masked by
whimsicality – which, of course, runs the risk of becoming too whim-
sical and thus of defeating its own object; the non-human world
stands in for the human; and what is fixed in the mind is not an event,
or any kind of narrative, but a picture: these characteristics of Heine's
mode in such a poem as this are also those of Nietzsche's in its most
typical manifestations:

Wer viel einst zu verkünden hat,
schweigt viel in sich hinein.

Wer einst den Blitz zu zünden hat,
muss lange – Wolke sein.

(He who has much to proclaim one day, stays silently much immersed within himself. He who has to kindle the lightning one day, must for a long time – be a cloud.)

Sternen-Moral
Vorausbestimmt zur Sternenbahn,
was geht dich, Stern, das Dunkel an?
Roll selig hin durch diese Zeit!
Ihr Elend sei dir fremd und weit!
Der fernsten Welt gehört dein Schein!
Mitleid soll Sünde für dich sein!
Nur *ein* Gebot gilt dir: sei rein!

(*Star morality.* Predestined to a starry orbit, what do you care for the darkness, star! Roll blissfully through this age! May its wretchedness stay remote from you! Your light belongs to the most distant world! Pity should be a sin for you! *One* command alone concerns you: be pure!)

Pinie und Blitz
Hoch wuchs ich über Mensch und Tier;
und sprech ich – niemand spricht mit mir.
Zu einsam wuchs ich und zu hoch –
ich warte: worauf wart ich doch?
Zu nah ist mir der Wolken Sitz, –
ich warte auf den ersten Blitz.

(*Pine-tree and lightning.* I grew high above man and animal; and if I speak – no one speaks with me. I grew too solitary and too high – I wait: but what am I waiting for? The seat of the clouds is too close to me – I wait for the first flash of lightning.)

Nietzsche began writing poetry as a boy and until about 1860 it was, together with composition, his main creative interest. He seems to have been seriously dedicated to training himself as a craftsman and was always dissatisfied with what he had done hitherto. But what survives of this juvenilia does not indicate any ability out of the ordinary: he desired to be a poet, but was not one except in the sense in which almost any educated German boy can produce acceptable verse if he wants to do so. To write verse – indeed, *good* verse – is far easier in German than it is in English. German is very rich in rhymes, and its sentence structure readily drops the rhyming words into the right place. Moreover, German prose rhythms and verse rhythms coincide much more often than is the case in English: 'Es war einmal ein König' is prose and verse, 'Once upon a time there was a king' is prose, and if you want to make it into verse you have to distort and contort it. The effects of these characteristics of the German language are to be felt wherever it is used, from the relative abundance of German 'folk poetry' compared with the relative paucity of English to the relative simplicity of Goethe's line compared with the relative complexity of Shakespeare's, not to speak of Milton's. In Nietzsche's day, the celebration of birthdays and other family anniversaries was usually attended by the composition and recitation of verses, and often by the performance of little plays or tableaux, and something of this still remains: the origin of the taste for such mummeries lies in the capacity for them – in the ability of large numbers of people who would not pretend to be 'poets' in any other sense to write tolerable verse. Nietzsche's own abilities in this line did not in his youth extend very far beyond this.

The period *Human, All Too Human* to *The Gay Science* was also the period of his finest verse: a consequence probably of the same 'breakthrough' which transformed his prose and, indeed, his thinking as such. To get a vivid impression of the kind of change his poetical values underwent you have only to compare what is probably the best, certainly the best-known, of his early poems with one of the epigrammatic pieces prefixed to *The Gay Science*:

Noch einmal, eh ich weiterziehe
und meine Blicke vorwärts sende,
heb ich vereinsamt meine Hände
zu dir empor, zu dem ich fliehe,
dem ich in tiefster Herzenstiefe
Altäre feierlich geweiht,
dass allezeit
mich deine Stimme wieder riefe.

(Once more, before I travel on and look along the way I am going, I raise my hands in solitude to you, my refuge, to whom I have solemnly dedicated altars in the deepest depths of my heart, that your voice may always call to me. 'To the Unknown God', first stanza.)

Für Tänzer
Glattes Eis
Ein Paradeis
Für den, der gut zu tanzen weiss.

(*For dancers.* Smooth ice is a paradise for him who knows how to dance well.) Comment is almost superfluous: the latter poem employs the natural capacities of the language with complete assurance for the construction of something original; the former struggles against them in an effort at originality.

He continued to write longer poems, but none of them is as memorable as his epigrams or the verses previously quoted: the only exception being 'An den Mistral' (To the Mistral), which is one of the best good-bad poems in German:

Mistral-Wind, du Wolken-Jäger,
Trübsal-Mörder, Himmels-Feger,
Brausender, wie lieb ich dich!
Sind wir zwei nicht eines Schosses
Erstlingsgabe, eines Loses
Vorbestimmte ewiglich?
Hier auf glatten Felsenwegen
Lauf ich tanzend dir entgegen,
Tanzend, wie du pfeifst und singst:
Der du ohne Schiff und Ruder
Als der Freiheit freister Bruder
Über wilde Meere springst.

(Mistral wind, you hunter of clouds, killer of affliction, scourer of the skies, how I love you! Are we two not the first fruit of one womb, eternally predestined for one fate? Here on smooth rocky paths I run, dancing, towards you, dancing to your piping and singing: you who, as freedom's freest brother, leap across turbulent seas without ship or rudder. ....) Notice again that it is *light* verse, with maximum emphasis on rhythmic effect: the same *type* of poem as 'The Bells'.

In *Zarathustra*, in addition to the 'prose poetry', we are offered a number of free verse poems, to which others were later added to form the *Dionysos-Dithyramben*, a collection made at the very end of 1888. I have no wish to denegrate these poems as such, for many people have clearly enjoyed them, but they are certainly not 'dithyrambic': on the contrary, their immobility is nearly incredible coming from the author of 'To the Mistral'. They contain some telling images, and if they are read as prose they can make a powerful impression as distraught monologues: but you have only to compare them with 'Ecce Homo' to feel their inferiority as works of art. The *heavy* hand has come down again: the *Dithyrambs of Dionysus* recall 'To the Unknown God'.

Nietzsche's best-known poem, set by Mahler and Delius, is 'O Mensch! Gib acht!' from *Zarathustra*; his most beautiful is a free-verse lyric sometimes called 'Venice', sometimes 'Gondola Song', and published in *Ecce Homo*:

> An der Brücke stand
> jüngst ich in brauner Nacht.
> Fernher kam Gesang;
> goldener Tropfen quols
> über die zitternde Fläche weg.
> Gondeln, Lichter, Musik –
> trunken schwamms in die Dämmrung hinaus . . .
> Meine Seele, ein Saitenspiel,
> sang sich, unsichtbar berührt,
> heimlich ein Gondellied dazu,
> zitternd vor bunter Seligkeit.
> – Hörte jemand ihr zu?

(Lately I stood at the bridge in the brown night. A song came from afar; a golden drop, it welled over the quivering surface. Gondolas, lights, music – drunken it swam out into the twilight . . . My soul, a stringed instrument, invisibly touched sang to itself a gondola song in reply, quivering in many-coloured happiness. Did anyone listen to it?) If the *Dionysos-Dithyramben* had been in any way like this our discussion of Nietzsche as a poet would have taken quite a different course.

So far as I know he wrote not a single love poem.

II: Philologica

'Classical philology' – the study of the language and, through that, the literature and life of Greece and Rome – was Nietzsche's profession: the first and only job he ever had was teaching classical philology at the University of Basel and Greek language at the high school associated with the university. He was never in any respect a professional philosopher, and he held no qualifications in philosophy.

In later life he asked himself why he had adopted this profession and not some other – that of a doctor, for example, or something else useful. The unfinished *Meditation* called 'We Philologists' opens with the observation that 'a man *chooses* a profession when he is not yet capable of choice: he does not know the various professions, he does not know himself'; and, although in this place he does not seem to have his own case in mind, it would not be long before he came to think that he too had chosen a profession without sufficient reflection.

The fact of the matter is that as a young man Nietzsche was not in general very independently minded: with the exception of his refusal to continue with the study of theology – an important exception, but still an exception – the course of his career until he left Basel in 1879 was determined wholly by forces external to him. He became a classical philologist because the curriculum at Pforta was weighted very heavily on to the side of classical languages and literature: for a pupil of Pforta possessing Nietzsche's intelligence *not* to have become an academic of some sort would have required very considerable independence of spirit. So far as one can judge from this distance of time, the education provided by Pforta school in the 1860s, while it would certainly civilize a young man and greatly widen his horizons, would also make him very bookish and desk-bound; and when he came to reflect on a career, he would be likely to assume that his obvious course was to go on to teach others what he himself had been taught – because what he had been taught could be put to no other use. The *most* obvious thing for a pupil of Pforta to become was, in fact, a teacher of classical languages. At Leipzig, Nietzsche was singled out by the philologist Friedrich Ritschl as being his best pupil, and Nietzsche again responded with an inner affirmation of an external judgment: he became the star classical scholar of Leipzig. His famous acquisition of the chair of classical philology at Basel at the age of twenty-four was, again, something into which he was propelled: he would, of course, never have contemplated applying for it himself at this age and while still not having obtained his doctorate in the subject; Ritschl recommended him, and told him he had done so only after learning that his recommendation was being seriously considered. Nietzsche was not, even at this time, at all blind to the fact that his life was moving along as if on rails – nevertheless, he made no serious effort to 'go off the rails'. He became a professor of classical philology and remained one for ten years: it was only when illness literally forced him to abandon this career that he forsook the path that had been laid down for him from the day he first attended school.

Now I do not say there is anything extraordinary, not to speak of reprehensible, in this course of conduct: but it explains why Nietzsche became a classical philologist, and why he later came to consider this profession, if not absolutely a mistake and waste of time, at least a waste of his particular powers. Of all the famous philosophers he is the least bookish, the least academic, and in his mature years he can hardly bring himself to speak of professorial philosophy without a sneer: yet classical philology is of all disciplines the *most* bookish – its 'materials' are nothing but books. Thus by the end of his active life he had developed a very ambivalent attitude towards books as such, towards book-learning, and towards sedentary occupations of any kind. 'Early in the morning, at the break of day, in all the freshness and dawn of one's strength, to read a book – I call that vicious!' (*EH*, II. 8).

Nietzsche's *philologica* consists of the work he did at Leipzig, on the basis of which he was awarded his doctorate, and his lectures during the ten years he was at Basel. Only the completest editions include it, and it is something of interest to classical scholars rather than students of Nietzsche. But the boundaries of 'classical philology' are – in German-speaking universities at least – capable of being stretched and extended almost at the will of the teacher, and in accordance with his predilection and interests; and since Nietzsche's predilection, even when he first went to Basel, was philosophy in general and Schopenhauer's in particular, what is strictly philology in his *philologica* shades into discussion of classical philosophy. He went to Basel, indeed, with the determination to be 'something more than a taskmaster to efficient philologists' (letter of 11 April 1869): and this is only one of many depreciations of philology to be found in his letters of this time. It is in part an expression of the ordinary young man's fear of and distaste for settling down, becoming limited, and having to shoulder responsibilities: Nietzsche seems to have thought he could dodge this by secretly indoctrinating his students with Schopenhaueranism, and thus doing 'something more' than teach classical philology – a notion which, as far as I can see, he never made the least attempt to translate into practice, perhaps because he discovered its impossibility.

But his tendency to look down on the discipline of which he was an accomplished practitioner is also explicable in terms of his own evolution. Exactly what a man constituted as Nietzsche was ought to have done with himself at the age of twenty-four I cannot presume to say, but I feel fairly confident that he ought not to have become a university professor, and I say that with the greater confidence in that Nietzsche himself clearly thought so. My strongest feeling is that a side of his genius which had to struggle for expression would have been immeasurably aided if he had studied medicine and become, as he later suggested he should have become, a physician: his own feeling in the late 1860s varied between transferring to philosophy and taking his degree in that subject, and going to Paris for a year and studying 'the divine can-can and the yellow poison absinthe', and either course would probably have done him more good than assuming the chair of classical philology in staid and steady Basel. Unquestionably it was a reaction against the prospect of continuing on in a respectable bourgeois existence which would contradict the growing tendency of his thought that led firstly to a deprecation of philology and then to the attempt to extend its boundary in the direction of philosophical discussion.

In this regard the most interesting of his *philologica* is the series of lectures on 'The Pre-Platonic Philosophers', given in 1872–3, and in which 'philology' is definitely extended to encompass what was currently one of his most deeply-felt interests, the Greek philosophers of the sixth century. By far the most influential of his early unpublished writings is his excursus on the so-called pre-Socratics, 'Philosophy in the Tragic Age of the Greeks', which belongs to the same period as 'The Pre-Platonic Philosophers' and may be said to have inaugurated the reassessment of these forefathers of philosophy which has now set them at a far greater height than they enjoyed previously: Nietzsche's understanding and appreciation of the line from Thales to Democritus was, indeed, so marked and, for his time, uncommon, that he came to be seen as their 'disciple' and continuator: a view which greatly exaggerates one side of him. The language of 'Philosophy in the Tragic Age of the Greeks', which is certainly not the language of the mature Nietzsche, is none the less an efficient medium for revealing what it was that attracted him to the pre-Socratics, at least initially. The opening sentence of his consideration of Heraclitus, for instance, reads: 'Into the midst of this mystical night in which Anaximander's problem of becoming was shrouded *Heraclitus* approached and illuminated it with a divine flash of lightning' (section 5). This is the language of *mystery*: you cannot write about Plato or Aristotle in these terms. The fragmentary state in which their writings survive, the oracular nature of much of what does still exist, our very imperfect knowledge of what they were really like and of the circumstances in which they lived, all encourage, or even make necessary, the exercise of the imagination when dealing with the pre-Socratics; and the language in which Nietzsche elects to deal with them reveals, to me at least, that it was the opportunity they offered for inventiveness, for creative reconstruction, which drew him to them.

Early in his career he almost wrecked it by publishing *The Birth of Tragedy*, which when it appeared was regarded as a work of classical philology produced by a classical philologist who had gone off his head. No citation of sources, no footnotes, no Greek, no caution, no 'scholarship' at all in the conventional sense: *The Birth of Tragedy* is, again, a work of creative imagination, and one which has since been vindicated – though one has to emphasize, in defence of its contemporary critics, that it has not vindicated *itself*, it does not contain the materials and evidence by which its conclusions can be checked, which is of the essence of scholarship. It is a work of 'intuition', and in this respect at least typical and revelatory of Nietzsche's way of thinking.

The *Concise Oxford Dictionary* defines 'intuition' as 'immediate apprehension by the mind without reasoning'. I think we ought to hesitate before accepting that definition, because it implies the existence of a means of apprehension by the mind which is something other than reasoning without saying what that means is. What, concretely, is 'an intuition'? It is a statement which I make to myself – or 'my mind' makes to me – for which I do not have any supporting reasons; that is to say, it is the conclusion of an argument with the premises missing or 'suppressed'. Are there grounds for supposing I have arrived at this conclusion by extra-rational means, by means, that is, of an unknown faculty of 'intuition'? To multiply 'faculties' is the last thing you should do; any explanation which covers the observed facts is preferable. One ought therefore to prefer the suggestion just offered: that intuition is a product of unconscious reasoning, *very fast* reasoning perhaps, and that a man 'gifted with intuition' is not a mystic keyed up to extrasensory perception or possessed of an extra faculty but a reasoner capable of reasoning with lightning speed. The difference between a true and a false intuition would then be that the former was borne out and the latter refuted by a reconstruction of the process of reasoning which led to it. As Schopenhauer said, the difference in mental capacity between man and man is so great that that which is plain sense to one may seem like a supernatural revelation to another; and a conclusion which strikes a man of 'intuition' with all the force of a proved proposition may seem like a wild guess to the rest of mankind until they have laboriously thought their way through to it. It seems to me that Nietzsche was 'gifted with intuition' to a high degree; that his notorious failure to 'give reasons' is in part attributable to impatience but in part to the fact that he does not always know what the reasons are; and that this capacity was first demonstrated in his 'intuitive' grasp of Hellenic culture, which led to his discovery of the ritual origin of Greek tragedy.

The Birth of Tragedy is also a product of that ambition to be 'something more' than a promoter of scholarship which in the end led Nietzsche to decry his whole career as classical philologist as a waste of his powers.

III: Compositions

As a boy and young man Nietzsche was an amateur composer. His compositional manuscripts still preserved extend over the twenty years 1854 to 1874. After the latter date he virtually ceased to indulge in this pastime, though in 1887 he completed the only composition he ventured to publish: Hymn to Life, a setting for chorus and orchestra of a poem by Lou Salomé.

Most of these manuscripts have remained unpublished and unperformed: even the most comprehensive editions of his works do not include them, and the most recent, whose justification lies in its intention to be the completest ever, ignores them (see the bibliography below). Songs for voice and piano were published in 1924 as volume one of a proposed edition of the musical works, but no further volumes appear to have been issued; and copies of the entire manuscript collection made for incorporation into the Historisch-kritische Gesamtausgabe were, together with a number of originals, destroyed in a bombing raid on Leipzig. A few items have been printed individually, but as a whole Nietzsche's compositions remain unknown except to students of the manuscripts themselves.

That they 'exhibit the rankest amateurism' (Ernest Newman, Life of Wagner, vol. IV (1947), p. 317) there is no need to doubt, though one might demur at the harsh word 'rankest', which clearly originates in Newman's view, expressed on the same page, that Nietzsche 'laboured under the strange delusion that he was a composer', which is not really the case: his attempts to get his compositions performed were very few and far between (it was Gast's compositions he tried to get performed), and he understood perfectly well that composition was for him hardly more than a hobby. More apposite is the conclusion of Frederick Love

(*Young Nietzsche and the Wagnerian Experience*, 1963) that Nietzsche's compositions are not imitations of Wagner, for this conclusion reinforces the view that Nietzsche's Wagnerian period involved a desertion of his true bent even in musical matters.

IV: Letters

Nietzsche was not a great letter writer, in the sense that his letters are not read for their own sake as 'literature'; but he was a very *good* one; his letters contain much matter, and a student will have an imperfect idea of him unless he has read a decent selection of them.

Arranged chronologically they provide a biography and 'physiognomy' of their author. In this regard, the letters of the 1860s and 1870s are of greater value than those of the 1880s (1888 excepted): during the earlier decades he is expressing more of himself and exposing more of his ideas, the reason being, presumably, that he is not then expressing himself fully in his books. Strictly biographical usefulness declines during the 1880s until 1888, the letters of which year are again of first-rate importance for his biography.

Arranged according to correspondents, they show how he was capable of adopting differing tones of voice depending on whom he was writing to. His letters to his mother and sister are almost always cheerful and in a sense 'harmless': they are chatty and uncomplaining, they play down his invalid condition and exaggerate the slightest improvement in it. They are the letters of a 'good son', and for that reason not, on the whole, very informative. He does not discuss philosophy with his mother, and only in a very simplistic way with his sister. His letters to Peter Gast, on the other hand, are full of self-revelation and of discussion of his work: Gast used to make fair copies of Nietzsche's manuscripts for transmission to the printer, and regarded himself (and was regarded by Nietzsche) as Nietzsche's collaborator; the letters to him therefore often go into what Nietzsche is engaged upon in quite minute detail. The sympathetic Franz Overbeck, to take a third case, receives the content of Nietzsche's bad days (as does to a less degree the less sympathetic Erwin Rohde): the letters to Overbeck are an account of his struggles against ill-health and depression, the measures he is taking against them, the occasions when he almost suffers defeat. Details of other correspondents, and of the falsifications perpetrated by Elizabeth Nietzsche, will be found in the bibliography.

About 2,800 of Nietzsche's letters have survived.

Bibliography

Nietzsche's Writings

There are many collected editions of varying degrees of completeness. The chief of them to date are:

Gesamtausgabe in Grossoktav (Leipzig, 1901–13), 2nd edn, 19 vols (index added as vol 20 in 1926). Vols 1–8 Werke, vols 9–16 Nachlass, vols 17–19 Philologica.

Musarionausgabe (Munich, 1920–9), 23 vols, Works, Nachlass, philologica, juvenilia are arranged in chronological order.

The Historisch-kritische Gesamtausgabe der Werke (Munich, 1933 ff.), arranges works and all other manuscripts in chronological order; but the edition was broken off at vol 5 (writings of 1868–9) and is unlikely to be resumed.

A well-printed and easily available edition of the works and the Wille zur Macht is provided by Kröners Taschenausgabe (Stuttgart, 1952 ff.).

From the point of view of shelf-space and easy portability, the most convenient edition to own is Werke in drei Bänden, herausgegeben von Karl Schlechta (Munich, 3rd edn 1965; plus index vol.). Vols 1 and 2 contain the Werke, vol. 3 contains a selection of juvenilia, Nachlass and letters.

Friedrich Nietzsches Werke des Zusammenbruchs, herausgegeben von Erich F. Podach (Heidelberg, 1961), provides manuscript versions of the Antichrist, Ecce Homo, and the Dionysos-Dithyramben.

Werke. Kritische Gesamtausgabe, herausgegeben von Giorgio Colli und Mazzino Montinari (Berlin, Paris and Milan). Abteilung I: Jugendschriften. Philologische Studien und Publikationen bis 1869. Abteilung II: Universitätsvorlesungen, philologische Studien und Publikationen von 1869 bis 1879. Abteilung III: Die Geburt der Tragödie. Unzeitgemässe Betrachtungen I–III. Nachgelassene Schriften und Fragmente von 1869 bis 1874. Abteilung IV: Unzeitgemässe Betrachtungen IV. Menschliches, Allzumenschliches I–II. Nachgelassene Fragmente von 1875–1879. Abteilung V: Morgenröthe. Idyllen aus Messina. Die fröhliche Wissenschaft. Nachgelassene Fragmente von Anfang 1880 bis Herbst 1882. Abteilung VI: Also sprach Zarathustra. Jenseits von Gut und Böse. Zur Genealogie der Moral. Der Fall Wagner. Götzen-Dämmerung. Der Antichrist. Ecce homo. Dionysos-Dithyramben. Nietzsche contra Wagner.

Abteilung VII: Nachgelassene Fragmente von November 1882 bis Sommer 1885. Abteilung VIII: Nachgelassene Fragmente von Herbst 1885 bis Januar 1889. This edition, now in course of publication, will, if it is true to its prospectus, be the first to include every surviving manuscript of Nietzsche's, reproduced without editorial emendation or interference: it will thus be the first truly complete edition and should replace all others as the foundation of Nietzsche studies. With critical apparatus, indexes, chronologies and facsimile reproductions, the edition is expected to comprise about thirty volumes.

All of Nietzsche's books have been translated into English. *The Complete Works of Friedrich Nietzsche*, edited by Oscar Levy (London and New York, 1909–13), 18 vols, offers translations of varying degrees of competence and acceptability. The extremes are perhaps Thomas Common's *Thus Spake Zarathustra*, which is not to be recommended and is, indeed, all but unreadable, and Helen Zimmern's *Beyond Good and Evil*, which frequently cannot be improved on, although even here there are unaccountable errors and lapses into incomprehensibility. The entire set was reprinted in 1964 by Russell and Russell, New York.

Two large volumes of translations, with very helpful notes and commentary, have been published by Walter Kaufmann: *The Portable Nietzsche* (New York, 1959), which contains *Thus Spoke Zarathustra, Twilight of the Idols, The Antichrist, Nietzsche contra Wagner*, selected letters, etc.; and *Basic Writings of Nietzsche* (New York, 1968), which contains *The Birth of Tragedy, Beyond Good and Evil, On the Genealogy of Morals, The Case of Wagner, Ecce Homo*, and selections from other works.

Individual translations include:

The Birth of Tragedy and *The Genealogy of Morals*, translated with an introduction by Francis Golffing (New York, 1956).

Thus Spoke Zarathustra, translated with an introduction and notes by R. J. Hollingdale (Harmondsworth, 1969).

Twilight of the Idols and *The Antichrist*, translated with an introduction and commentary by R. J. Hollingdale (Harmondsworth, 1969).

The Will to Power, translated by Walter Kaufmann and R. J. Hollingdale, edited by Walter Kaufmann (New York and London, 1968).

Nietzsche's Letters

The most complete collection so far is *Friedrich Nietzsches Gesammelte Briefe* (5 vols in 6, Berlin and Leipzig, 1900–9, and later edns). But there are many letters since published which are not included, and some falsifications have been exposed (see, e.g., the Philologischer Nachbericht to Schlechta's edition (in vol. III). Important additional letters appear in:

Friedrich Nietzsches Briefe an Peter Gast (Leipzig, 1908).

Friedrich Nietzsches Briefwechsel mit Franz Overbeck (Leipzig, 1916).

Bibliography

The *Historisch-kritische Gesamtausgabe der Briefe* (Munich, 1933 ff.) produced four vols, but then, like the companion edition of the *Werke*, it was broken off.

Briefwechsel. Kritische Gesamtausgabe, herausgegeben von Giorgio Colli und Mazzino Montinari (Berlin, Paris and Milan). Abteilung I: Nietzsches Briefe. Abteilung II: Briefe an Nietzsche. Abteilung III: Zeitgenössische Briefe über Nietzsche und Lebenszeugnisse. As in the corresponding edition of the *Werke*, this edition of letters by, to and about Nietzsche, publication of which has only just begun, aims at the greatest possible completeness. It is anticipated that text and apparatus will fill about twenty volumes. If its prospectus is realized, it will likewise supersede all previous editions.

There exists no complete translation of the letters. Three recent selections are:

Unpublished Letters, translated and edited by Kurt E. Leidecker (New York and London, 1960).

Nietzsche: a Self-Portrait from his Letters, translated and edited by P. Fuss and H. Shapiro (Cambridge, Mass. and London, 1971).

Selected Letters of Friedrich Nietzsche, translated and edited by Christopher Middleton (Chicago, 1969).

Books about Nietzsche

The Nietzsche literature is very large: it is probably too large by now for any one person to read it all, even if that were desirable. The most complete bibliography is provided by the *International Nietzsche Bibliography*, edited by H. W. Reichert and Karl Schlechta (Chapel Hill, N.C., 1960).

There exist three large-scale studies which I think students would agree are the principal studies of Nietzsche at present available in English and required reading for anyone seriously concerned with him. They are:

Karl Jaspers, *Nietzsche: an Introduction to the Understanding of his Philosophical Activity* (Chicago, 1965);

Walter Kaufmann, *Nietzsche: Philosopher, Psychologist, Antichrist* (Princeton and London, 3rd edn 1968);

George A. Morgan Jr, *What Nietzsche Means* (Cambridge, Mass., 1941; New York, 1965.)

The present selection concentrates on the 'classics' of the literature, on recent rather than early work, and on studies currently in print.

Andler, Charles, *Nietzsche, sa vie et sa pensée* (6 vols, Paris, 1920–31).

Andreas-Salomé, Lou, *Friedrich Nietzsche in seinen Werken* (Vienna, 1911).

Andreas-Salomé, Lou, *Lebensrückblick*, herausgegeben E. Pfeiffer (Zurich and Wiesbaden, 1957).

Bernoulli, Carl Albrecht, *Franz Overbeck und Friedrich Nietzsche: eine Freund-schaft* (2 vols, Jena, 1908).

Blackham, Harold, *Six Existentialist Thinkers* (London, 1952). Chapter on Nietzsche.

Blunck, Richard, *Friedrich Nietzsche: Kindheit und Jugend* (Basle, 1953).

Brandes, George, *Friedrich Nietzsche* (London, 1914). Essays and correspondence.

Brann, Hellmut Walther, *Nietzsche und die Frauen* (Leipzig, 1931).

Brinton, Crane, *Nietzsche* (Cambridge, Mass., 1941; New York, new edn, 1965).

Danto, Arthur C., *Nietzsche as Philosopher* (New York, 1965).

Deussen, Paul, *Erinnerungen an Friedrich Nietzsche* (Leipzig, 1901).

Fink, Eugen, *Nietzsches Philosophie* (Stuttgart, 1960).

Giesz, Ludwig, *Nietzsche: Existentialismus und Wille zur Macht* (Stuttgart, 1950).

Grau, Gerd-Günther, *Christlicher Glaube und intellectuelle Redlichkeit: eine religions-philosophische Studie über Nietzsche* (Frankfurt a/M., 1958).

Heidegger, Martin, 'Nietzsches Wort "Gott ist tot"' in *Holzwege* (Frankfurt a/M., 1950).

Heidegger, Martin, 'Wer ist Nietzsches Zarathustra?' in *Vorträge und Aufsätze* (Pfullingen, 1954).

Heidegger, Martin, *Nietzsche* (2 vols, Pfullingen, 1961). Writings and lectures of 1936–46.

Heller, Erich, *The Disinherited Mind* (London, 1952). Three chapters on Nietzsche.

Heller, Peter, *Dialectics and Nihilism: Essays on Lessing, Nietzsche, Mann and Kafka* (Amherst, Mass., 1966).

Hildebrandt, Kurt, *Gesundheit und Krankheit in Nietzsches Leben und Werk* (Berlin, 1926).

Hofmiller, Josef, *Friedrich Nietzsche* (Hamburg, 2nd edn 1947).

Hollingdale, R. J., *Nietzsche: the Man and his Philosophy* (London and Baton Rouge, La., 1965).

Hubben, W., *Dostoevsky, Kierkegaard, Nietzsche and Kafka* (London and New York, 1962).

Jaspers, Karl, *Nietzsche and Christianity* (Chicago, 1961).

Kaufmann, Walter, *From Shakespeare to Existentialism* (New York, 1959). Five chapters on Nietzsche.

Klages, Ludwig, *Die psychologische Errungenschaften Friedrich Nietzsches* (Leipzig, 3rd edn 1930).

Knight, A. H. J., *Some Aspects of the Life and Work of Nietzsche, and Particularly of his Connection with Greek Literature and Thought* (1933, reprinted New York, 1967).

Lavrin, Janko, *Nietzsche: a Biographical Introduction* (London, 1972).

Lea, F. A., *The Tragic Philosopher* (London, new edn 1973).

Love, Frederick R., *Young Nietzsche and the Wagnerian Experience* (Chapel Hill, N.C., 1963).

Löwith, Karl, *From Hegel to Nietzsche: the Revolution in Nineteenth-Century Thought* (New York and London, 1965).

Löwith, Karl, *Nietzsches Philosophie der ewigen Wiederkunft des Gleichen* (Stuttgart, revised edn 1956).

Mann, Thomas, *Nietzsche's Philosophy in the Light of Contemporary Events* (Washington D.C., 1947).

Martin, Alfred von, *Nietzsche und Burckhardt* (Munich, 4th edn 1947).

Mencken, H. L., *The Philosophy of Friedrich Nietzsche* (Port Washington, N.Y., 3rd edn 1913).

Mittasch, Alwin, *Friedrich Nietzsche als Naturphilosoph* (Stuttgart, 1952).

Müller-Lauter, Wolfgang, *Nietzsche: seine Philosophie der Gegensätze und die Gegensätze seiner Philosophie* (Berlin, 1971).

Nicholls, R. A., *Nietzsche in the Early Works of Thomas Mann* (Berkeley, Calif., 1955).

Podach, Erich F., *The Madness of Nietzsche* (London, 1931).

Podach, Erich F., *Gestalten um Nietzsche* (Weimar, 1932).

Podach, Erich F., *Friedrich Nietzsche und Lou Salomé: ihre Begegnung* (Zurich, 1938).

Podach, Erich F., *Der kranke Nietzsche: Briefe seiner Mutter an Franz Overbeck* (Vienna, 1937).

Reyburn, H. A., *Nietzsche: the Story of a Human Philosopher* (London, 1948).

Salin, Edgar, *Jacob Burckhardt und Nietzsche* (Basle, 2nd edn 1948).

Schlechta, Karl, *Nietzsches grosser Mittag* (Frankfurt a/M., 1954).

Schlechta, Karl, *Der Fall Nietzsche: Aufsätze und Vorträge* (Munich, 2nd edn 1959).

Simmel, Georg, *Schopenhauer und Nietzsche* (Leipzig, 3rd edn 1923).

Stern, J. P., *Idylls and Realities: Studies in Nineteenth Century German Literature* (London, 1971). Chapter on *The Birth of Tragedy*.

Vaihinger, Hans, *The Philosophy of 'As If'* (New York, 1924). Chapter on 'Nietzsche and his Doctrine of Conscious Illusion'.

Wein, Hermann, *Positives Antichristentum* (The Hague, 1962).

Wolf, Hans M., *Friedrich Nietzsche: der Weg zum Nichts* (Berne, 1956).

Index

Index